ECOLOGY:

AN INTRODUCTION
FOR NON-SCIENCE MAJORS

Dr. Harold R. Hungerford

Art Work by:

Adam Cartwright
Pam Kincheloe
Harold Hungerford
Suzanne Hungerford

Layout and Design by:
Dr. Trudi L. Volk
and
Adam Cartwright

1997, 2003

ISBN 1-58874-268-7

Published by

Stipes Publishing L.L.C.
204 W. University Ave.
Champaign, Illinois 61820

TABLE OF CONTENTS

Acknowledgments

Mostly unread, "Acknowledgments" are found on millions of sheets of paper in millions of term papers, textbooks, monographs, theses, and dissertations. Still, there exists a need for me to acknowledge the contributions made to this work because not do so would be to take credit for some things for which I am really not eligible.

A case in point: Editing!!! Heaven forbid that a singular should really be a plural, or "framer" should really be "farmer", or "effect" should be "affect". I always make the mistake of asking experts like Drs. Trudi Volk and Bill Bluhm to read manuscripts for errors. Never learning a most important lesson, my ego is constantly beleaguered with, "Uh-oh, there is another one!". Not only does the ego suffer, these mistakes on my part lead to the loss of valuable time given that I cannot possibly dismiss their findings and, thusly, must go back to the computer and fix the darned things. Even Pat Hungerford takes delight in sneaking a peek at a manuscript and informing me of the errors of my ways. Alas! But, fortunately, many errors disappear because of the work done by these people!

Art work! Although Suzanne Hungerford and I did a good deal of the art work in initial drafts of this book, much of the really neat art work was done by Pam Kincheloe, Adam Cartwright, and others whose talents must not go unsung. I cannot express how delighted I am with Pam's work and, furthermore, hope that she will stay talented and in good health. Some of her work herein is not signed. However, you can tell which is hers - a cardinal, quail, wolf, heron, fly, . . . and others. Nor can I dismiss the dramatic drawings done by Adam Cartwright. If you want real drama in art work, look for that done by him. It literally jumps from the page into your mind. You will be able to tell which is his. And, too, much of the formatting is Adam's as well, especially the color pages.

Ideas! Where do they all come from? Certainly, some are original but as I wallow a bit in nostalgia, I think of long and fascinating discussions on ecology with Dr. Ben Peyton of Michigan State University who helped stimulate the desire to develop an introductory book on ecology for adult learners. It - or something like it - needs to be available to non-science majors everywhere!

And, too, teaching so many, many Ecology Workshops for Teachers with Dr. Jerry Culen (now of the University of Florida) was bound to stimulate prescriptive utterances that wound up here as well as some which did not. I think we taught together summers for eight (8) long years at Southern Illinois University at Carbondale - long enough for his ideas to become hybridized with mine and, therefore, probably appear here in some form. And, too, he has made direct contributions to the book and I doubt that these have been credited appropriately.

After "retiring" from the summer workshops with Jerry Culen, Dr. Gerry Saunders taught the Ecology Workshop for Teachers and he, too, made many valuable contributions to this publication. It is substantially improved because of the effort he put into it and I thank Gerry sincerely ! And now this workshop is in the able hands of Dr. Bill Bluhm who is doing fine things with the concepts and activities.

For those who have read or used the threatened and endangered animals case study [Stipes Publishing Co., 1996 Ed.], there will be some entries in this book that look familiar, particularly in the last chapter. Some of this material was developed in consort with Dave Hagengruber, a young man with a brilliant mind and a tremendous potential for enormously successful work in environmental education.

Others who can take credit or have to share blame with Ben, Jerry, Dave and Gerry include such people as Doug Knapp, John Ramsey, Durward Allen, Carl Bollwinkel, Clifford Knapp, Delores Roth, G. Tyler Miller, and also my father who, every so often, was able to take a few moments from his teaching schedule to show me how to use a shotgun, how to fish the Kankakee River, how to long for the days when huge flocks of mallards blackened the sky, and how to appreciate a natural river system long since damaged by selfish and ecologically-illiterate people.

I cannot give that original river system back to me nor to the people of Indiana and Illinois. Nor can I live my youth again. But maybe - just maybe - a few mature or maturing learners somewhere, sometime, will get help from this document and find a way to communicate to others just how important, complicated, and precious their ecological environment is! I hope so!

Harold R. Hungerford
April 4, 2003

AN INTRODUCTION

WHAT IS ECOLOGY?

WHO ARE ECOLOGISTS?

1

An Anecdote

The day had turned out to be pleasantly warm and sunny. She felt good about being in the forest today because yesterday had been a rainy one. She and her young field assistant from the university had to quit early yesterday to avoid being drenched in this southern Illinois forest. The young man working with her seemed anxious to get to work also. She knew that he could only help her a few more days because he had to take summer courses in the Forestry Department during June, July, and August.

The two of them had set up a series of large squares called quadrats in a line through the heart of this forest. The work was being paid for by a grant from an environmental organization interested in purchasing this tract of timber. By the time they finished counting the mature and immature trees in each of the quadrats, they would have a pretty good idea what the entire forest was like. But, they would still put the information into the computer to make certain that the data were as scientific as possible.

She started counting the mature white oaks in Quadrat No. 2. There were only two in this 100 square meter quadrat. Interestingly, these were the only mature trees in this quadrat. But, they were huge! There were also two young shagbark hickory trees and one aging red bud tree in the understory. The hickory trees might be able to reach maturity if something happened to the white oaks in the next ten or twenty years. She knew that the red bud tree would never reach the top of the forest. Red buds and several other tree species in southern Illinois were called understory trees because of this growth pattern.

Having completed a plotting of the understory trees, they turned their attention to the seedlings beneath the understory. There were several dozen of them. There were white oaks, scarlet oaks, shagbark hickories, pignut hickories, red buds, dogwoods, and even a couple sassafras seedlings. They both knew that almost all these seedlings would eventually die because they simply couldn't compete with the larger understory and canopy trees shading them. But, they were there even so, ready to grow and replace the larger trees if given a chance to do so.

This forest, on the surface, looked much like any other hardwood forest in southern Illinois. But, it was somewhat unique because it probably had never been timbered. Uncut forests, called "virgin forests", were really rare now and the environmental organization wanted to preserve it before the present owners felt forced to timber it for financial reasons.

Preserving a truly mature hardwood forest was preserving more than just trees and both of them knew this. It was also preserving the wildflowers, vines, and shrubs of this forest type. And, too, it was preserving habitat for resident birds and migratory birds as well as for forest mammals, reptiles, amphibians and a host of other animals such as insects. If this forest turned out to be as unique as it appeared on the surface, a lot of other scientists and educators could use it for research and educational purposes. It was large enough so that people could study in it if the forest was managed properly.

It took the better part of a week to plot all of the forest layers in each quadrat on the worksheets she had prepared. The data would be put into a computer which would prepare a printout of each layer of each quadrat and a summary profile of all of the quadrats taken together. These data tables would be interpreted by the ecologist and the entire report made available to the interested organization. She hypothesized that the organization would be very interested in purchasing this forest because of the data she and her assistant were collecting. She hoped this was the case because both of them had become very impressed by this woodland in the short time they had studied it.

Ecology Defined

ECOLOGY is the science that studies interrelationships within and between plant and animal populations, and with the non-living environment.

The purpose of this book is to help the reader better understand the science of ecology! It is also a very basic introduction to ecological concepts for those mature and maturing learners who do not have a science specialization yet need or want an introduction to the science of ecology and at least some of its crucial environmental connections.

3

The term "ecology" is easily one of the most misunderstood and misused terms in the English language. The word is abused in newspapers, magazines, on television, and in everyday life among far too many environmentalists. Hopefully, the contents of this book will help you better understand what the term "ecology" means and, maybe, what it doesn't!

It is very important for the reader to understand that ecology is a science. Ecology is the science that studies the interrelationships that exist within and between populations of plants and animals. It is also the science that attempts to determine how entire living systems operate - what makes them work and what factors threaten them. It is also the science that tries to determine the role of humans in the environment from a scientific standpoint.

Ecologists are interested in collecting evidence or information that will, eventually, help all humans understand the role of every living thing in the makeup of the planet earth. Ecologists search constantly for data that give us better information about how populations and other living systems work.

> *Ecology is the study of the structure and function of nature.*
> C. Kupchella & M. Hyland, 1986

Ecologists also attempt to find out how to keep natural environments healthy and productive. Ecological information can help humans preserve and wisely use the resources of this planet. Although ecologists have learned a great deal about these things in the last 100 years, a great deal remains to be learned.

Each chapter in this book begins with an "anecdote" - mostly scenarios written to introduce the reader to the chapter's content. The anecdotes are meant to be stimulating but, in some cases, they can be sad or depressing. More importantly, perhaps, I might have tripped over my own ethic and entered the realm of anthropomorphism in one or two of these. If I am guilty of being anthropomorphic, so be it. However, it is not done with intent! Apologies to my readers if, in fact, apologies are needed.

As you progress in this text you will get a better idea of the kinds of things ecologists study. I hope that you will find ecology as exciting as I do. I also hope that the time spent here will help you understand more about your own role in the vast community of living things.

Harold R. Hungerford

In the late 1960's the general public was hardly aware of the term *ecology*. As a topic of interest ecology stirred little public discussion and as a science it had none of the glamour of molecular biology. By 1970 ecology had become a household word, but it was misunderstood, misused, and equated with environmental science. Too many failed to understand that ecology refers to the interrelations of an organism with its environment and that this includes man.

Robert L. Smith, 1974

CHAPTER I

AN ECOLOGICAL ANECDOTE:

A LESSON FROM OUR PAST

Note: Chapter I has, in large part, been taken from an earlier unpublished version of this ecology book. It also appears in a document published by Stipes Publishing Company entitled, *Threatened and Endangered Animals* by Hagengruber and Hungerford (1996).

An Ecological Anecdote:

A Lesson From Our Past

Part I

It was an unusually hot day for April. The year was 1869. It had rained hard the night before and the humidity was high. The two men in buckskins sweated heavily as they made their way to the top of the knoll overlooking a broad grassy valley. The big bearded man with the broad-brimmed hat cursed softly as he caught his foot on a piece of granite rock hidden by green grass plants nearly a foot high. Although winter was still a clear memory, the big man's face was well tanned from many weeks in the sun on the plains of the Oklahoma Territory. His buckskins were cracked and filthy. He needed new ones. And, neither he nor his skinner smelled very good. It had been a long time since their last baths.

The skinner was a shorter man but it was obvious that there was great strength in his upper body. Also dressed in buckskins, his clothing had a greasy look and there was dried blood on much of him. He carried a pair of knives in sheathes on his belt. One of the knives had a wide blade, curved upward at the pointed end. The other was smaller, more like a dagger. Both were sharpened to a razor's edge. In fact, when the skinner shaved, he shaved with the shorter one.

The two men had little love for each other even though their lives were thoroughly intertwined. The skinner was simply hired help and his job was a hard one. He and

another skinner, who was back a mile or so with the mules and wagons, skinned the bison (buffalo) and cured the hides. They also loaded the hides on the wagons for the long trip to the rail head far to the north in Dodge City. The big man was the hunter and the boss, and he would make decisions that would tell whether he could make a profit and pay the skinners their wages.

The hunter and the skinners had picked up the buffalo herd north of the Red River on the Texas border a few weeks earlier. The herd was moving slowly northward, feeding on the rich green grasses of the Oklahoma prairie. The hunters simply followed the buffalo, taking as many hides as could be skinned, dried and transported.

As the buffalo hunter and the skinner peered over the crest of the knoll, they gazed down on only forty or fifty animals. Evidently this group had left the main herd a day or so earlier and moved into this shallow green valley by themselves. The hunter shrugged his shoulders silently, knowing he could kill more than enough to keep his skinners busy and could catch up with the main herd later.

The hunter slowly went to his knees with his Sharps rifle in his right hand. He then inched forward until his elbows rested in the soft soil behind a smooth but small boulder. He reached into his side pocket and withdrew a handful of the large cartridges the big bore of the rifle took. The cartridges were placed in a pile on the ground to his right. The rifle was very heavy and he rested the long barrel on the granite boulder.

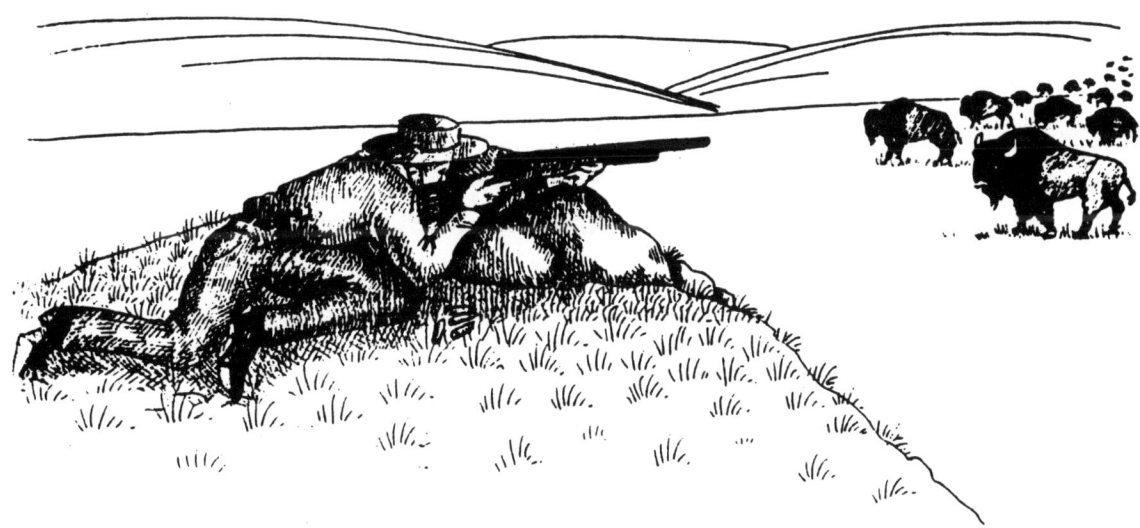

The skinner, now beside the hunter on the knoll, pointed to a yearling calf at the edge of the herd. He knew that the young heifer would skin easily and also yield the most tender meat in the herd. They needed the meat because they had run out a day or two earlier. The hunter nodded, took aim and shot. The yearling's legs crumpled and he lay dead in a heap on the Oklahoma prairie.

The hunter knew that the sound of the rifle and the dying bison would probably not bolt the herd. The animals would mill about nervously but probably stay long enough to insure a good kill. If any of the animals looked like they might run, they were killed quickly. He slipped another cartridge into the breech of the rifle and swung the barrel toward a cow heavy with calf. He barely felt the strong recoil but the cow felt the bullet tear through her lungs. She stood there for a few seconds blowing blood-flecked froth from her nostrils as she died. She rolled over on her side and her calf died soon afterwards inside her.

The killing went on for some time until enough bison lay dead or dying to keep the skinners busy for hours. These few represented only a drop in the bucket when one realizes that there may have originally been as many as 60,000,000 buffalo west of the Mississippi River. But the killing was going on everywhere on the plains where the hunters could get the hides to a rail head for shipment eastward. And, too, the killing went on in some places simply for sport and in others to reduce the Indians' food supply. Those killed for sport or for political reasons were often just left to rot. Not even the hides were taken.

Part II

There were four huge herds of buffalo on the Great Plains. Each had its own migration pattern, following the greening of the prairie grasses northward in the spring and southward to milder winters when the weather turned cold. This southern herd our hunter was after ranged from Texas northward to southwestern Kansas where its range overlapped the Arkansas Herd. The Arkansas Herd could be found from the Oklahoma panhandle as far north as the southwestern corner of what is now Nebraska. Northward into Wyoming and South Dakota ranged what was called the Republican Herd. Still northward into North Dakota, Montana, and Canada was the Northern Herd.

The southern or Texas Herd was huge. Between 1872 and 1874 almost four million buffalo were killed out of it by white hunters and Indians. By 1879 the Texas Herd was gone and the plains of Oklahoma, Texas, and Kansas were littered with the bleached bones of millions of bison left to rot after their hides had been removed.

The end of the buffalo also spelled doom for the Plains Indians. In the first quarter of the 19th Century there were probably 300,000 Indians on the Great Plains totally dependent on the bison. There were the Puncahs, the Mandans, the Minatarees, and Ricarees as well as others like the Sioux, more well known in terms of history. The tribes had evolved with the bison and the Indian knew no other lifestyle. Whether on horseback on on foot, the Plains Indians were able to survive because of the enormous herds of buffalo that swept north and south each year.

For the Indian the bison meant meat, hides for clothing and shelter, armour in the form of shields that were arrow-proof, glue, jewelry, hair dressing and sinew. Further, the dried dung fueled fires that kept them warm on cold evenings on the prairie. Fall hunts allowed tons of meat to be dried to keep the tribes in foodstuffs through the winter.

During the days of plenty in spring and fall, feasts were commonplace in both Indian encampments and the camps of the trappers and fur traders. At these times, only the choicest cuts of meat were used with odd assortments of pieces being used with relish. Favorite cuts included the hump, the tongue and the intestines. It was not unusual for an individual to sit down to a feast of the choicest cuts and consume perhaps eight pounds of meat before quitting. At these times the wolves and coyotes of the plains were bloated with all they could eat because the bulk of the buffalos was left unused by the feasting humans.

The coming of the white man to the Great Plains changed all of this in a matter of a few short decades. The Texas Herd was the first to go and by 1883 the Republican and Northern Herds had been slaughtered to the point that it was uneconomical to hunt commercially.

In these few, short decades one can imagine what happened to the Indian. He went from an independent, healthy human being to one totally dependent on the whims of the white man. *Those that had not been exterminated were herded into seemingly worthless pieces of real estate and fed with "government beef". New and terrible conditions brought about a breakdown in the culture and social structure of the tribes from which, to this very day, they have not recovered. The greed and savagery of the white man on the Great Plains tends to be a forgotten part of our heritage but it was very real and, in part, came about purposefully to push the Indian out of the way so that the plains could be ranched, farmed, and mined. We not only dedicate ourselves to forgetting this part of our history, we also seem dedicated to forgetting what happened to the Great Plains ecology in a few short decades with the coming of the white man.*

Part III

The Great Plains of North America covered a huge mass of land. The Great Plains stretched from the Mississippi River on the east to the Rocky Mountains on the West. North and south, these plains existed from Texas northward into Canada. Most of the plains consisted of grasslands. There were the tall grasses to the east and the short grasses in the dryer, western portions of the Great Plains. The kinds of grasses that grew in different regions were controlled largely by the amount of rainfall - higher to the east and lower in the west.

For tens of thousands of years, the plains saw not one white man. These were the years during which a fascinating aboriginal American developed a very special relationship with the plains and with the animals that lived there. This relationship was a fairly simple one in ecological terms. The basic relationship consisted of the following parts: (1) the soil of the plains, (2) the grasses of the plains, (3) the bison (buffalo), and (4) the Indian. All of these parts were interrelated. The ecologist might write these interrelationships like this: soil <-> grass <-> buffalo <-> Indian. What does this mean?

It means simply this. The grasses were dependent on the soil of the plains, the buffalo were dependent on the grasses, and the Indian upon the buffalo. We can also say that the Indian was, indirectly, dependent on the grasses and the soil as well. This soil <-> grass <-> buffalo <-> Indian relationship is fairly simple in ecological terms (there are far more complicated ones elsewhere). But, even though very simple, it was destroyed by greedy men selling hides and those who wanted the Indians and buffalo removed from the plains so that this huge land area could be used for other things.

10

There is a lesson to be learned from all of this if we are intelligent enough to learn it. Nowhere is this lesson so well stated as in Durward Allen's book entitled Our Wildlife Legacy. Dr. Allen writes:

" . . . this soil-grass-buffalo-Indian relationship is a simplified replica of what modern men face in living on the earth's resources. Each item in the system is dynamic and exists by compromise with the others. When any one fails to compromise, there is trouble for the whole. The buffalo was an essential link between Indian and soil; and when the herds were destroyed, the result was immediate. Winter blizzards howled across empty campsites where only a decade before they had drummed against the taut sides of lodges." *

---

* - Durward L. Allen. *Our Wildlife Legacy*. New York: Funk and Wagnalls Company. 1954. p 17.

Nebraska's Last Buffalo

Soon after the roundup of 1881, while I was out riding one day, I came across a trail that I took to be cow-calf tracks, and followed to see whose they were, and when I came in sight of them, I almost fell off my horse with astonishment, to find it was a herd of buffalo. There were twenty-eight grown ones and five calves in the herd. That country had been ridden over for four years by cowboys and hunters by the hundred, and no one had ever dreamed of seeing any buffalo there.

Frank was at the ranch and his daughter, a girl of twelve was there. Ed North, son of my older brother was also there. . . . Ed had never seen a wild buffalo before, and of course wanted to kill one. When we made a dash at them they ran off in two bunches, and Ed and I went after one bunch, and pretty soon he killed a three year old heifer. Frank and his daughter Stella ran after the other bunch and cut out a calf, which they chased around until it was so tired it could not run, but Frank had no rope and he didn't want to kill it, so let it go. . . . . This band of buffalo was later killed . . . and I think they were the last buffalo ever seen on the North side of the Platte River in Nebraska.

From *Man Of The Plains* by Luther North

Activity 1.1

A Few Things to Think About

1. Although Chapter I is just a beginning, the title says that this Chapter is about a lesson from our past. What do you think this lesson is?

2. Try to communicate how each element in the soil <-> grass <-> buffalo <-> Indian relationship is connected to each of the others in an ecological sense.

3. Economics often affect decisions that we make about natural resources. How did economics affect the soil <-> grass <-> buffalo <-> Indian relationship?

4. You will recall that, in 1889, there were only 551 buffalo left in the United States. This small number was down from as many as 60,000,000 or so just a few decades earlier. If there had been a concept called "endangered species" in 1889, the buffalo would have been placed on the list of endangered species in an instant. Given what you read in the story and what is given you below, try to construct an explanation for the buffalo's population crash (decline). In other words, what were the reasons for the buffalo becoming a severely endangered species?

> *In the 1870's there were those in the Congress of the United States that wrote legislation making it illegal for anyone to kill a female buffalo or more male buffaloes than could be used for food or commercial purposes. This bill was debated heatedly in and out of Congress. Some of those who supported the bill felt that it was immoral to try to starve the Indian into submission. There were others that said that wild, savage Indians should not be given any consideration compared to the poor, civilized settlers who simply wanted to use the buffalo's grass to graze their sheep and cattle. Even the Secretary of the Interior said that he would be glad when the last buffalo was gone. Still, the bill was passed in 1874. It was sent to President Ulysses S. Grant for his signature. He never signed it into law.*

Once again, your task with No. 4 is to explain in some detail why the buffalo became a severely endangered species.

5. If time permits, you might want to compare this part of the history of the United States to what is happening to wildife on the grasslands of Africa or to the tropical rainforests around the world. There are some similarities (and some differences). Still, you might question whether this "lesson from our past" has been learned by the world's leaders and citizens.

CHAPTER II

PATTERNS OF LIFE ON EARTH: LIVING SYSTEMS

Learner Objectives

During or subsequent to any and/or all interactions with this Chapter, you will be expected to be able to . . .

1. . . . define the term **ecosystem** and provide a minimum of five examples. For each example you will cite evidence to defend its selection as an example.

2. . . . define the term **ecosystem concept** (although ambiguous at times it is particularly powerful when analyzing living systems from an ecological perspective).

3. . . . define the term **community** and provide a minimum of five examples. For each example be able to cite evidence to defend the use of that example.

4. . . . define the term **microcommunity** and state specifically how microcommunities differ from both communities and ecosystems.

5. . . . define and/or describe what is meant by the term **biosphere**.

6. . . . define the term **biome** and provide a minimum of four examples. In each instance, defend the rationale behind giving that example biome status.

7. . . . explain why the geographic area represented by a biome is much greater than an ecosystem representing that biome. Further, be able to substantiate that explanation with accurate examples.

8. . . . diagram a continuum which shows the increasing levels of organizational complexity in the biosphere. This diagram must include at least the following: biome, species population, microcommunity, individual, biosphere, and community.

9. . . . describe the general relationships existing between latitudes and biomes. You will be expected to use correctly the following terms: latitude, biomes, temperature, soil development, and precipitation. Further, be able to provide at least two reasons why North America, in part, violates this biome-latitude relationship.

10. . . . list at least six abiotic variables that greatly influence the character of an ecosystem and explain how each can contribute to the overall development of an ecosystem.

11. . . . defend the idea that energy is a major variable involved in the integrity of an eco-system over time.

12. . . . define the term **habitat**. Explain how habitat is related to the survival of species populations in an ecosystem. Provide examples of this relationship.

13. . . . define the term niche and explain why the concept of niche is a very complicated one. Also, differentiate between the concepts of **habitat** and **niche**.

14. . . . define the term **species population** providing several accurate examples.

15. . . . compute **population density** for real or surrogate data.

16. . . . explain why the species population is an organizational pattern in the ecosystem.

17. . . . using your own observations made in the laboratory or in the field, describe a species population in terms of its being a pattern of life in an ecosystem, in terms of its interrelationships with other species populations, and in terms of interrelationships between individual members of that species population.

18. . . . diagram, name, and/or describe the layers found in a typical deciduous forest. Explain why the ideas associated with layering are useful but arbitrary.

19. . . . discuss and/or describe how animal species are associated with particular forest layers. Be able to incorporate the niche concept into this discussion. Further, be able to provide examples of animal species which are related to layers in a typical deciduous forest.

20. . . . discuss how a variety of biotic variables in a deciduous forest affect the abiotic variables one can observe there.

21. . . . discuss why both biotic and abiotic variables contribute to the overall character of an ecosystem. Be able to provide legitimate examples to exemplify the discussion.

22. . . . describe what is meant by the fallen log microcommunity. Defend the idea that this microcommunity does, indeed, fit the microcommunity concept and contributes significantly to the character and stability of the larger ecosystem with which it is associated.

23. . . .provide at least two examples of microcommunities other than the fallen log. Be able to describe one of these in some detail.

24. . . . be able to correctly state the ideas inherent in the generalizations stated by the authors regarding patterns of life in the biosphere, e.g., patterns of life exist along a continuum . . . Further, be able to prepare a rationale that explains why each of these is a sound generalization.

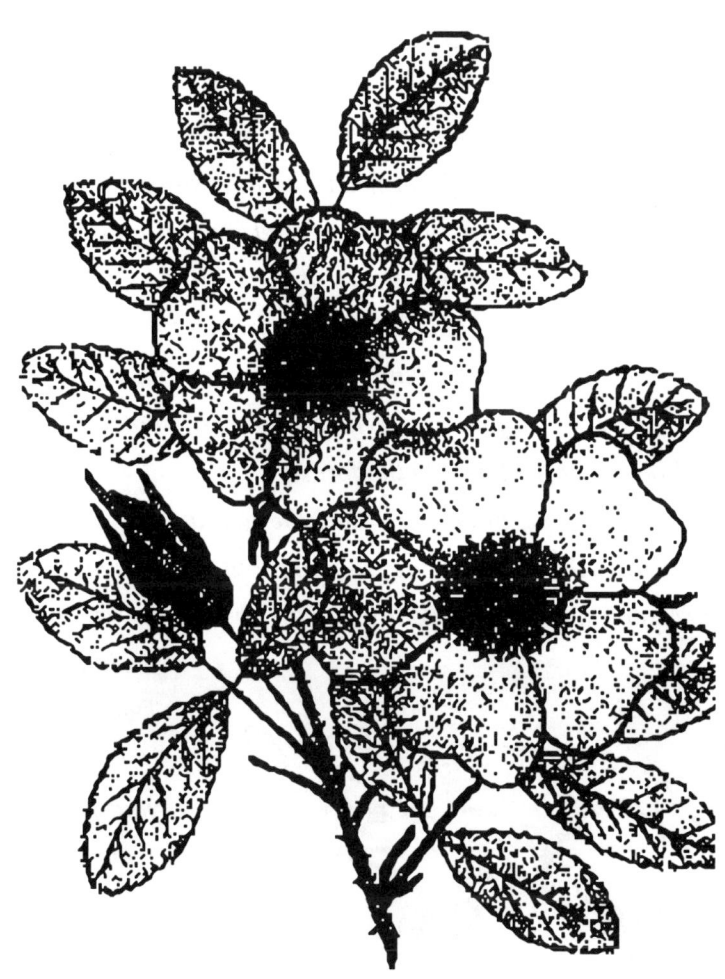

An Anecdote

The Red Fox Through the Year

Staying just at the edge of the ecotone, he walked slowly and, in human terms, deliberately next to the drying grass of late autumn. His pointed ears cocked intently, he watched to his left almost all of the time. Suddenly he stopped as if frozen in his tracks. His attention was riveted upon an ever so slight rustle he had heard coming from a clump of brownish-green grass. The sound came again. He slowly turned his body toward the sound, stepping cautiously as he did so, his body tense with excitement. He leaped stiff-legged and pounced on the grass hump. He moved the grass aside with a paw. Lightning-fast jaws clamped shut on the mouse, killing it quickly. He tossed the mouse into the air, caught it again and swallowed it whole. He would repeat this scenario several more times this windless autumn afternoon. Toward the end of the day, he would construct a cache of mice under a pile of leaves inside the ecotone. This mouse storage system would act as a reservoir of food as autumn turned into winter and food became increasingly scarce.

The fox was well over two years old, having been born two years ago this past March in a den only three miles from where he now stood. Home was the Shawnee National Forest - large blocks of hardwoods which covered over a quarter of a million acres and extended from the Mississippi River to the shores of the Ohio River in southern Illinois. Actually, his territory was only a small part of that forest. His search for food during the winter often took him several miles into the forest or surrounding farm lands but he always returned to the territory he was most familiar with - a mix of oak-hickory forest, ecotones, rocky streams, farm ponds and small farms still being worked next to the forest.

Autumn, of course, finds the fox hunting alone. He hunted for himself as well as for his offspring throughout the summer but the juvenile foxes had now been taught to hunt for themselves. His association with them now is only casual and he crosses paths with them

periodically as they establish their own territories. Two of the four have already been killed - one by a bobcat and the other by an automobile as the youngster tried to cross a moonlit highway. In any event, it would appear - speaking again in human terms - as though he prefers the independence he will have until February, when he will find a female and mate again.

Probably, our attention here should focus not on the fox but on the environments in which he lives. His "home" is the deciduous forest biome of North America - an immense area found between the Mississippi River and the Atlantic Ocean. It was once said that a squirrel could climb to the top of a tree at the edge of the Mississippi River and travel to the shore of the Atlantic without touching the ground. It is doubtful that this happened but, most certainly, the squirrel would have had to come to the ground rarely.

Today, the squirrel couldn't even come close to making the journey through the tree tops. Still, there are areas left where one can look out from high ground, over a spectacle of tree tops and a sea of leaves that reach as far as the eye can see. Mostly, the forest has been harvested and re-harvested and, in places, the land cleared for agriculture. Some of the farmlands have since been abandoned but numerous family farms still exist and are tilled in a number of different ways. At the edges of these farms where the forest is more or less mature, grows an "edge community" composed of hardwood trees and "pioneer trees" such as sassafras and persimmon. The edge community is a thick and, in places, seemingly impenetrable margin of woody plants. This woodland community is called an ecotone by the ecologist - a place where different living systems meet and intermingle.

Our fox, then, interacts with a number of sharply different environments. In fact, it is the nature of this diversity that helps this animal survive. The intermingling of the living systems creates environments which produce a vast array of energy sources for the fox. As we have already seen, the fox may hunt an abandoned farm field for mice. It will also pick and eat strawberries, wild grapes, blackberries and other fruit as it ripens. It will dig through the snow under fruit trees in orchards for apples. Insects as well as frogs and turtle eggs make up a substantial part of his diet during warm weather. Carrion in the form of dead wildlife or livestock is used quite often, particularly in the cooler seasons of the year. The diet of the fox is an opportunistic one - whatever is available and palatable, regardless of the source, will be used as food.

The fox can use the forest itself as sanctuary against packs of coyotes and wild dogs. It can place its den in the forest, in the thick growth of the ecotone, or even out in an abandoned field in a reconditioned burrow left by a groundhog. The fox is definitely an animal of mixed environments and does very well in them, unlike some other mammals who need one particular kind of environment. When we consider the vast differences that exist between forests, fields, farm ponds, streams, and ecotones we begin to see the tremendous capacity the red fox has for adapting. Its role in the environment - its niche - is a very broad one and its survival (when sought after by hunters, trappers, coyotes, feral dogs, eagles, bobcats and other predators) is almost as amazing as the diversity within which it lives.

Patterns, Patterns, and More Patterns

"Patterns of life" - a major theme in ecology. Whether small communities of plants and animals interacting in a fallen log, or a temporary pool of water on a forest floor, or huge ecosystems covering much of the earth's surface such as the marine ecosystems, patterns of life dominate this planet.

The photographs that you will see early in this chapter and accompanying prose are presented for you to serve as an advance organizer for what is to follow. This section should help focus your attention on ecological concepts such as, *biosphere, biomes, ecosystem, community, interactions, energy flow, population dynamics*. It will also give you a pictorial reference that you can return to over and over again if need be. What appears on these pages is, to a great extent, a major theme in ecology - patterns of life on the planet Earth.

A word of caution is needed here, however. We do give names to ecosystems. We might call a place in Florida where pine trees grow far apart a *savanna*. This is a perfectly good name for a pattern of life because *savannas* are typically places where trees grow widely scattered with grass growing between them. Sometimes there are islands of trees surrounded by the grasses such as the historic oak savannas of northeastern Illinois. Sometimes the trees are widely interspersed with the grasses such as on the Serengeti in Tanzania. However, if you stepped into what we often call a *Florida pine flatwoods* you might think it a pine forest - some people do. Or, you might see some grasses among the other shrubs and call it a *pine savanna* - some people do. What, then, is the point? The point is simply that the names of patterns are arbitrary. They are arbitrary for us and quite often for the ecologist as well. Still, this, in no way, makes them any less important. Names of patterns allow us to identify most of them and talk about all of them. Even though we might disagree as to where a *coniferous forest* ends and a *tundra* begins, we still find the names for these patterns extremely helpful.

The writer has taken some liberties early in this chapter, in an attempt to make the concepts easier for you. For example, the notion of "pattern" has been simplified, perhaps to excess. Many kinds of "patterns" exist. Some plant and animal interactions are rather small and might be called *microcommunities*; some larger ones are seen only in terms of the animal and plant populations present and might be called *communities*; still others would include the plants, the animals, and the nonliving factors and use the term *ecosystem*; and some would take into account combinations of similar, yet different, ecosystems and call these *biomes*. It all depends upon on who is doing the looking, i.e., how the observer views the different patterns. We will clean up the meaning of all of these terms for you as you progress through this book. In the meantime, if you can, look upon the patterns represented here with the awe that arises when one realizes the dynamic complexities that exist within each.

Deciduous Forest

The vast oak-hickory forests of eastern North America have, in large part, been replaced by farms or by second growth forests. Even so, it is still possible to find some splendid stretches of hardwood forests in Illinois, Missouri, Indiana and elsewhere in the midwest. Some of these are in the Shawnee National Forest in southern Illinois where this photograph was taken. Here we find magnificent oaks, a variety of hickories, dogwood, sweet gum, sycamore, scattered walnut trees, black cherry, etc. Living here on the forest floor can also be found a wide variety of plants and animals. This splendid array would include the DeKay's snake often found in decaying logs, the blusher mushroom found with decaying vegetation, and the catbird which often nests in the shrubs of the forest. *Photos courtesy H. R. Hungerford.*

Tropical Rain Forest

Tropical rain forest ecosystems are found in many parts of the globe. The vastness of this wet pattern has been diminished due to deforestation in Asia, South America and elsewhere. Even so, many thousands of acres remain. The rain forest photo on this page was taken on what is commonly referred to as the "big island" in the state of Hawaii, namely the island of Hawaii.

The rain forest is usually characterized by very tall trees and a great deal of diversity with much of the life of the forest living in the canopy or the upper reaches of the trees themselves. The tree ferns seen here inhabit the rain forest in Hawaii Volcanoes National Park on Hawaii. The spectacular jungle fowl did not originate in Hawaii but they did on other continents that have rain forests.

Grasslands

Grasslands are among the most fascinating of all of the patterns of life. Across North America, from east to west, are found tallgrass prairies, midgrass prairies, and shortgrass prairies controlled largely by rainfall. Grasslands support amazing numbers of plants and animals, particularly in the eastern parts of their range where the tall grass prairies once dominated the landscape. The bison and prairie dogs seen here were photographed in western Oklahoma on a midgrass prairie.

The main photograph on this page was taken in east central Illinois in late summer. The tall lavender colored plants are blazing star. This species is joined by a variety of grasses and other flowering plants. Some of the grasses on this tallgrass prairie (e.g., big bluestem) grow taller than a tall man can stand. These spectacular grasses gave rise to the term "sea of grass" because, in pioneer days when there were millions of acres of tall grasslands, the "sea" seemed to undulate in huge waves, driven by the winds that coursed over the prairie.

Photos courtesy H. R. Hungerford.

Swamps

We usually think of swamps as tropical in nature. Often they are. However, there are also temperate swamps as well. The aerial view to the left is of the Larue Swamp in southern Illinois. This swamp is rapidly filling in due to the tremendous amount of vegetation that it supports. Each year tons of organic matter fall to the bottom to decompose and a new layer of soil is formed. However, during its existence as a pattern of life, it supports an amazing variety of plants and animals, some of which are unique to the area.

The other scene (above) is of the famous Corkscrew Swamp near Immokalee, Florida. As with the Larue Swamp, it is a very rich ecosystem. Corkscrew is famous for its orchids and bromeliads. Among its many other residents are the endangered wood stork and alligator.

Photo courtesy H. R. Hungerford

22

Alpine-Subalpine

The San Juan Mountains of southern Colorado are some of the most spectacular in the United States. Few roads penetrate the wilderness portion of these mountains. When one approaches the tree line, two patterns emerge. One is the sub-alpine ecosystem where spruce trees are fairly common and rugged bristle cone pines are sometimes found. Here, in late summer, the flowering plants put on a wonderful display. They are joined by ptarmigans, hummingbirds, marmots, rock rabbits, and other less obvious animals.

Above the tree line the environment takes on a very rugged appearance where no trees can survive and only a handful of hardy flowering plants such as the alpine spring beauty (above) grow close to the ground. This is the alpine biome which can be found in the United States at the very tops of the highest mountains.

Photo courtesy H. R. Hungerford.

Marine

The oceans of planet earth are as varied as any kind of life pattern. From the tropical seas of the Atlantic and Pacific to the oceans at the poles and beyond we find astounding plant and animal ecosystems. On this page we see where a coniferous forest meets the sea in the state of Washington. The marine environment here is a tidal flat which, of course, is very rich in marine life. Of interest are also the sand-dominated environments (beaches) so popular with swimmers and beach-combers. Here we often find the threatened or endangered animals and plants which are part of, or live very close to, the sea. And from the sea comes food for millions of human beings. Shrimp, oysters, clams, crabs, lobsters, squid, scallops, and fish like the grouper seen here are just part of this harvest.

The Savanna

The savanna is an interesting pattern of life and not as uncommon as one might imagine. There are savannas in North and South America as well as Africa and elsewhere. A savanna is characterized by widely scattered trees interspersed with grass. The huge savanna which is pictured on this page is the very famous one in Kenya and Tanzania known as the Serengeti.

Often, the savanna is characterized by large hoofed animals and those carnivores that feed on these plant eaters. Nowhere is this better illustrated than on the Serengeti with its huge herds of zebras, wildebeests, gazelles, and smaller mammals which serve as food sources for lions, leopards, cheetahs, hyenas, and other predators as well as the many scavengers that live there.

Sonoran Desert

The "desert" is simply a pattern of life controlled by a lack of available water. Some deserts are hot but some can also be found in cold climates where precipitation is a limiting factor.

Sometimes called a cactus "forest", giant saguaro cacti dominate the Sonoran Desert ecosystem in southwest Arizona and parts of Mexico. The saguaro cactus plus many other cactus species, birds, mammals, insects, reptiles, and even some grasses interact to produce a dynamic desert ecosystem. In this environment are displayed rather amazing plant and animal adaptations to heat and drought. Here one also finds the red-flowering ocotillo, large yuccas, many insects, and birds.

The Sonoran Desert is a famous desert pattern but the huge Chihuahuan Desert of Mexico and West Texas is equally fascinating with some truly spectacular scenery along the Rio Grande River of Texas and Mexico. There, in the remoteness of that region, one can find mountian lions and black bears.

Photos courtesy H. R. Hungerford.

Many millions of years ago huge redwood trees covered much of North America. Today's climate is much different than it was then and this restricts the range of the three existing species of redwoods. This page contains photos from Muir Woods National Monument in California. These particular redwoods are the coast redwoods which need the moisture that is available to them along the coastline of northern California. Muir Woods is one of the stands of the remaining redwoods. This monument is named for John Muir, a noted conservationist of the 19th Century. The redwoods are the tallest living things on earth - one of them in Muir Woods stands over 365 feet. Photo courtesy H. R. Hungerford.

This photo shows another view from within Muir Woods National Monument. In addition to the coast redwoods which are visible in this photo, some of the other variables in this rich and fascinating pattern of life can be viewed. Among the most notable variables are the ferns which grace the banks of this rocky stream. In addition, a host of mosses and lichens grow on any hardwood tree available in this moist environment. This stream - known as Redwood Creek - flows year round and provides moisture for a number of plant and animal species and also a habitat for crayfish, salamanders and fish including salmon which move upstream to spawn during periods of high water during the spawning season. Photo courtesy H. R. Hungerford.

27

The photos on this page were both taken in the Florida Everglades National Park at the southern end of Florida. The Everglades ecosystem has shrunk considerably over time due to agriculture and other forms of human development. Numerous environments can be found in the Park. Included would be mangrove swamps, freshwater marshes, pinelands, shallow marine environments, and hardwood hammocks. In this photo we see pine trees in the distance and, in the foreground, the sawgrass which is very typical in this ecosystem. The pines and the other broad-leaved trees seen in the middle distance are probably growing on a raised "island" only a few inches above the surrounding terrain. The Everglades is a region where mere inches in altitude control the plant communities found there. Photo courtesy H. R. Hungerford.

In the Everglades, an abundance of dwarf cypress trees can be found along with the sawgrass. In places these cypress trees are so successful that they make up what are called dwarf cypress prairies. Some believe that these prairies create a strange - even bizarre - landscape. However, combined with these small trees can be found other plants besides the sawgrass. One might expect to find pickerel weed, arrowhead, and bladderwort among others. Where the water is deeper - or quite deep in limestone solution cavities - one can find small fishes, the large apple snail and other aquatic organisms. This deeper water makes these prairies very important during dry periods because birds and other predators can hunt for food here. Photo courtesy H. R. Hungerford.

Patterns of Life on Earth:
Living Systems

If you have had even limited contact with the science of ecology, you probably have at least an initial, working concept of the living system called an ECOSYSTEM. You probably know, for example, that a naturally-existing ecosystem contains numerous populations of organisms. You might understand that these organisms interact with each other and with abiotic (nonliving) variables. Some of these interactions are competitive and some are not. You may also know that food energy flows through the system and is of critical importance to the ecosystem. And, hopefully, you know that the ecosystem is more or less stable even though the dynamics operating within the system are certainly not static.

However, beyond this initial concept of an ecosystem, you may find it difficult to bring order out of a seemingly endless array of variables. For example, you probably find it difficult to determine where the boundary of one ecosystem ends and another begins. You may have asked yourself whether you could ever grasp the totality of the living systems in the region in which you live - let alone the continent or the world. Yes, it is complex and it may not be of much comfort to know that the professional ecologist would be the first to admit that we know so very little about living systems.

Still, the ecologist does know a great deal about how ecosystems operate and more is being learned every day. Further, lay citizens who are interested in the environment contribute to this body of knowledge constantly. As more knowledge accumulates, new generalizations are stated and old generalizations improved or modified. This is all very good you say, but how does one organize this information into a meaningful format - one that ultimately makes sense to you?

You should have inferred by this time that I am extremely interested in your becoming familiar with the term "ecosystem". This interest stems from the fact that I believe that the ideas associated with this term are of critical importance to both the professional and the lay citizen. Why is this? First of all, the concept of "ecosystem" is manageable. It can be developed fairly quickly and it makes sense. It makes sense because it permits us to look at a living system as a whole - an entity that is self-sustaining (for the most part) and self-contained (for the most part).

> *Ecosystems* have definition in space and time. They are also defined by their species populations which interact with each other and with the abiotic variables so crucial to an ecosystem's characteristics.

It is important to note that, even though the ecosystem is a most useful term, it is also an arbitrary one. It is arbitrary because it can be applied to a number of living systems - both large and small. There may be ecosystems operating within ecosystems! Still, once we have decided on the particular unit or ecosystem we want to look at, we have defined the limits of the system and can get down to the business at hand.

An example might help. In one instance, we might want to look at an entire hardwood forest as the ecosystem unit. Its parameters may be a bit fuzzy but we do have a concept of what constitutes a hardwood forest. This permits us to look at that system as an ecosystem. But, within that forest operate numerous other, small units or subsystems which, themselves, can be referred to as ecosystems. A fallen, rotting log would be one example. A temporary, rain-filled depression could be another. A water-filled tree cavity could be still another. These units or subsystems can be called ecosystems because each has its own species populations and these populations interact with each other and with abiotic variables (as well as with the larger forest ecosystem).

Another term is also prominent with respect to living systems in ecology. This is the term COMMUNITY. The community concept includes only the plant and animal populations and their interactions. Abiotic variables are not considered when using the term "community".

The community concept is a very useful one but not nearly as powerful as the ecosystem simply because the concept of ecosystems deals with living systems in a more holistic manner. However, it should be pointed out that there are times when an individual wants or needs to look at interacting populations without regard to the abiotic variables. When this is the case, the community is ideal.

Actually, what we are looking at here are patterns of life on the planet earth. Many such patterns exist. Further, *these patterns of life exist at different organizational levels*, some relatively simple and some which are very complex. The community is only one such pattern or organizational level.

A subsystem or subcomponent of a community might be the fallen, rotting log. We could term this log a MICROCOMMUNITY - a simpler level of organization. In both instances, however, the community and the microcommunity would be considered as ecosystems once the abiotic variables are considered.

The community and microcommunity organizational levels cannot be used to name all of the patterns of life on the planet. There are still larger patterns. We call these large patterns BIOMES and the BIOSPHERE. There are also smaller patterns. We call these SPECIES POPULATIONS and INDIVIDUAL organisms. Frustrating? Sure! But, right now frustration is a key element in your own pattern of life. However, you will not feel frustrated when such a classification system becomes useful to you. And, you will find it useful!

> **Ecological terms result from arbitrary decisions made by human beings in order to try to bring order out of chaos!**

Certainly, ecological terms are function of arbitrary decisions made by human beings interested in bringing order to the universe of scientific information. Although arbitrary, the decisions are usually logical, i.e., they provide us with a means of communicating information in ecology and a basis for classifying that information. Thinking about classification and communication for a moment should reveal that this is a mechanism that permits us to bring order out of what could be chaos. Try to imagine, then, how much more orderly things would appear if we could somehow classify patterns of life into organizational levels - each one being less complex than the preceding one (or more complex if you wish to reverse the order).

The key terms we will be dealing with in this chapter can be thusly arranged - diagrammed to help organize your thinking. Such a diagram is found on the following page. Needless to say, you are not expected to have a handle to each of these terms right now. However, you will find it extremely useful to keep referring back to this diagram as you proceed. Please do so.

The Planet Earth : Organizational Levels

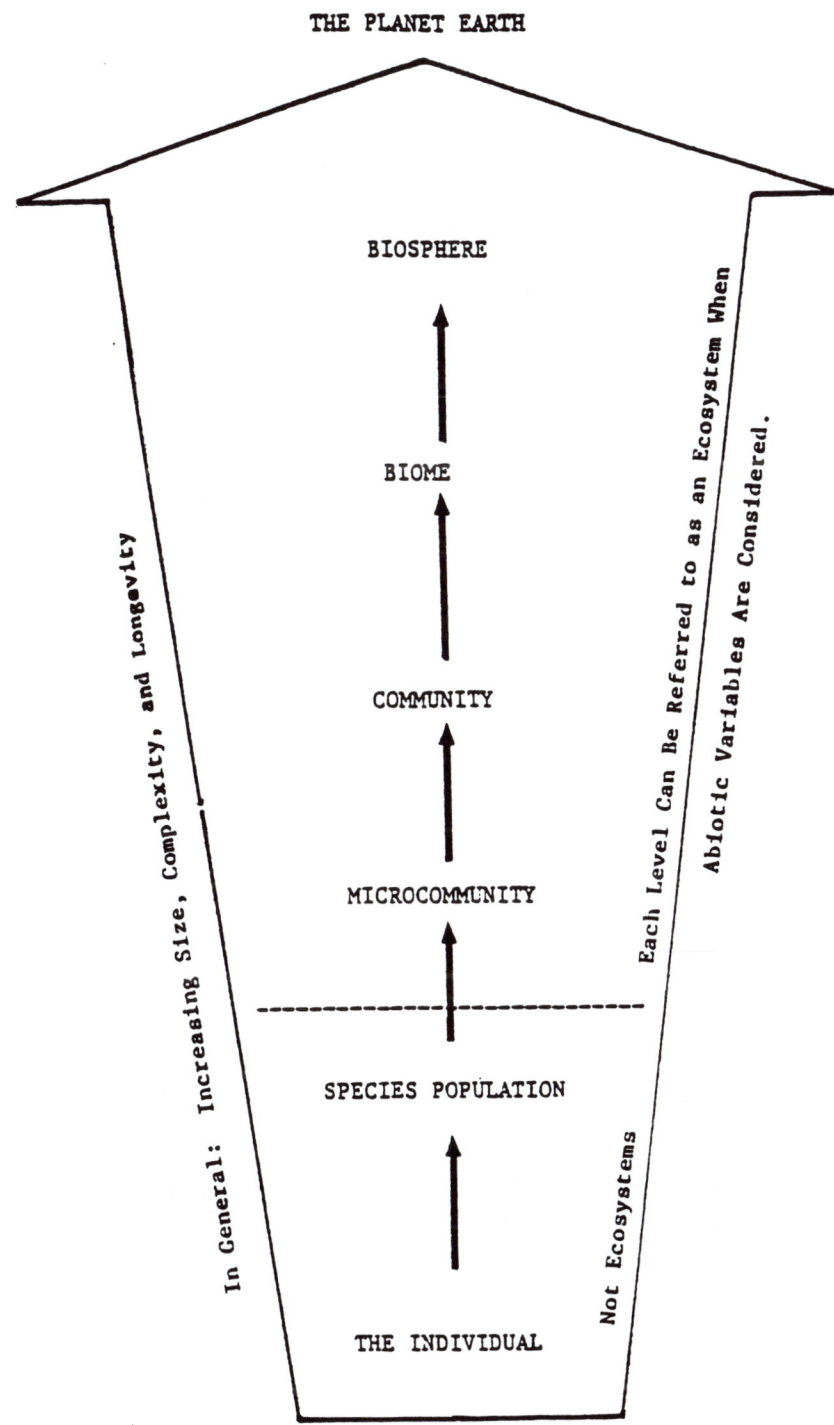

A schematic diagram of increasing levels of organizational complexity in the biosphere. All of the organizational levels or patterns of life are interrelated. Further, these organizational levels exist along a continuum and do not function as separate and autonomous entities.

The Biosphere

The earth as a habitat for living things is highly restricted in its ability to provide homes for plants and/or animals. You think not? Let's look at a few numbers.

The earth is 12,756 kilometers in diameter (about 8,000 miles). From this figure, estimate the average width, in kilometers, of the region around the earth which contains abundant life. Would you say 50 kilometers? Just what *is* your estimate?

How high up a mountain would you expect to find abundant life? Mt. Everest is only about 10 kilometers high. How abundant would life be on the peak of Mt. Everest? Why do you think so? Almost all of the earth's atmosphere lies below 30 kilometers (about 20 miles). How much of this height is suitable for life?

The greatest ocean depth on earth is only 11 kilometers. How much life would you expect to find there? Why?

Now, if you assume that most life forms exist below the elevation of Mt. Everest (10 kilometers) and somewhere above the deepest ocean (11 kilometers) you will wind up with a shell or a layer of life somewhere around 20 kilometers in width. More importantly, most ecosystems will be found in a shell of less than 2 kilometers in width. Certainly there are deep sea life forms, and there are organisms that can live at high altitudes. However, their numbers are minuscule compared to those that simply cannot survive in harsh abiotic conditions.

All of this means that **most life forms are restricted to a very small and unique layer on the planet earth**. This layer or shell surrounding the earth in which living things can successfully survive is called the BIOSPHERE. One can easily infer that life exists only where conditions are suitable. The variables that permit life to be successful are, in actuality, restricted to that area within the biosphere. And, when you consider the depth of the biosphere compared to the diameter of the earth you must realize that life is much more tenuous than most human beings believe.

> **Biosphere - The layer or shell surrounding the earth in which living things can successfully survive.**

Scientists have some very interesting perspectives about the biosphere. One of these is the theory that all interactions taking place in the biosphere are somehow interrelated. This theory is based on numerous observations of interrelationships existing across smaller ecosystems - some interrelationships that are quite direct and some which are indirect. If you stop and think about it, you will probably conclude that this theory has frightening implications for man.

The biosphere is definitely narrow and delicately balanced. However, with regard to known methods of scientific investigation, it is eminently difficult to study. Therefore, ecologists often turn to a smaller pattern of living systems.

Biomes

As one views the biosphere in its entirety he or she sees an astounding diversity of life. From the sparse deserts of northern Africa to the lush tropical rain forests of central America, one notes a profusion of varying life forms. At first, the same scene appears quite chaotic. However, a person attempting to bring some semblance of order out of this confusing situation would be able to identify some patterns of life which indicate order in the biosphere.

Biome - A major unit within the biosphere which typically contains a uniform type of vegetation.

Ecologists, too, in an attempt to make sense out of the distribution of living systems, have set about to classify the biosphere into functional units. These units are extremely large and complex. Each unit is individually represented by a *major ecosystem.* In these major ecosystems, the unit is usually represented by a *uniform type of vegetation.* Put another way, *the unit contains a similar array of living systems.* These units are called BIOMES.

The scientists who map biomes are called biogeographers. It is the business of biogeographers to determine the extent and boundaries of biomes. Interestingly, all biogeographers are not in agreement as to the exact dimensions and types of biomes found in the world. The same holds true for the United States as well. Precision in this field is difficult but, by the same token, any responsible classification of biomes is helpful in breaking the biosphere up into more manageable units.

Below you will find a simplified biome distribution map for mainland United States. The marine biome has been excluded from this map and we find that there are five terrestrial (land-based) biomes represented there.

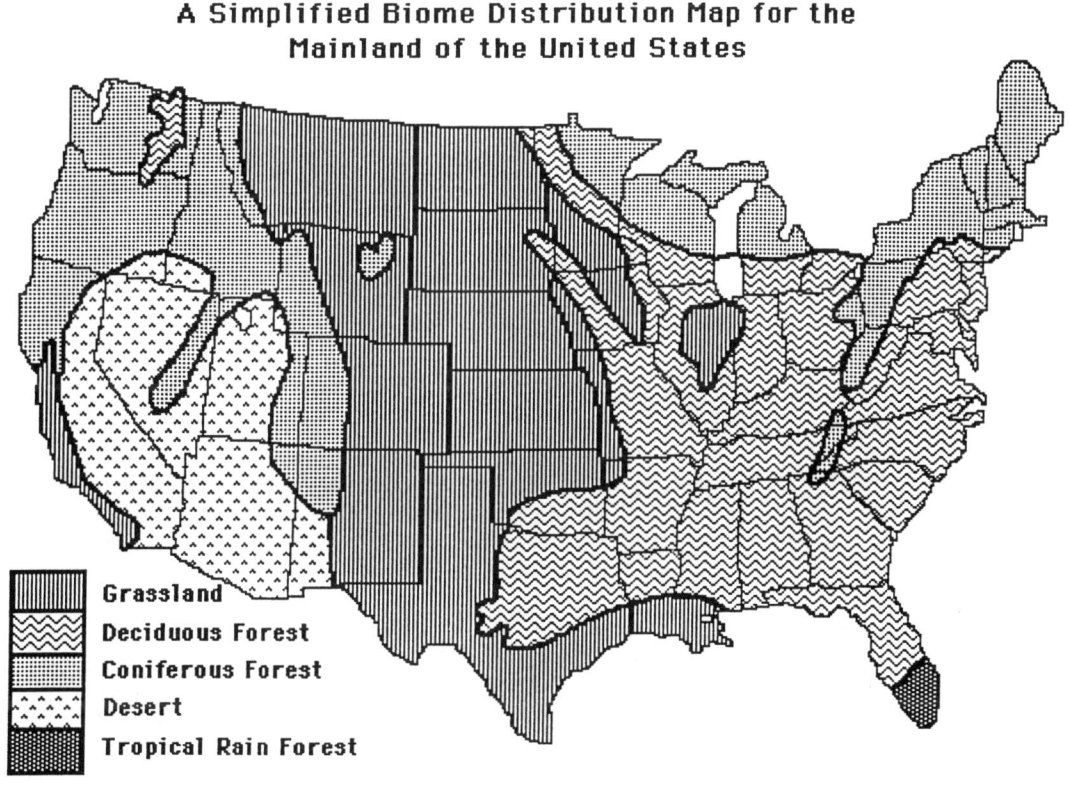

A Simplified Biome Distribution Map for the Mainland of the United States

Grassland
Deciduous Forest
Coniferous Forest
Desert
Tropical Rain Forest

33

Let's take a brief look at North American terrestrial biomes and some of the characteristics of each. The chart below includes the tundra biome which will not be found on the map on the previous page. Even so, it might be helpful to refer back to the map while reading the information that follows.

Typical Terrestrial Biomes of
The United States(Excluding Hawaii) and Southern Canada

U.S. Biome	VEGETATIVE TYPE	OTHER CHARACTERISTICS
Deciduous Forest	Deciduous trees such as oak, maple, beech, hickory, and tulip poplar.	Found in temperate regions where precipitation exceeds evaporation. Rainfall will normally range from 90-100 cm per year. One of the typical biomes of the Eastern U.S.
Grassland	A variety of grasses depending on location. Other herbs are also numerous.	Found in temperate regions where evaporation exceeds precipitation but where annual rainfall is still extensive enough to support grasses (30 - 90 cm/year).
Desert	Cacti, shrubs, sparse grasses, other herbs.	Found in a variety of temperature extremes. Both cool and hot deserts occur in the U.S. The key variable seems to be annual precipitation (20 - 30 cm/year).
Coniferous Forest	Larch, spruce, and fir.	Found in northern climates or areas that represent northern climate variables. The temperature is usually colder than for the deciduous forest and precipitation is moderate. The coniferous forest biome stretches in a band several hundred km wide across all North America (mostly in Canada). This biome dips down into the U.S. in mountainous regions.
Tundra	Lichen, grasses, sedges, dwarf willow, and cranberry.	The tundra stretches across North America. in a wide band north of the coniferous forest biome. The tundra biome can also be found on high mountain peaks in lower latitudes. The tundra climate is cold, rigorous and has a very short growing season.
Tropical Rain Forest	A variety of tall trees with large numbers of climbing plants. In Florida one can expect to find plants represented by the cabbage palm, cypress, strangler fig, pop ash, custard apple, and swamp maple.	The tropical rain forest is found in the continental U.S. only in the southern tip of Florida. However, it is a common in Central and South America. The rain forest is found in regions of mild winters, high temperatures, and heavy rainfall (+ 110 cm/yearly).

It is obvious that climate is a key variable in the distribution of biomes. Further, annual precipitation is of immense importance in helping determine the distribution of biomes. Temperature is another key variable. However, in many instances, temperature and precipitation are interrelated variables and work in consort to help control the distribution of biomes.

The Effects of Temperature and Rainfall on the Development of Ecosystems

Rainfall in Centimeters

Northern Coniferous Forest Example: The spruce forests of Canada and Alaska	**Temperate Deciduous Forest** Example: The oak-hickory forests of the Midwest	**Tropical Rainforest** Example: The rainforest of Central and South America
Cold Grassland Example: The Arctic tundra	**Temperate Grassland** Example: The tall, mid, and short grass prairies of North America	**Tropical Grassland** Example: The tropical savannas of East Africa
Cool Desert Example: The Gobi Desert of Asia	**Temperate Desert** Example: The Sonoran Desert of North America	**Tropical Desert** Example: The Sahara Desert of North Africa

120
110
100
90
80
70
60
50
40
30
20
10
0

Temperature

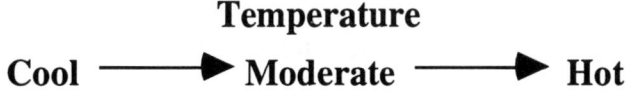

Cool ⟶ Moderate ⟶ Hot

Although there are many exceptions to the rule - and one of the exceptions is the United States - biomes tend to change in broad bands from the equator to the poles. An attempt to diagram these changes for the northern hemisphere is presented below.

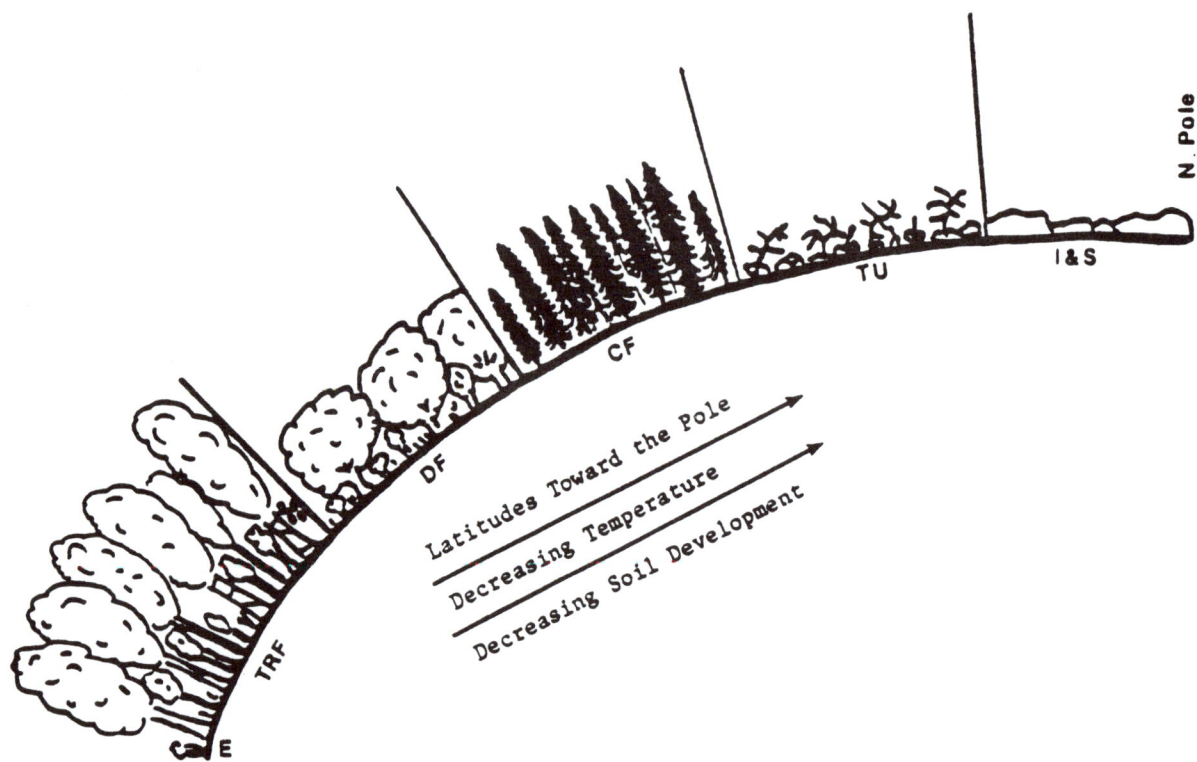

A generalized diagram showing the changing biomes as one proceeds from the Equator to the North Pole. Associated variables are also shown on the diagram. Key: TRS = Tropical Rain Forest; DF = Deciduous Forest; CF = Coniferous Forest; TU = Tundra; I&S = Ice and Snow.

Initially, one might think that biomes would be found in broad bands running east and west across the United States. However, this is far from the way things are. In the United States there are a number of variables that keep this generalization from being absolutely true. Why is the United States so different? These differences are largely a function of variables that influence precipitation. The deciduous forest biome of the eastern, southern, and midwestern United States is largely a function of the precipitation brought in from the Atlantic and northward from the Gulf of Mexico. The grasslands biome to the west is largely a function of decreasing precipitation. In fact, as one travels west through this biome he or she can observe grass plants becoming shorter and shorter. Decreasing moisture mandates that short grass species replace those taller grass species to the east. Not only do the grasses become shorter, they become sparser, i.e., greater and greater distances occur between members of the population. As spacing becomes pronounced, new plants appear and, in the Southwest, the grasslands eventually change into desert. This desert stretches to California and, again, this is largely a function of precipitation.

You may wonder why moisture cannot move eastward from the Pacific Ocean. If it did, perhaps the desert regions would not exist. Moisture does, in fact move eastward from the Pacific. However, as the moist air moves eastward over California, it comes in contact with tall mountains. In order to move over the mountains, the moist air must rise. As the air rises, it cools. Cool air cannot hold as much moisture as warm air. Soon the air becomes so chilled that the moisture is lost as precipitation (rain or snow). Thus, the mountains provide what is called a "rain shadow". One side of the mountain range is wet and the other side is desert. This phenomenon is diagrammed below.

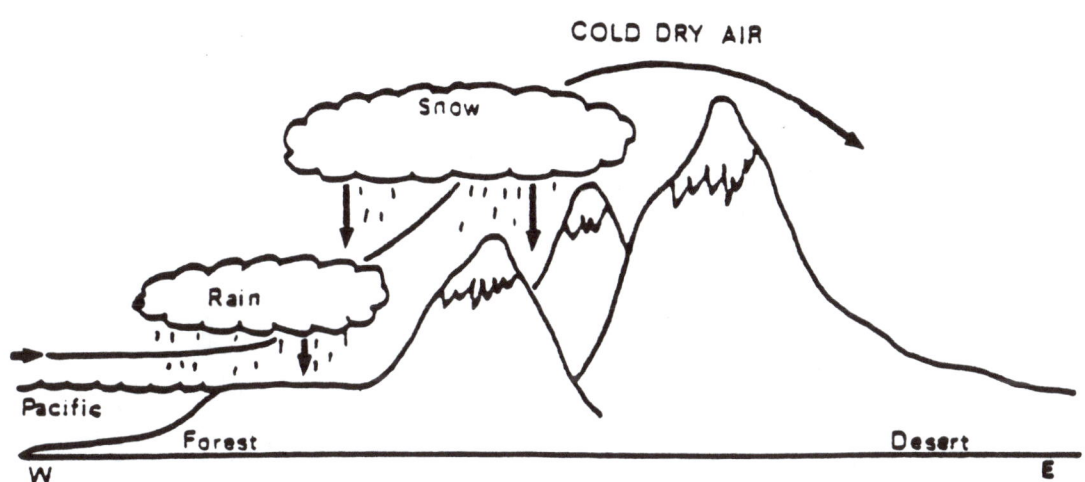

The Rain Shadow Phenomenon

The variables described above, along with many others, make the North America biome picture complex. However, it becomes more complex when one looks carefully at a particular biome. Suddenly it becomes obvious that things may not be all that orderly! It is apparent that the desert is not all desert - the deciduous forest is not all hardwood trees - the coniferous forest not all conifers - the prairie not all waving fields of grass. What is the bog doing in the Michigan forest? What is the slough doing on the Dakota prairie? What is the swamp doing in the Illinois deciduous forest? What are the Everglades doing in the Florida tropical rain forest biome?

No, all is not simple and as orderly as you might like! A diversity of smaller ecosystems thrives in every biome. It is a matter of living systems within living systems - each system with its own unique characteristics - each available for study in a particular way. Even though we might find it frustrating in our effort to sort out the pieces, it is probably this very diversity that promotes the integrity (survival) of the entire biosphere. And, this is an idea that we tend to forget.

The Community Concept

Community - An organizational unit which includes plant and animal populations and their interactions within a specified area or region.

Thus far in this chapter we have dealt with some very large ecological patterns, the biosphere and the biome. If you are still concerned about the immensity of these terms you are probably in good company. Ecologists have found it useful to refer to a smaller, more manageable pattern. That pattern is the COMMUNITY. (As noted earlier, when the community is considered along with the abiotic variables involved, the concept once again becomes that of the ecosystem).

If we were to take a late spring walk together down a country road in - say southern Illinois, southern Indiana, or western Kentucky, we might see a number of different environments. Knowing that we were in the deciduous forest biome, we would be on the lookout for a forest of hardwood trees and some of its associated organisms. There it is! Large oaks and hickories dominate the scene with wild cherry, flowering dogwood, and red bud growing around and beneath the oaks and hickories. A catbird flies from the branches of the wild cherry tree to a woody shrub. Two male cardinals cry out to each other as they communicate nesting territories. A squirrel races across brown leaves on the forest floor and up a black oak tree. A millipede slowly travels the surface of a rotting log and takes a detour around a slug tracking "slime" across a blanket of lichens. The forest is truly a magnificent ecological system.

A bit further down the road we come to a large field which has been cleared from the forest and planted to alfalfa. The alfalfa is in bloom and bumble bees are flying to and from the flowering plants. A meadowlark sings from a fence post and a cottontail rabbit peers at us from the edge of the alfalfa.

The field has a rolling topography. At one side of the field, at the end of a short valley-like feature, a farmer has constructed an earthen dam. Behind this dam is a large farm pond which is used for watering livestock. The edge of the pond bristles with cattails and a red-winged blackbird cries its lusty "Kong-ka-ree" from the top of last year's seed head. A muskrat swims from the cattails to a den inside the dam, while dozens of dragonflies fly back and forth over the pond seeking out gnats and mosquitoes.

Over the next hill we come to another field, one that once was farmed but is now abandoned. It appears to have been abandoned less than twenty years or so because we can see tall grasses and other herbs growing amidst sassafras, persimmon, and smooth sumac trees. A black snake crosses the road in front of us and enters the field. A white-tailed deer looks at us intently from a distance. There is a good chance that she has a fawn hidden close by. An indigo bunting perches on the telephone wires next to the field and a rather rare blue-winged warbler flies from tree to tree looking, perhaps, for insects.

All of this in the deciduous forest biome? Absolutely! And much, much more!

As we look back on our walk we recall that each one of these areas - the forest, the alfalfa field, the pond, and the abandoned field - had its own individuality - its own integrity if you prefer. Each had its own particular populations of plants. Each had its own populations of animals. These plant and animal populations interact, are interdependent, and contribute heavily to each other's survival. Each one of these separate ecological units we will call a community -- each one functions in the deciduous forest biome.

In defining a community, we must take several things into consideration including the idea that a community is an association of plant and animal populations that occurs naturally in a given area. Further, these populations are interactive and interdependent. In addition, the populations contribute to each other's survival.

Another very important characteristic of a community is that its populations are all tied into energy exchanges. Some populations collect as well as consume energy, some only consume energy, and all dissipate energy. Energy exchanges in a community result in abundant deaths of individuals and the replacement of lost members, usually by reproduction. This, of course, results in fluctuating population densities. In many communities, population densities also vary due to immigration and/or emigration. And, too, populations will fluctuate greatly due to seasonal and other environmental influences.

This, then, is the community. In review, you will see that the major variables in the community are the *interacting populations of plants and animals*. And, all other things being equal, the key to the continuance of the community is *energy*.

Here we look down at the top (canopy) of a small portion of the deciduous forest biome in North America. This particular scene is of an oak-hickory ecosystem in Union County, Illinois. It very likely represents what most of the eastern part of the United States looked like two centuries ago. Looking at this scene reminds one of a familiar and popular historical concept concerning the deciduous forest in North America - that being that a squirrel could climb to the top of an oak tree on the bank of the Mississippi River and travel to the Atlantic Ocean without ever touching the ground.

The community in turn is influenced by and influences a large number of abiotic variables. Such variables as topography, soil type, insolation, available minerals, moisture, precipitation, and temperature weigh heavily on the stability of the community. Therefore, it is highly appropriate to consider the abiotic variables when studying interacting populations of organisms. Doing so allows us to view the entire ecological system - the ecosystem.

39

The numbers of organisms in a given community can be staggering, particularly if you take into consideration the microscopic organisms (e.g., bacteria of decay) as well as the macroscopic organisms. Populations, in some instances, are literally uncountable and estimates of numbers can be open to considerable error. In a given community, there can be hundreds of different plant species, hundreds of animal species, and a myriad of microscopic organisms (protists). The interesting thing here is that each organism is found in an environment that is suited to its survival. This environment is called the **habitat** of that organism

> **Habitat - Refers to where an organism lives; includes the immediate environment of that organism with both biotic and abiotic variables.**

Thus, the habitat is where the organism lives. It includes the immediate environment of that organism with both biotic and abiotic variables entering the picture.

As you probably already know, the habitats needed by different organisms may differ considerably. This can be true even among species which are closely related. In some instances where an organism's habitat is restricted or modified the organism becomes extinct. This is because many organisms are unable to adjust rapidly to new or changing environmental conditions. This is probably one of the reasons for the extinction of the passenger pigeon, the eastern woods bison and numerous other organisms. If a particular habitat is severely restricted, any organism that is adapted specifically to it is very susceptible to the activities of man or major natural catastrophe. Both of these variables, for example, threaten the last remaining wild population of whooping cranes. Man has severely restricted the habitat available for the whoopers. Its wintering habitat of coastal, salt water marshes is now restricted largely to a small area on the gulf coast of Texas (Aransas National Wildlife Refuge). Wildlife biologists are greatly concerned that a major storm could decimate the wintering, breeding pairs - or, that a major oil slick could critically modify the environment needed by the crane.

The concept of habitat goes further than being related to the overall community. Habitats differ within communities so that different organisms are found in different parts of the ecosystem. Again, the variables associated with this phenomenon are both living and nonliving. This diversity of habitats within the ecosystems will soon be discussed when we look at the different components of a deciduous forest ecosystem.

Sometimes, beginning ecology students become a bit confused with where an organism *lives* in the community and what the organism *does* in the community. What the organisms does or its role in the community is called its NICHE. The niche, then, refers to the organism's function in the community. It is the sum total of its interactions in the ecosystem. Because an organism's role is so closely related to producing or consuming food energy , niches are often related to this variable.

Some organisms are said to have food producing niches (e.g., trees, shrubs, and herbs), some are said to have herbivore niches (e.g. plant lice, grasshoppers, deer, and rabbits), and some are said to have carnivore niches (e.g., owls, lions, bull snakes, and lizards), some are said to have scavenger niches (e.g., vultures and millipedes), some are said to have decomposer niches (e.g., decay bacteria and mushrooms), etc.. The concept of energy-related niches is perfectly alright except it doesn't go quite far enough. An organism's niche would also involve the space it occupies, the type and location of habitat, and all other interactions taking place between it and its habitat.

N iche - refers to an organism's function in the community.

Ecologists have collected evidence to indicate that no two organisms can occupy the same niche in a community for a extended period of time. When two organisms appear to occupy the same niche in the same community they will, upon inspection, be found to have differences in one or more elements of their environmental interactions. This is a very difficult concept for some beginning ecology students to grasp but it is a key concept in the field of ecology.

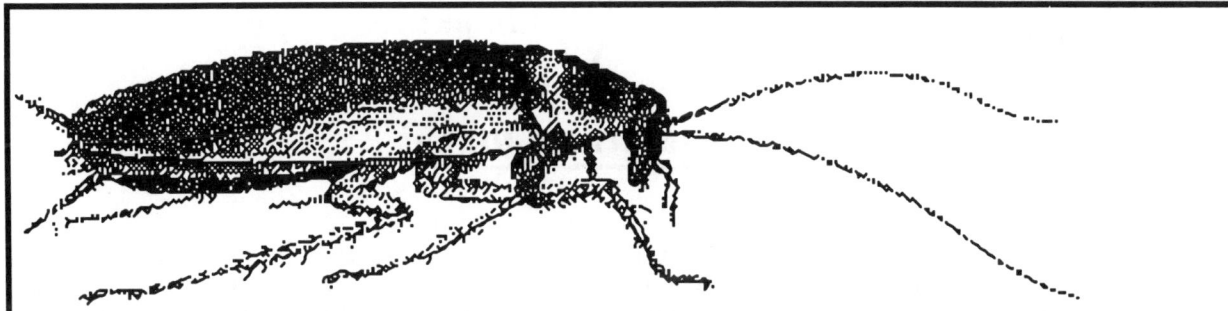

A cockroach. Interestingly, all animals and plants - even cockroaches - have discrete roles in ecological systems. These roles are called niches. Given the definition of "niche", how might you describe the one of the common household cockroach?

41

Generalized vs Specialized Niches: Some Examples

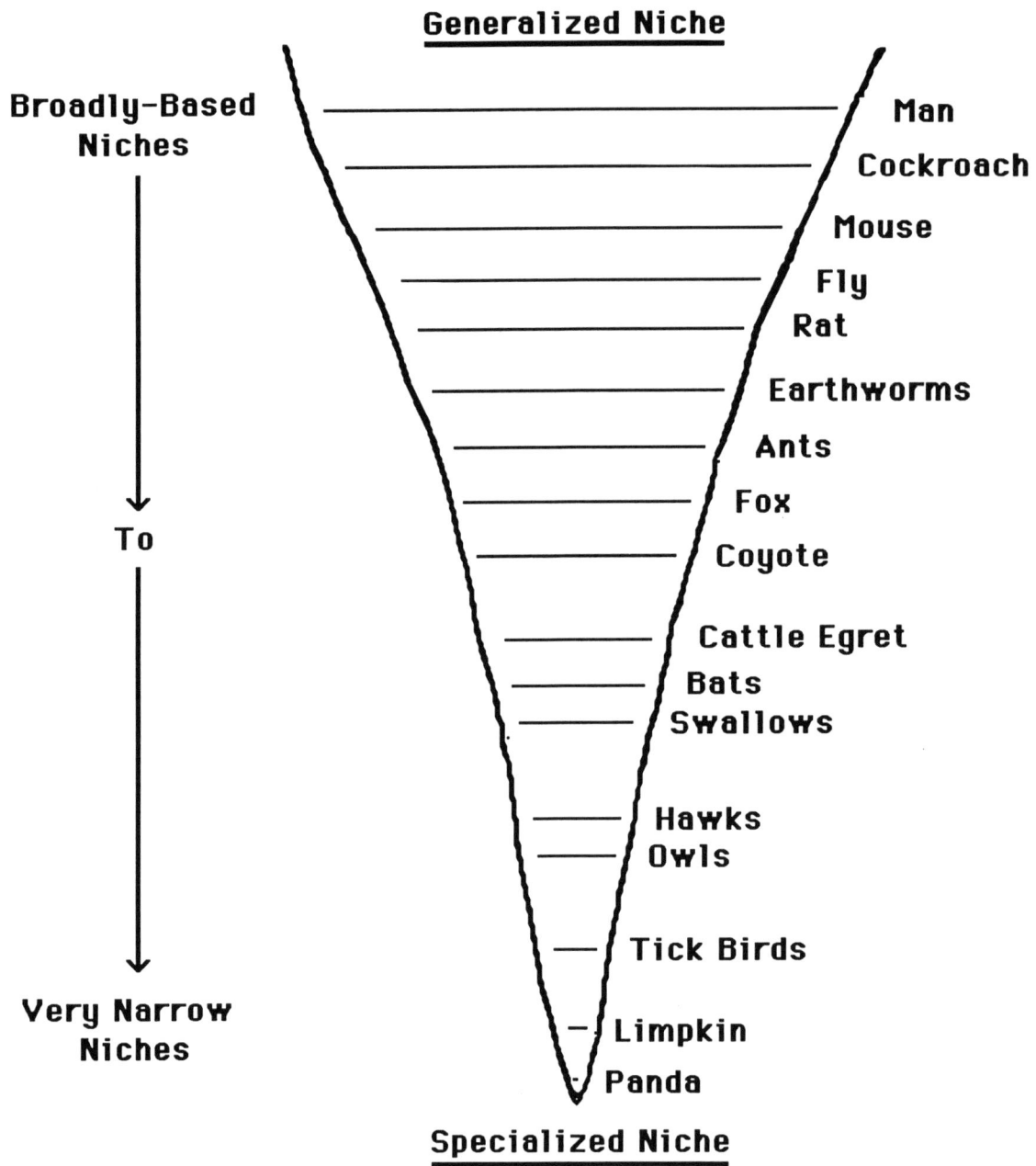

Generalized Niche

Broadly-Based Niches

To

Very Narrow Niches

Man
Cockroach
Mouse
Fly
Rat
Earthworms
Ants
Fox
Coyote
Cattle Egret
Bats
Swallows
Hawks
Owls
Tick Birds
Limpkin
Panda

Specialized Niche

The niche is thought of as an organism's role in the ecosystem as well as where it fits in the space-time dimensions. In theory, each organism's niche is characterized by such things as its required living space, climatic tolerances, food needs, etc. When you stop and think about it, it becomes obvious that some organisms are adapted to very specialized (narrow) niches and some to very broad ones. This has dramatic implications for the organism and its survival in an ecological sense. The above figure attempts to illustrate niches that exist along a continuum from very specialized to very broad.

The Species Population

Communities are patterns of life organized from interacting groups of organisms. These groups themselves represent a pattern of life called SPECIES POPULATIONS. A species population may be defined as a group of individuals of the same kind, living together in a particular space at a particular time. To define a specific population, we must not only identify its type, but its space and time as well. For example, a species population might be the

> **Species population - A group of individuals of the same kind, living together in a particular space at a particular time.**

skunks in a specific Indiana deciduous forest during the summer of 1993. Or it could refer to the red oak seedlings or shagbark hickories in that same forest and year.

Species populations are more than just groups - they are systems as well, and have characteristics of their own. These will be dealt with in greater detail in a later chapter, but a brief summary of these characteristics might be helpful.

One important characteristic is the number of individuals in the population . . . not only the total number in the population, but the ratio of individuals compared to available space. This latter measurement is called POPULATION DENSITY. For example, knowing that there are 100 skunks in a southern Indiana deciduous forest in the summer of 1993 describes one characteristic of the skunk population. This might be made more meaningful if we knew the density of skunks per km^2 of the forest. In addition to geographical space, time, and size (population density), species populations also have characteristics such as birth rates, death rates, emigration rates and immigration rates. These characteristics interact to maintain the integrity of the species population system and cause the population to function as a unit in and of itself.

Population density involves plants as well as animals. In this ohia forest on the island of Hawaii, the ecologist might be interested in determining the number of mature ohia trees per hectare. Knowing this population density might provide a clue as to the overall health of the ecosystem. Furthermore, the forest seen in this photograph is also an official bird sanctuary. A number of threatened and endangered birds are very dependent on the ohia forest. Photo courtesy H.R. Hungerford.

The species population, as a organizational pattern in ecology, has tremendous implications not only for itself but for the larger pattern within which it functions. A population of white-tail deer associated with the oak-hickory forest has its own set of internal dynamic relationships--that is, individuals interact with each other. Further, this population has a set of dynamic relationships with the rest of the forest community. And, too, all other biotic and abiotic variables in the forest system relate back to the deer. The white-tail deer population is simply a part of the forest ecosystem including all of the associated interrelationships. One can diagram these interrelationships as seen here. This figure provides only a simplified schematic representation of some of the interrelationships that are possible. In actuality, the white-tail deer is noted for traveling to and from a number of different ecosystems, e.g., the mature forest, immature forest, a marsh, or a pond. It is easy to see that identifying the sum total of all interrelationships possible would be a most difficult, if not impossible, task. This, however, does not

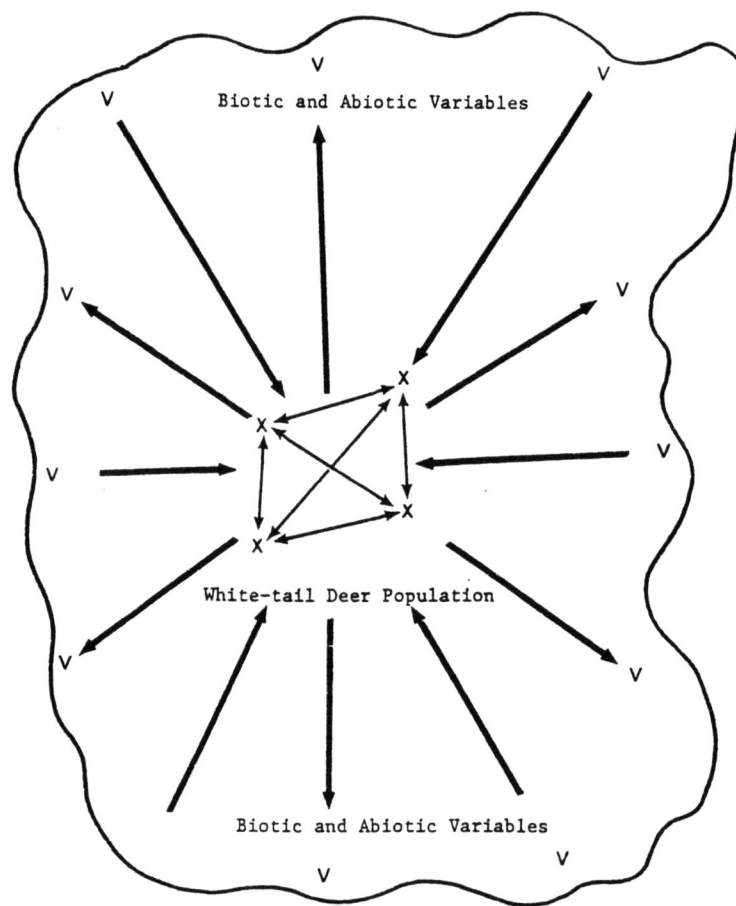

This figure is an attempt to diagram a few of the interrelationships that take place between deer and the greater ecosystem. The small box in the center represents interactions within the deer herd itself. Arrows leading away from and to the box represent interrelationships with other variables (V) in the environment. Thus, this species population experiences dynamics within itself, and between it and both biotic and abiotic variables in the larger ecosystem.

diminish the importance of the species population. Instead, it tends to reflect not only its importance but the complexity of the dynamics involved as well.

A Look at a Deciduous Forest Community/Ecosystem

Because the deciduous forest biome is so extensive in North America it is appropriate to look at a deciduous forest ecosystem as an example of both the community and the ecosystem. The particular forest ecosystem described in this section is an oak-hickory forest located in the Midwest. The oak-hickory forest is so extensive in the deciduous forest biome that it makes it an excellent example. The organisms and the abiotic factors described are typical.

The same general format used below could apply to almost any deciduous forest ecosystem in the United States except that the various niches might be filled by different species of plants and animals. For example, the dominant tree species might be beech and maple rather than oak and hickory.

Layering in the forest

Due to the many plant adaptations found in a deciduous forest, the forest community tends to be layered or stratified. Ecologists have been quick to grasp this idea because it provides a means for classifying the plant life from an ecological perspective - a classification system based on strata.

The line drawing on the next page demonstrates the layering in a mature or nearly mature oak-hickory deciduous forest. The uppermost layer is called the canopy. The trees that make up the canopy are the dominant forest tree species in the community and the forest is named for these species. The canopy is that layer of the forest that receives the most insolation (light energy). The canopy is arranged so that millions upon millions of leaves are exposed to direct sunlight, facilitating photosynthesis. The canopy trees are, then, a major food producing source for the community.

The oak-hickory forest may have a wide assortment of oak species and hickory species making up the canopy. Here and there other trees may reach the canopy but these are not representative of the dominant tree species.

A characteristic of typical understory tree species is that they are shade tolerant. The light entering the understory or filtering through the canopy is much less than that received by canopy trees. Therefore, the trees growing in the understory must be able to survive in a region of relatively low light intensity. Some tree species are unable to do this.

Poison Ivy

Understory tree species are adapted for growth in the shade of the canopy trees. You should be quick to infer that the canopy replacement trees in a mature deciduous forest are able to grow effectively in both high intensity and low intensity light situations. This, of course, permits the mature forest to stabilize and maintain its integrity over long periods of time.

The layer beneath the canopy is called the shrub layer. Shrubs are woody plants with numerous stems. This layer can be from 90-200 cm high. In our particular forest community, the shrub layer might be represented by the goose-berry or the spicebush. It might even be represented by the interesting poison ivy (seen to the left) which can grow as a vine or a shrub. However, it is not uncommon for the shrub layer to be sparse or even absent. Whether or not the shrub layer is prevalent will depend upon a number of variables, including the amount of sunlight filtering down through the understory. Forests with open spaces in the canopy and understory can have a thick and almost imprenetrable shrub layer.

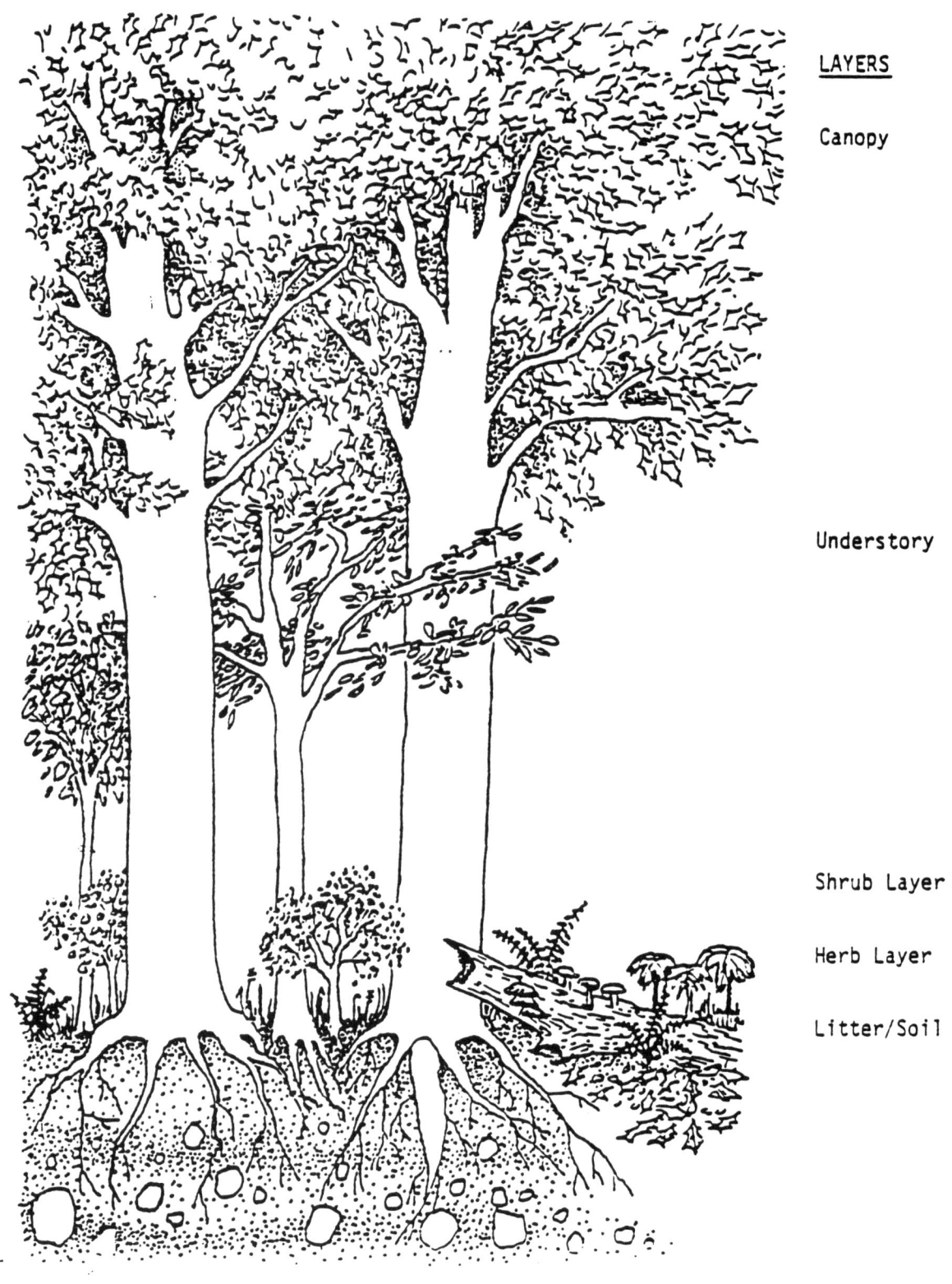

LAYERS

Canopy

Understory

Shrub Layer

Herb Layer

Litter/Soil

Layering in an oak-hickory deciduous forest

46

Now that you have read about layering and have seen a diagram that represents layering, can you identify layering in the real thing? Here is a photo of a midwestern oak-hickory forest. It is a fairly young forest, having been timbered in the past. However, there is a canopy, an understory, signs of a shrub layer, and a well-defined soil and litter layer. A decaying stump is seen in the foreground. As you read further, about associated animal life in the forest, think about what you might find here.

Beneath the shrub layer (in those communities where shrubs exist) is found the herb layer. The herb layer is composed of many kinds of soft-stemmed plants. In this particular forest the herbs one might find include trillium, violets, ginger, a variety of orchids, spring beauties, and numerous species of fern. The herb layer is well known for its ability to grow rapidly during the early spring before leaves appear on the canopy and understory trees. This adaptation permits the herbs to reproduce and produce much of the food needed for their survival. After the leaves appear on the canopy trees, the ability of the herbs to carry on photosynthesis is greatly reduced. The herb layer differs in different areas of the forest but it is a very typical forest community layer.

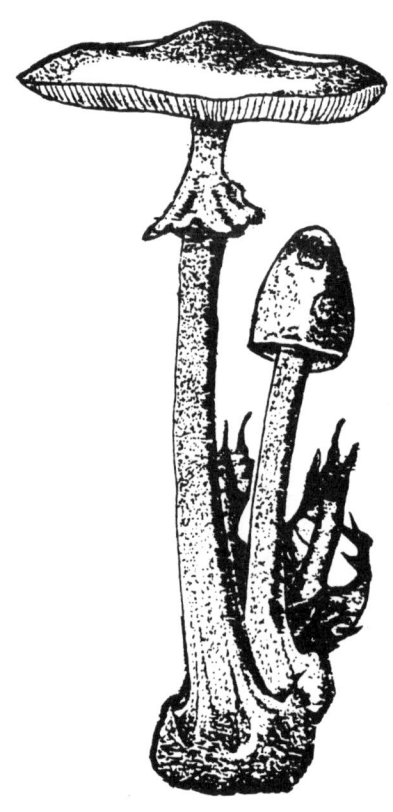

The bottom layer of the deciduous forest is the soil and litter layer. Perhaps a ton or more of animal wastes and plant debris collects on each acre of the forest floor each year. The debris includes leaves, stems, branches, tree trunks, animal wastes, and the dead bodies of numerous animals. In fact, there may be a number of identifiable strata in this layer alone. Within these strata are found an interesting array of small animals, many of which are invertebrates such as insects, spiders, centipedes and such. Although the decay of leaves can be a relatively slow process it goes on almost constantly. It is here that the bacteria of decay are found in extremely large numbers. And, after spring or summer rain, mushrooms appear which indicate that they have been at work, helping to break down dead plant material. The poisonous mushroom, the deadly amanita, is seen to the left.

Beneath and intermingled with the litter will be found the soil in which the forest plants are growing. The soil is a mixture of rock fragments, minerals, and organic matter.

Organic matter is most abundant in the upper soil layers. The rock particles tend to be small near the surface and become larger as depth increases. Decay organisms can still be found in the soil as can numerous other organisms.

Interestingly, the soils found with different plant communities can differ considerably. The midwest deciduous forest soil is likely to be brown in color where prairie soil in adjacent regions is likely to be dark - almost black - in color.

The acidity of the soil can also be influenced by the plant community growing on it. The oak-hickory forest is likely to have a moderately acid soil whereas a coniferous forest's soil is likely to be even more acidic. This acidity is a function of the kind of material being decayed on the forest floor (in the litter layer) as well as a number of other variables including the rock material from which the soil particles originated.

Associated Animal Life

It would be logical to assume that each layer of the oak-hickory forest would have its own representative animal forms. Indeed, this is the case. Animals are typically associated with particular layers although many will interact with two or more layers at particular times.

The illustration above provides examples of some of the birds found in particular strata of a Midwestern oak-hickory forest. These are by no means the only birds found in these layers. Similarly, many other kinds of animals can be found associated with one or more layers of the forest.

Besides the scarlet tanager, we could expect to find a number of smaller insect-eating warblers in the canopy layer. The presence of these birds indicates that there must be large populations of insects here as well. This is precisely the case and tree hoppers, aphids, caterpillars, and numerous beetles can be found here. Spiders are also here. Even mammals such as the flying squirrel are not uncommon.

In the understory we can observe the red-eyed vireo and the blue-gray gnatcatcher. Again, insect populations are numerous with tent caterpillars, wood-borers, and aphids being typical understory inhabitants. A gray squirrel may be found here at times although this mammal interacts with several layers. It is also in this region of the forest where one

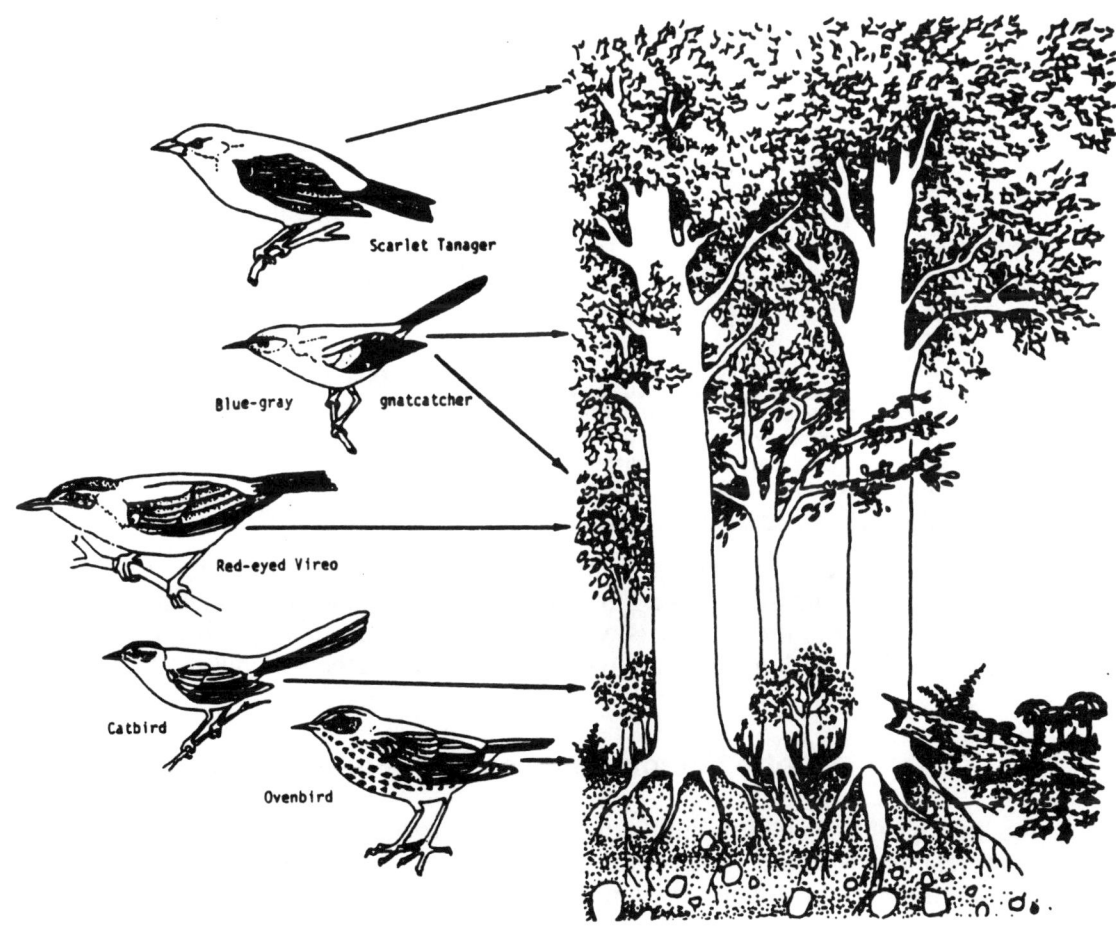

Scarlet Tanager

Blue-gray gnatcatcher

Red-eyed Vireo

Catbird

Ovenbird

49

would expect to find woodpeckers inhabiting and interacting with both the understory trees and the trunks of the larger canopy trees.

The shrub layer finds the catbird and the cardinal nesting in the cover of woody stems of shrub thickets. Again, numerous insects and spiders are present and many other animals interact on a part-time basis. Included would be deer, snakes, and a number of rodents. Interestingly, the shrub layer often provides excellent cover for other animals that are typically members of the forest floor. Overhanging shrub branches provide excellent habitat for ground-nesting birds and entrances for chipmunk burrows.

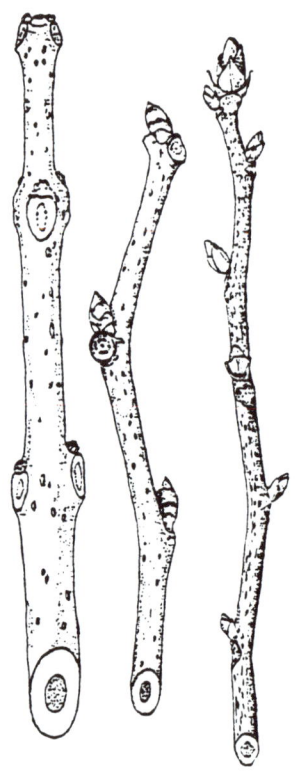

These twigs in winter condition give the term "deciduous" meaning. The ability of many deciduous species to shed leaves during autumn in preparation for winter permits them to live in moderate to cool climates. The twigs here represent catalpa, mulberry, and hickory.

It is somewhat difficult to discuss the animals of the herb layer without also including many that also roam the surface of the litter layer. The rabbit, for example, will eat a variety of herbs but raises its young in the litter layer. The same general condition exists for numerous other animals. The Kentucky warbler and the ovenbird nest on the forest floor but most certainly feed on insects there and in other layers. Of course, similar circumstances surround the lives of numerous salamanders, frogs, toads, snakes, and mice. And yet, as we move into the soil and litter layer itself we will find still another assortment of animal life.

Typically, the animals of the soil and litter layer are quite small. Many are microscopic or nearly so. A few, however, like snails, earthworms, millipedes, and centipedes are very easy to observe. The tiny organisms here are represented by populations running into the millions. Included would be mites, nematodes, springtails, and a variety of other small creatures.

A couple of important ideas emerge from our discussion of forest layering. One of these is that each layer of the deciduous forest has a fairly representative assortment of animals associated with it. Another is that some of these animals will travel back and forth across layers. And, in keeping with a basic principle of ecology, each animal has a particular niche which it is filling.

Abiotic Factors and the Deciduous Forest

If you should find yourself hiking along a country road on a warm, sunny day in June near a deciduous forest you would be in a position to observe directly some dramatic abiotic variables. First of all, out there on the country road in full sunlight, it is quite warm. Whatever wind there is tends to strike you with most or all of its velocity. The air is relatively dry and the sunlight may seem intense. But, as you continue your hike you pass by a mature oak-hickory forest. You decide to walk into the forest several meters. All of a sudden you realize that you are in an environment much different than that out on the country road.

On this warm, sunny day in June you observe that the woodland environment is much cooler than in the direct sunlight. Further, it is much darker inside the forest than out in the open. There is little breeze inside this ecosystem because the forest trees serve as an effective barrier to air movement. In addition, it seems more humid within the forest. Although it is cooler here, it also becomes obvious that the amount of moisture in the air is greater than out in the open.

Abiotic variables most certainly influence the character of an ecosystem. However, the variables you have just observed are abiotic variables that have been influence *by* the forest community. The forest itself produces a characteristic environment that is the sum total of a number of interacting abiotic variables. Those you observed when you walked into this oak-hickory forest were light, wind, humidity, and temperature. Of course, there are others as well but the important point here is that **an ecosystem is both influenced by and influences abiotic variables.**

It is somewhat difficult to discuss the abiotic variables associated with the oak-hickory forest without considering seasonal differences. The season of the year has considerable impact on the abiotic character of this ecosystem. The same holds true for the time of day. The environment in the deciduous forest during the daylight hours is quite different than that existing there at night. Consider, as an example, the effect that direct sunlight might have on both the canopy and the interior of the forest as the day heats up. The interior of the forest, although shaded by the canopy, will become warmer and the humidity level would increase. It is not our intent to describe all of these varying abiotic conditions. However, it is important to understand that the community interacts with abiotic variables and that these interactions can have a considerable influence on the environment.

Once again, let us return to the oak-hickory forest at midday on a sunny day in June. The canopy leaves represent the region receiving the most light. The understory trees are shaded but have some advantage in terms of their height. However, light falls off drastically as lower elevations are reached. The herb layer is, for the most part, bathed in eternal shade during June. Well over 95% of the light energy is absorbed by or reflected back into the atmosphere by the layers above the herbs. It becomes increasingly obvious that the herbs are benefited by their ability to grow and reproduce before the canopy trees have fully developed their leaves in the spring.

You will recall how humid the forest's interior seemed. There are a couple of reasons for this. The most important deals with the fact that all of the leaves of forest plants are continually giving off water. This water evaporates into the air causing the humidity to rise. Too, some water will evaporate from the soil and litter layers. This adds to the moisture. Because of the lack of air movement in the forest, the moist air tends to remain in place creating a constantly humid environment.

When it rains on this forest, millions of leaves are available to cushion the impact of the rain drops. This is one reason why soil erosion is so minimal on forested land. However, it is interesting to note that not all of a rainfall enters the forest soil beneath the canopy. Some of it is trapped by the leaves and some of this water evaporates back into the atmosphere. What doesn't evaporate will run down the stems, branches, and trunks of the trees. This water soaks into the ground at the base of the tree. This phenomenon is called "stemflow". Sometimes more water reaches the soil through stemflow than through direct contact of raindrops on the forest floor. This can help explain why, in some forests, herbs tend to accumulate around tree trunk bases. However, during a heavy storm shower, the force of the rain will bend leaves downward. This permits most of the rain to find its way through the canopy. In fact, during heavy storms, more water will find its way directly to the forest floor between trees than by stemflow.

Temperature in the June oak-hickory forest is stratified along lines that are synonymous with forest layers. The canopy is the warmest because the canopy leaves collect most of the light falling on the forest. The understory is somewhat cooler, the shrub layer cooler yet, and the soil is the coolest layer of all. At night the temperature differences are negligible and, during a daytime rain shower, temperature differences are minimal. Might you be able to hypothesize reasons for this?

> **Remember, the ecosystem influences and is influenced by abiotic variables! This is a truly important concept in ecology!**

The difference between wind velocity inside the oak-hickory forest and outside in the open is an easily understood phenomenon. The forest, in spring and summer in particular, acts as a natural buffer, forcing much of the moving air up and over the canopy. Inside the forest itself, wind velocity continues to decrease layer by layer. The wind velocity on the forest floor may be less than 5% of what it is above the canopy. When one stops to consider this situation, the impact of the forest on wind is quite dramatic. It is little wonder that homes built inside a forest or on the south side of a forest use much less heat energy in the winter than those built out in the open. Of course, the differences in wind velocity are not as great during the winter but the differences are substantial. Would the differences be even more noticeable if the forest was coniferous? Why?

In addition, numerous chemicals besides water constitute critical abiotic variables in the ecosystems. A few examples would be nitrogen, carbon, oxygen, and phosphorus. These elements, like water, flow through the ecosystem in cycle-like patterns. Each plays an important role in the survival of plants and animals in the ecosystem. In many instances, green plants take in and transform these elements into complex chemical molecules. Some of these are then broken down by the plants themselves or by consumers and released back into the ecosystem. In other instances, they are locked up in the bodies and wastes of plants and animals and must be released anew by decomposers acting on dead tissue or the wastes from living organisms.

The Microcommunity

The microcommunity as a pattern of life is simply another step along the continuum of organizational levels and exists as one of the most fascinating concepts in ecology. It is an interesting concept because a small but complete microcommunity can function dynamically within a much larger community and yet remain an integral part of that larger community.

Let's look at an example of a microcommunity. A wind storm sweeps into our now familiar oak-hickory forest. A dead limb of about 15 cm in diameter is torn off of an oak tree. Because the limb had already died, bacteria and other organisms had started to decompose the woody tissue inside. Now the dead stub is exposed, surrounded by living, healthy oak bark. Over the next several months - even years - the decay process continues. Eventually, perhaps a red-headed or a pileated woodpecker will search for insect larvae here and further disturb the site.

Eventually, a cavity is formed. Within that cavity is a rudimentary soil in which very small animals find a suitable habitat. Decay organisms continue to attack the dead tissue and larger insects appear to search out food and shelter. Eventually, the bottom of the cavity may retain a few centimeters of water for long periods after a rain. If this is the case we should be able to find numerous animals there including aquatic worms, beetles, and the larvae of tree hole mosquitoes. Yes, there are species of mosquitoes that specialize in breeding in wet trees holes! And, amazingly, one might even find a small frog or toad living in the tree hole. In any event, this tree hole can become a small but complex and dynamic community/ecosystem.

One more pattern of life is the *ecotone* - an very real ecosystem and one that is very dependent on abiotic factors for its development. What is seen here is an ecotone in western Kentucky. An ecotone is the pattern of life that develops where a deciduous forest community ends and a cultivated field begins. Undisturbed, the ecotone presents a wall of leaves to the sunlight that is available outside the forest itself. A surprising array of species exists here as well as numerous birds, reptiles, and mammals. The ecotone is a very rich ecosystem. Can you think of reasons why the ecotone develops where the forest stops? Photo courtesy H. R. Hungerford.

Microcommunities are not at all uncommon. Another, important one will be associated with the limb that broke off of the oak tree and the trunk of the large oak that fell to the forest floor a number of years ago. A dead, fallen tree trunk provides a suitable habitat for numerous organisms and is commonly called the fallen log microcommunity.

A large tree trunk will take decades to disappear from the scene. Throughout the years, numerous organisms may spend their entire lives on, in, and/or around the fallen trunk. As the years pass by the decay process modifies the log considerably and this microcommunity changes character and adjusts to the changing conditions. Eventually, of course, the log is fully decomposed and the minerals that were once an important part of the living tree's life history are now reincorporated into the soil of the forest. Here they are available for use by a new generation of oaks and hickories (or other community members).

While the fallen log microcommunity is in existence, however, numerous populations interact there. Of course, the millions of bacteria are too small to be seen with the naked eye but their role in decomposition is evident. Very tiny anthropods such as mites and springtails live here in droves, feeding and being fed upon. Even smaller protozoans and minute worms live here and in the soil around the log, highly dependent on moisture retained in the ecosystem. And, if moisture conditions are appropriate, the very primitive slime mold will grow from spores which have fallen on the log and the slime mold's glistening, sometimes colorful body will spread out over the surface of the log as it searches for organic matter upon which to feed. Mushroom mycelia will grow profusely through the dead wood, digesting the once-living wood with powerful enzymes. Lichens and mosses will take up residence on the surface of the log, following an opportunistic life style which includes growing on any suitable substratum.

Many years ago this large, decaying tree trunk was a healthy, growing member of an oak-hickory forest in Kankakee County, Illinois. Today it represents a microcommunity within the larger forest community. While it exists, the food energy stored in its tissue will provide tremendous potential for numerous decay organisms. And, the log itself (a microcommunity) will act as a habitat for many other plant and animal species.

Termites are active within the fallen log, digesting the wood itself, with the help of protozoans in their digestive tracts. A colony of black, carpenter ants finds the dead wood of the log an excellent place to set up their cooperative society. They will produce a series of chambers within the log - areas for living and reproduction. When they eventually depart, the abandoned chambers will be taken over by a host of other small animals and fungus plants. The scavengers such as sow bugs and millipedes find suitable plant debris on which to feed while the carnivorous centipedes and DeKay's snake search out small invertebrate animals appropriate to their diets. At night, a raccoon may use the log as a part of a trail through the forest, as a place to rest or dry itself, or simply as a vantage point from which to see the surrounding terrain. Numerous other kinds of animals and plants (numbering into the hundreds) interact in a myriad of ways, filling the many niches to be found in, on, and/or around the fallen log.

The time of greatest activity in this microecosystem is during the spring and summer seasons. It is then that both moisture and temperature conditions are within an optimum range for community activity. Even so, some activity takes place in fall and winter. In the winter, a surprising number of small animals seek out the protection of the fallen log as a place of hibernation. Hibernating animals include beetles, bugs, toads, salamanders, snakes, and numerous other organisms including the log's regular inhabitants.

Microcommunities can occur not only in forests but in all ecosystems. On page 57 you will find a sketch of a small but dynamic community found associated with the flower head (umbel) of the common milkweed plant. This microcommunity is extremely short-lived, having a life expectancy of less than two weeks. The common milkweed may produce several umbels during June or July and each one becomes a microecosystem. This living system is composed of a surprising array and number of insects and spiders. Numerous energy exchanges take place in this system including at least one that goes beyond the plant eating level. This energy exchange involves the honeybees which feed upon the nectar produced by the flowers and the crab spider which kills and consumes one or more of the bees (see the figure on the next page). When the flowers of the umbel die the community changes drastically and only those organisms remain that can interact successfully with leaves, stems, roots, and fruit.

In order to gain some understanding of the complexity of such a temporary but dynamic ecosystem, data are presented in the following table. This table records typical numbers of arthropods found on an umbel during peak activity. It must be noted that these data are representative only. Populations could be fewer or greater (total population numbers have been recorded in excess of 400 arthropods on a single umbel).

**Typical Arthropod Population Densities
On One Umbel of the Common Milkweed.**

Key	Organism	Typical Population Density
A	Butterflies	4
B	Ants	12
C	Thrips	250
D	Milkweed Beetles	4
E	Milkweed Bugs	2
F	Honey Bees	8
G	Crab Spiders	1
H	Other Arthropods	20
	Total =	301

In summary, the microcommunity is an important concept in ecology. Even though relatively short-lived, the microcommunity displays many of the same dynamics observed in the larger, more permanent communities. Too, the abiotic variables are important and contribute to the need for viewing this as being complex. Some organisms associated with this system live out their entire lives there. Some members are only part time members. This phenomenon, however, is also observed in larger community systems. The microecosystem is a part of a larger ecosystem and it is undoubtedly necessary for the larger ecosystem to exist before the microecosystem can do so.

56

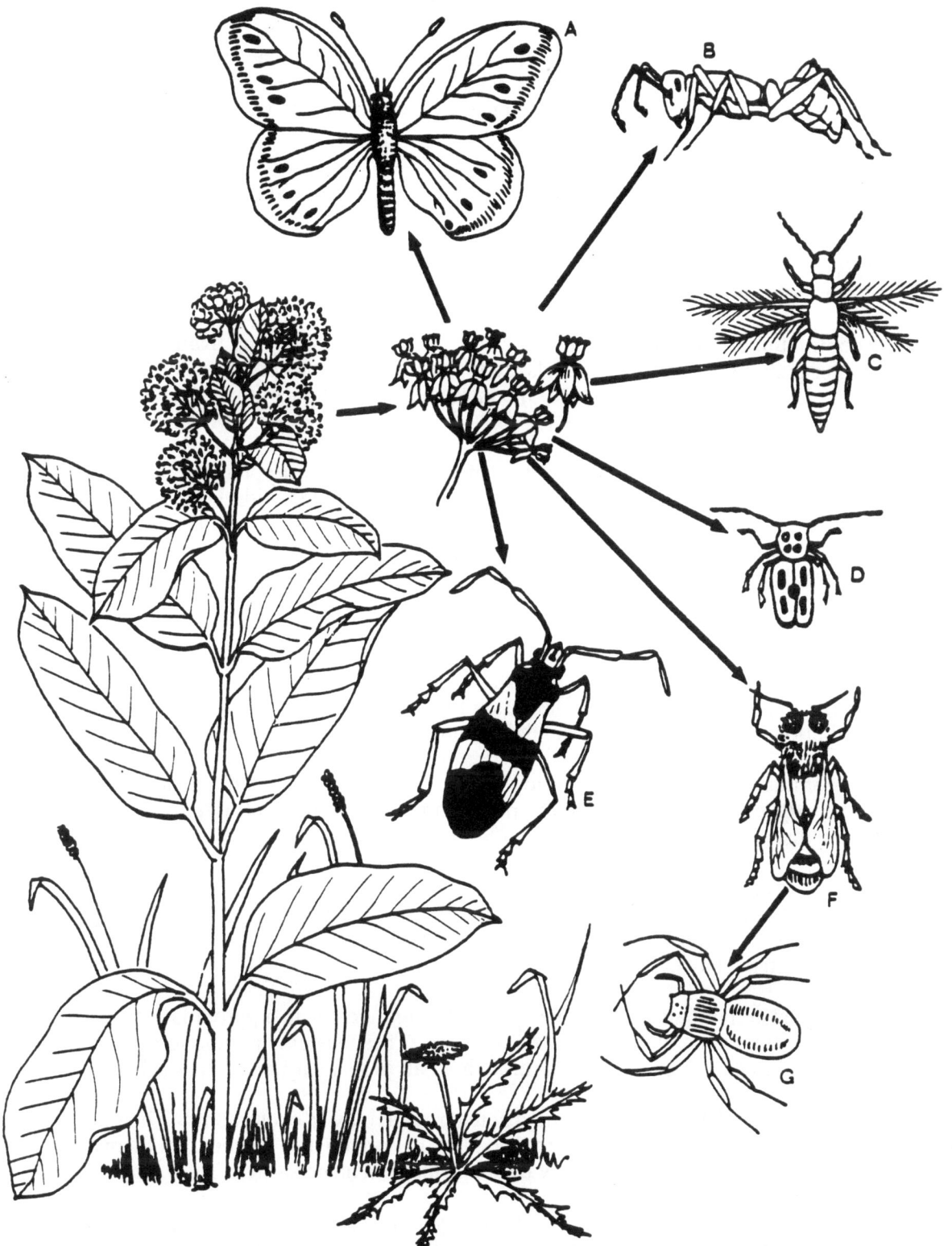

A typical microcommunity associated with the umbel of the common milkweed plant includes the flower head itself, butterflies, ants, thrips, milkweed beetles, milkweed bugs, honey bees, crab spiders, and other arthropods.

In Summary

The intent of Chapter II is to provide you with some very basic concepts which will permit you to understand and apply the many ideas introduced throughout this worktext. Important concepts which have been introduced in Chapter II and ones with which you should feel comfortable are:

1. Living systems are, in reality, patterns of life in which organisms interact on the planet earth. Different patterns can be described as having differing organizational levels.

2. Different organizational levels of living systems do not represent autonomous entities but exist along a continuum of intimately related patterns of life.

3. A continuum of organizational levels can be thought of as moving from complex to simpler patterns of life. These levels are represented by concepts associated with the terms: (A) biosphere; (B) biome; (C) community; (D) microcommunity; (E) species population; and (F) the individual.

4. The biosphere, biome, community, and microcommunity can be treated as ecosystems when the abiotic (nonliving) variables associated with those systems are considered.

5. Biotic and abiotic variables interact with each other in all ecosystems.

6. The biosphere exists tenuously as a shallow film surrounding the planet earth.

7. Biomes represent huge ecosystems in the biosphere which are usually dominated by uniform types of vegetation. There is a high correlation between the consistent distribution of abiotic variables and the dominant vegetation in each biome.

8. The community represents a particular but smaller pattern of life than does the biome. the community, like the biome, is comprised of interacting populations of organisms.

9. The microcommunity represents a much smaller pattern of life than does the community even though it can also be described as being comprised of interacting populations of organisms. The microcommunity, unlike the community in which it exists, is often relatively short lived.

10. A group of individuals of the same species living together in a particular space at a particular time is called a species population. These species population must be considered to be a dynamic system throughout all of its many interrelationships.

11. Every organism has a definitive and discrete role to play in ecosystems. The role of a particular species in an ecosystem is called that organism's "niche". In theory, at least, no two species can fill exactly the same niche in an ecosystem.

12. The terms used to describe various living systems or organizational levels of life (e.g., the community) are arbitrarily assigned to units that appear to represent definable entities within and including the biosphere.

13. The continuum represented by the various patterns of life presented in Chapter II can be characterized by a number of fairly sound generalizations. In some instances, however, definite exceptions can be observed. These generalizations are:

A. Patterns of life tend to exist along a size continuum with the individual organism the smallest and the biosphere the largest.

B. As size increases along the continuum, complexity of patterns also increases.

C. As size increases along the continuum, longevity also tends to increase (e.g., biomes tend to remain in existence longer than a community).

A beach/dune ecosystem along the Gulf Coast of Florida. The ever shifting sands of the shore are stabilized, in part, by the grass called sea oats. Where undisturbed by human intervention, this ecosystem is quite a bit richer than appears superficially. Its contact with the sea makes for some dramatic interrelationships. The sea oats seen in the foreground are very popular with tourists and residents alike for use in flower arrangements. Therefore, they have become so scarce in places as to force officials to pass laws prohibiting the picking of this grass. Photo courtesy H. R. Hungerford.

Activity 2.1

Predator Birds And Toothpick Worms: A Lesson In Adaptation

Focus: This activity will demonstrate how a species' physical adaptations influence its survival in a given environment.

To the Instructor: This is an activity to demonstrate the adaptation called "protective coloration". This, of course, is a common adaptation in many ecosystems and the advantages it gives to those organisms that have it are made obvious in this activity.

The activity can be done at any time of the year as long as there is a grassy area available and no snow cover. Needless to say, spring and summer can be ideal. In any event, it is recommended that the instructor (or other person in charge) use regular toothpicks and vegetable dye. Five hundred (500) toothpicks are often used: 100 red, 100 yellow, 100 blue, 100 green, and 100 natural (straw colored). An outside area is chosen that typifies the grassy condition of the lawn. The area might be 5 X 5 meters or larger. Twine is used as a border.

The instructor or his/her agent distributes the 500 "worms" within the area. The class is asked to gather around the perimeter of the area. Two to four "predator birds" are selected from the group and told that they will have one minute to prey on the "worms". They are to pick up every "worm" that they can see in that one minute. The collected toothpicks are turned in to the instructor or his/her agent. Other "predators" are then chosen to go into the area and try to retrieve as many of the "worms" as possible. These are collected but *not* counted as part of the activity.

The worksheet is completed, the frequency distribution noted, and a discussion (or assignment) ensues.

Directions to the Participants: Colored "worms" (colored toothpicks) have been distributed in a predetermined nearby area. A team of predators (participants) will hunt and collect "worms" (the prey organisms) for one minute. The team will then sort its "worm catch" by color and report the data. A data sheet can be found on the next page.

Discussion:

1. Describe the characteristics of the environment (e.g., its size, plants, color patterns, etc.) in which the "worms" live.

2. Which type of "prey" was most frequently found by the "predators" (students)?

The color: _____. Infer why this occurred.

3. Which type of "prey" was least frequently found by the "predators"?

The color: _____. Infer why this occurred.

4. Over time, which color of "worm" is more likely to survive in this environment as an intact, stable population?

The color: _____. Why do you think so?

5. An **adaptation** is a behavior (i.e., a way in which the organism acts) OR a physical characteristic (i.e., a body structure or other physical attribute) which provides a competitive advantage for a particular organism living in a particular environment. What adaptation(s) seem(s) to affect how frequently a "prey species" is found in this activity?

Adaptation(s): _____

Is this or are these behavioral or physical characteristics?

6. What environmental changes could take place in this area which would **favor** another worm color (or increase predation on the one which is most protected now)?

7. What real-life examples can you think of from naturally-existing ecosystems, e.g., a deciduous forest, a prairie, a pond, a swamp, a desert.

DATA COLLECTION SHEET

Number of Worms Preyed Upon (By Color)

Predators	Red	Yellow	Blue	Green	Natural
Predator 1	_____	_____	_____	_____	_____
Predator 2	_____	_____	_____	_____	_____
Predator 3	_____	_____	_____	_____	_____
Predator 4	_____	_____	_____	_____	_____
Total:	_____	_____	_____	_____	_____
% of Total	_____	_____	_____	_____	_____

Activity 2.2

Abiotics - A Two Way Analysis

Intent : The intent of this activity is for you to take a hard look at important nonliving (abiotic) variables and determine, as best you can: (1) whether the variable impacts on communities in isolation or in consort with other variables, (2) whether the variable has a major role in establishing tolerance gradients (optimum ranges of tolerance for organisms) in the ecosystem, (3) what its major effects are in the ecosystem, and (4) whether or not this variable can be influenced by the community itself.

All in all, this is a kind of synthesis activity concerning abiotic variables. It is not a particularly easy one to complete but it is an important one if we are to understand the ecosystem concept in some depth. It will be almost impossible to tease out all of the influences and interactions that are associated with each variable but this is perfectly alright. There is a lot left to be learned about these things by the professional scientists as well.

Procedures: We would heartily suggest your doing this activity out-of-doors as you observe one or more natural ecosystems, e.g., a hardwood forest, a fresh water pond, a grassland, a desert, a bog, an alpine meadow, a coniferous forest. We would also suggest that it might be more interesting to do this with someone else or with a small group of interested learners. In this way many more observations are possible.

If you wish, a few basic tools might be helpful. You might want to consider using one or more of the following: thermometer, light meter, hygrometer, rock hammer, Ph meter/paper, meter stick, compass.

ABIOTICS - A TWO WAY ANALYSIS

The Abiotic Variable	By and large, this variable effects communities. . .			This variable has a major role in establishing tolerance gradients (optimum range of tolerances)? YES OR NO	Examples of major effects on communities:	Can this abiotic variable be influenced by the community? If yes, provide at least one example.
	Individually	In consort with another variable	Both			
1. Climate						
2. Seasonal Change						
3. Annual Precipitation						
4. Available Moisture						
5. Evaporation						
6. Humidity						

The Abiotic Variable	By and large, this variable effects communities. . .			This variable has a major role in establishing tolerance gradients (optimum range of tolerances)?	Examples of major effects on communities:	Can this abiotic variable be influenced by the community? If yes, provide at least one example.
	Individually	In consort with another variable	Both	YES OR NO		
7. Heat Energy Present (Temperature)						
8. Insolation						
9. Substrate (Bed Rock)						
10. Soil (both depth & type)						
11. Acidity/ Alkalinity (ph)						
12. Elevation (in particular, gross changes in elevation)						

The Abiotic Variable	By and large, this variable effects communities. . .			This variable has a major role in establishing tolerance gradients (optimum range of tolerances)? YES OR NO	Examples of major effects on communities:	Can this abiotic variable be influenced by the community? If yes, provide at least one example.
	Individually	In consort with another variable	Both			
13. Topography						
14. Air Movements; Direction and Velocity						
15. Man's Works (Concrete Asphalt, Structures, etc.)						
Others:						

Activity 2.3

The Old Log Inn!

Intent of this activity:

It is often quite difficult to maintenance the collection of data concerning a community of interacting organisms over a long period of time. This is especially true for those who are not full-time ecology researchers. How, then, can long term observations be made when one is not available to go into the field on a regular basis? It's simple. Bring the community to the observer!

The intent of this activity is to expand and improve concepts concerning the community. In actuality, a microcommunity is used but the principles involved are very similar. One note of caution, however, by bringing the community inside we run the risk of modifying a number of variables. This threat should be seriously considered when and if this activity is carried out. What might some of these variables be?

Procedures:

Obtain a large plastic tray, pan, or small wading pool. Place it inside in a shady spot (a little diffused light is certainly appropriate - even recommended). Locate a rotting log that will fit inside the tray - or, cut a section from a rotting log that will fit. Bring the log into the room, place it in the tray, and pour a shallow film of water into the tray (this will permit the log to maintain moisture intake, similar to its situation in the soil and litter layer of the forest). Because the log may give rise to a variety of things like mold spores, centipedes, and adult insects, you may wish to construct a cover within which these organisms can be contained. This cover, however, should permit some ventilation to occur. As time goes by, you may find that the room environment is dryer than that in the woods. A periodic "rain" from a sprinkling may be desired.

The Old Log Inn is now a member of a "human ecosystem". What species populations can be observed as the days pass? What interactions can be observed between members of the same population? Between members of different populations? What evidence accumulates to indicate the presence of organisms not directly observed? What interactions can you observe that appear to contribute to the deterioration of the microcommunity, i.e., the decay and decomposition of the log? Is there evidence of the presence of decomposers, e.g., slime mold, bacteria, or mushrooms? If so, what is the evidence? Is there any evidence that nutrients are being recycled within the ecosystem itself? If so, what is the evidence? Is there an odor? What might account for this? These are but a few of the questions that can be considered as time passes.

The observations can take place over whatever time parameters seem appropriate to you and/or your instructor. However, the key element in this process is to synthesize an overall picture of the log as a dynamic microcommunity and/or microecosystem. Although this activity can be worthwhile in and of itself, it would also be of value to travel to the forest ecosystem and inspect first hand a number of fallen log microecosystems. This would permit more data collection for the synthesis process and make it more effective.

It is recommended that the "Old Log Inn" be returned to its natural ecosystem when observations have been completed. A number of species populations could then continue their normal activities in the "home environment".

Activity 2.4

Getting Out With The Ticks And Chiggers
- Or -
Observing A Living Ecosystem

Intent of this activity:

It is always a good idea for students of ecology to take a hard look at a living ecosystem in their area. An observation, data collection exercise such as this one will provide some clues to a few of the things that make a living system "tick". You can use this initial experience with a living system as a point of reference as your knowledge increases. You may also find it interesting to come back to this activity in a few weeks as sort of a self-evaluation of how far you have come over a relatively short period of time. You might be pleasantly surprised.

Procedures:

Travel to a living system that seems to be similar overall and one that exists in the region where you live. If it is a terrestrial environment, walk into it an spend some time just observing the things around you. Don't worry too much about the names of things in the environment. Instead, try to observe the system from a number of different perspectives. The questions which follow will help you focus your observations to the best of your ability. Note, however, that this exercise will take more than a few minutes to complete.

Date Observations Were Made: _____

1. What would you call this living system? Is it a hardwood forest? A vacant lot? A prairie? A temporary pond? A desert? Just what is it you are observing?

2. Do you believe that this environment is dominant in the region in which you live? In other words, is this an extensive living system in the region? Yes _____ No_____ Provide your reasons for answering as you did.

3. Where is this living system located? Provide some evidence as to its location.

4. Can you identify the <u>specific boundaries</u> of this system? What might be some of the difficulties encountered in sharply defining the system's boundaries?

5. What are the general characteristics you see when you observe the overall character of this system? If a drawing would help supplement your description, feel free to make one.

6. What are the nonliving (abiotic) factors that seem to be controlling the character of this system? For example, what might be the influence of topography? Bed rock? Humidity? Rainfall? Air temperature? Soil temperature? Insolation? Etc.? Now how do these abiotic factors appear to be controlling the character of this living system?

7. What populations of plant and/or animals can you observe here? What is your evidence?

8. Living organisms may be referred to as "biotic factors". Can you identify any biotic factors which seem to heavily influence the overall character of the system?

9. Is there any evidence that layering or zones of life exist in this particular system? If so, how would you describe them? If layers or zones exist, you may wish to sketch and label these.

10. Can you observe any evidence of competition between members of a given population, e.g., between red-winged blackbirds in a marsh? Yes_____ No____. If evidence exists, what is it?

11. Can you observe any evidence of competition between members of two different species populations? Yes_____ No_____. If evidence exists, what is it?

12. What other kinds of interactions between members of different populations can you observe here besides competition? For example, a fungus plant growing on a tree stump would be appropriate. How is each organism affected by the other?

13. What evidence exists, if any, to indicate that food energy flows through the system? If you can observe evidence of this and you want to diagram same, please do.

14. What evidence exists, if any, to indicate that this environment is more or less stable?

15. Some people might want to apply the term "static" to this environment. The term "static" can be defined as showing little change, lack of animation or progression; quiescent. How do you feel about applying the term "static" to this system" Please explain.

16. Do humans, in any way, play a role in this living system? Yes____ No_____. What is the evidence?

17. Why do you think that it is legitimate to call this system . . . this forest . . . . or pond . . . or vacant lot . . . or whatever, and ECOSYSTEM? Think a bit about the term and the situation you are observing before answering.

CHAPTER III

ENERGY:

THE STUFF
THAT DRIVES
ECOSYSTEMS

Learner Objectives for Chapter III

After all of your interactions with Chapter III, you will be expected to be able to . . .

1. . . . explain why we typically gain fewer units of energy from the food we eat than it takes to get that food to our table.

2. . . . state the **first law of energy** and relate this energy law to Objective No. 1 above.

3. . . . state the **second law of energy** and construct a human food chain (different from one in the text) scenario which illustrates it.

4. . . . provide an example of **entropy** in an energy-related system and explain why entropy is associated with that system.

5. . . . write a short paragraph explaining why energy does, in fact, drive ecosystems.

6. . . . explain where energy originates within an ecosystem and how it travels through the ecosystem (citing examples of this energy flow).

7. . . . construct and label a valid four step **food chain** - one that does not include human beings.

8. . . . construct both two and three step food chains in which man is involved and compare them in terms of: (1) energy pyramids, and (2) entropy.

9. . . . construct, label and describe a diagram which illustrates how energy and nutrients move through ecosystems. Included in this diagram must be: (1) the sun, (2) producers, (3) herbivores, (4) carnivores, (5) decomposers, and (6) nutrients.

10. . . . infer and communicate why an ecosystem might be able to survive over time even though there were there no carnivores present in it. Also, infer and communicate why primary consumers might be necessary in an ecosystem for it to survive over time. (Note: The responses for these are not to be found in the text. These are some things for you to think about.)

11. . . . identify or state what group of organisms comprise the bulk of the **decomposers**.

12. . . . explain why catfish serve as a more efficient food source for humans than do beef cattle (in terms of the energy pyramid).

13. . . . explain: **net primary productivity**.

14. . . . identify or name three major ecosystems that have a high net primary productivity.

15. . . . explain why the ocean is so productive even though it has a low net primary productivity.

16. . . . explain why it is crucial for humans to begin conserving ecosystems which have a high net primary productivity.

An Anecdote

It was May and the water temperature had warmed a great deal due to the sun's rays the past month or so. The higher water temperature had turned the pond into a frenzy of animal and plant activity. No longer were the plants and animals in a state of near inactivity due to the cold temperatures of winter.

This one-acre farm pond in Missouri sloped gently up toward shore from a depth of twelve feet. It was an old pond, the small drainage valley having been dammed in 1950. Because of its age, the shallower areas had a wealth of plants growing beneath the surface. In some places, plants like cattails grew profusely at the water's edge. Nearby, the arrow-shaped leaves of the sagittaria rise above the water's surface.

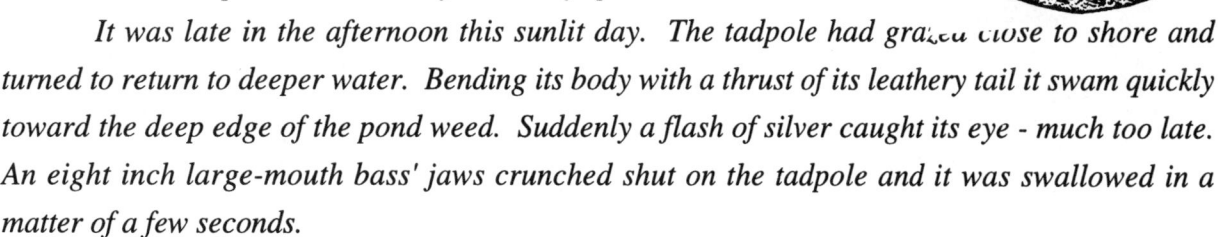

Pond weed also grew in this farm pond. Its long stems were rooted in the muck of the bottom. Thick, small green leaves floated in mats on the water's surface and, in May, flowers would appear at or above the surface.

Among the stems of the pond weed also grew strands of green algae which sometimes formed ball-like clumps beneath the surface. Other plants grew here too but the pond weed and algae seemed to dominate.

Into the "jungle" of green plants came water insects, harmless water snakes, toads, frogs, and small bass and bluegills. The thick cover provided a very good habitat for all these creatures. Many food chains and webs were going on here. One of these involved tadpoles which thrived here, grazing on the green algae and converting the algae to their own body parts.

One particular bullfrog tadpole had hatched the summer before and had spent the winter in the pond. It needed a large body before it transformed to the bullfrog. Bullfrog offspring need months of growth before they can become air-breathers. This tadpole and others seemed to be constantly feeding during the seasons in which food was available and the water temperature suitable for their life processes.

It was late in the afternoon this sunlit day. The tadpole had grazed close to shore and turned to return to deeper water. Bending its body with a thrust of its leathery tail it swam quickly toward the deep edge of the pond weed. Suddenly a flash of silver caught its eye - much too late. An eight inch large-mouth bass' jaws crunched shut on the tadpole and it was swallowed in a matter of a few seconds.

Instead of swimming quickly to deeper water, the bass lay quietly next to the pond weed while the tadpole's body entered the bass' stomach. The bass failed to notice a large dark gray leg enter the water next to it ever so gently.

The bass died quickly as the long, sharp bill penetrated its entire body cavity. The 38 inch great-blue heron lifted its head from the water, bass body attached. The heron quickly lifted the fish high in the air, turned the fish's head downward and swallowed it. A few thrusts of the long neck pushed the fish to the stomach.

The heron no longer needed to continue hunting for food. It bent its long legs at the knees, slung its body low and pushed hard against the muddy pond bottom.. With a loud "squawk" it thrust itself into the air, climbed into the sky and headed for its roost. It would not go hungry this night.

In the pond, life would continue. Pond weeds would grow, tadpoles would grow and mature, bass would hunt their prey, and great-blue herons would visit here again. The pond ecosystem was still intact.

A. CARTWRIGHT © 1993

Some Concepts About 'Energy'

Energy!!! There seems to be lots of it around. There is electrical energy, heat energy, solar energy, mechanical energy, thermonuclear energy, food energy, and more.

Somewhere in your education, someone probably lectured on or gave you an assignment on the energy needs of your own body. You were told or read that it takes energy to run that "machine" called the human body. Indeed, this is true. You either take in energy at some level over time or you die. It is that simple. But, how much do you know about this energy. Where does it come from? What is this energy used for? Is it 100% efficient? Does the human body "waste" energy? If so, where does it go?

And, what of ecosystems? What is the relationship between ecosystems and energy? Where does an ecosystem's energy come from? What is it used for? Is the ecosystem 100% efficient? And, what of the organisms in the ecosystem? What are the relationships between organisms in an ecosystem and energy? On and on!

An example! You walk into the supermarket to buy groceries. Although you don't particularly like carrots, your mother taught you that they were good for you so you pass up the doughnuts and go to the frozen food section and find a package of sliced carrots. Now, carrots are not particularly sophisticated things are they? Sure, they contain some vitamins and other nutrients (remember, they are good for you) and, of course, some stored *energy*. Now, if you are terribly conservative in your use of energy, you will take them right home, thaw them, heat them up and eat them. Aren't you proud? Certainly, your body is happier and your mother is most certainly happier! You then go about your daily living (human activities), utilizing the nutrients and expending he energy that was contained in those carrots.

To continue our example . . . suppose that somewhere in the past, a professor or high school teacher or textbook suggested that certain kinds of energy should be used sparingly. So . . . you

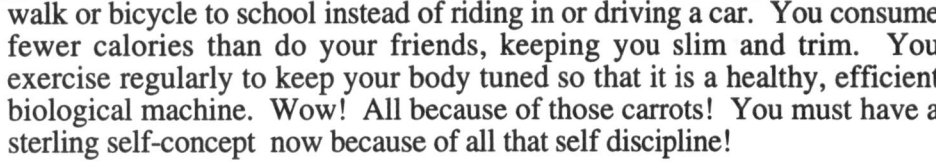

walk or bicycle to school instead of riding in or driving a car. You consume fewer calories than do your friends, keeping you slim and trim. You exercise regularly to keep your body tuned so that it is a healthy, efficient biological machine. Wow! All because of those carrots! You must have a sterling self-concept now because of all that self discipline!

But, wait a minute! Remember, you bought *frozen, sliced carrots!* You didn't go out into your own garden and pull carrots out of the ground, wash them off, slice them up and eat them raw. Shame on you! If you had done it this way you could really, really have a sterling self-concept! You could then have explained why you were such a good person by eating your carrots this way instead of going to the supermarket, buying frozen carrots, and preparing and eating them.

Now, what's this all about? Why the fuss over frozen carrots? Doesn't "everybody" go the supermarket and buy frozen carrots? Since "everybody" is doing it, it must be OK. Well . . . it's not really O.K. if conserving energy is important. Let's talk about this for a moment here.

The focus of Chapter III is on energy, its uses for individuals and ecosystems, and on its efficiency. This may seem strange right now but bear with the writer and try to sort some of these things out. Now, back to carrots. The billions of people on the earth must eat (you are one of these)! Eating provides the energy needed to live. Buying and eating frozen carrots is really a very inefficient way of getting needed energy.

Let's Trace Those Carrots from Seeds to Your Table

Those frozen carrots had to be grown somewhere. Let's assume they were grown in northern Indiana on a commercial vegetable farm. Seeds were sown in the ground (in much the same way you would sow them in your own garden). Warm soil helped to germinate the seeds and pretty soon green shoots appeared in super long rows - hundreds of long rows side by side. The sunlight in northern Indiana allowed the green shoots to carry on photosynthesis (the food producing process in green plants). In a few weeks the yellow roots (carrots) began to develop beneath the green foliage. The farmer stimulated this growth by applying commercial fertilizer to the many rows of carrots (commercial fertilizer comes from petroleum). A machine cultivated the carrots (using petroleum products). Another machine helped harvest the carrots (using petroleum products). Another machine washed the carrots (probably using electrical energy which came from coal, petroleum, or nuclear energy). Still another machine sliced the carrots (again, more energy). Another machine packaged the carrots (more energy). The carrots were then quick frozen (more energy). The frozen carrots were transported, probably by truck, to a distributor (energy for the truck and the freezer unit on the truck). The distributor transported the frozen carrots to the supermarket (more energy). The grocer kept them frozen in one of the huge freezers in the supermarket (more energy). You drive to the market to get groceries (more energy). You buy the carrots and take them home via the car (more energy). You probably toss them into your own freezer (more energy). When ready to eat them you take them out and you might defrost them in the microwave or on the stove in hot water (more energy). You then heat them to a desired temperature (more energy) and, finally, you eat them. How many separate energy usages are there? Yes a lot of them!

More About Those Carrots and Energy!

It gets a bit more complicated now. Hang in there and get a couple of very important concepts.

When you buy frozen carrots, how close can you come to getting one unit of energy for each unit of energy expended in growing, processing, transportation, and purchasing? The energy ratio is probably something on the order of 16 - 1. This means that **16 units of energy had to be expended on those frozen carrots for the 1 unit of energy you got from them.** In the above paragraph, you noted that a lot of the energy expended was produced from coal or petroleum. Coal and petroleum are **finite resources**. Once used they cannot be replaced. Beginning to get the idea?

What if you had grown the carrots in your own garden, harvested them yourself, and eaten them raw? The energy ratio here is close to 1:1 or 2:1. Even if you had processed them somehow - even freezing them in your home freezer, the energy ratio would have been much better than 16:1. The convenience of commercially frozen carrots is energy intensive and most people think nothing of it. In fact, there are people who don't even consider that carrots come from anywhere except the supermarket. Be that as it may, we pay a very dear price (in terms of energy and the biosphere) for those frozen carrots. There is an old adage in science related to energy and it goes something like this: **"You can't get something for nothing - or, it takes energy to get energy"**. This is the **first law of energy**. In order to get those carrots at the supermarket's freezer, we pay a very dear price in terms of energy. It simply takes a "ton" of energy to get those carrots to the table!

Now, what about the **second law of energy**? The second law of energy tells us: **"You can't break even ... or, a system tends toward increasing disorder with respect to energy (sometimes simply called entropy)."** Well now, this is a bit more difficult, but not if we look at those frozen carrots again. Just how efficient do you think those farm machines, trucks, freezers, processing machines, etc. really are? Do they use energy efficiently? Hold your breath here (but not too long, please). The energy ratio for a truck transporting those carrots, using gasoline as fuel, may be about 10:1. This means that we get one unit of useful energy from 10 units of energy in the gasoline. Other machines work at a rate better or worse than this.

Where do the nine (9) units of lost energy go? Can't you guess? Sure, they are lost as heat. Lost? Yes, lost! Does the temperature gauge on your car tell you the engine is hot when you drive a number of miles? Is the hood of your car hot after you take a trip? The heat produced by the engine (and the other moving parts of the car) is radiated out into the atmosphere. Here we are at the first law of energy again - we are not getting something for nothing - our car is "wasting" energy. It is not very efficient!

But, the second law of energy tells us about entropy - the increasing disorder in a system. Let's go back to those carrots again. The production, processing, packaging, freezing, transportation, etc. of those carrots is really a "system". Throughout that system, energy is lost in the form of heat. Thus, the system, as a whole, expends massive amounts of heat energy in order to do a relatively small amount of "needed" work. This "energy disorder" in the "carrot system" is a great example of **entropy** - increasing disorder of a system. Can you think of other examples of entropy in human technological systems?

Energy and Ecosystems

Energy drives ecosystems !!! It is terribly important for you to remember this and also to understand why it is true.

If you stop and think about it for a few moments, it isn't too hard to realize that, without energy, an ecosystem would collapse and become nonexistent. A myriad of activities go on within the living things in an ecosystem and all of this activity demands an energy expenditure. Thus, energy does, indeed, drive ecosystems. Now, where does this energy come from?

Energy drives ecosystems!

All ecosystems, in one way or another, are driven with solar energy - sunlight if you will. Light is the one form of energy that can be converted by green plants (called **producers**) to food energy. This is done in a very complicated process called photosynthesis. You probably remember a teacher or professor telling you that, during photosynthesis, carbon dioxide and water are combined in the presence of sunlight to produce sugar molecules. The green plant uses the sugar molecules to carry on life processes. The green plant can take the sugar molecules and convert them to other more complex molecules that are needed for living.

We could go on and on about how miraculous the green plant really is (and this is very, very true) but suffice to say that **the green plant allows all life to succeed on this small planet of ours by serving as the basis for the energy transfers that must take place in order for animals and plants to live here.**

When we think of the green plant (the **producer**) we probably think of grass in the yard or the leaves on a shade tree. That's perfectly alright except that these are terrestrial organisms. In aquatic environments, the green plants are usually algae, typically minute plant cells containing chlorophyll. Many different kinds of algae grow in fresh and salt water environments just as many kinds of trees inhabit a deciduous forest. So, food production takes place on land and in the water.

When parts of green plants are consumed by plant eaters (called **primary consumers** or **herbivores** or **first-order consumers**), the energy stored in the plant tissue is released by the animals involved. This is what happens when the cow is eating grass in the pasture. This is what happens when the wild mouse feeds on grass seeds on the prairie. This is also what happens when the snail grazes on fresh water or marine plants. So, we have come from sunlight to photosynthesis to consumption by primary consumers.

Producer: **An organism which has the ability to produce food energy (in most cases, producers are green plants using carbon dioxide, water, and sunlight).**

Consumer: **An organism which feeds on a second organism, utilizing the food energy stored in the tissues of that other plant or animal. A first order consumer (herbivore) feeds on plant tissue. Second order consumers (carnivores) feed on first order consumers. Third order consumers may feed on both first and second order consumers.**

Decomposer: **An organism which obtains energy by breaking down the complex molecules of wastes and dead bodies into simpler chemicals which it uses, or which are released into soil or water.**

Does it all end there? No! The cow is butchered and eaten by your brother-in-law and his family. The wild mouse might be caught and eaten by a coyote or a red-tailed hawk. The coyote or the hawk have to eat too and they cannot eat plant life for energy. These kinds of animals are called **carnivores** or **secondary consumers** or **second order consumers**.

Does it end here? No! Some secondary consumers are eaten by **tertiary consumers** - other **carnivores** or **third order consumers**. Well, you can see that we could go on and on, but it must stop somewhere and you will soon learn why. Before going to that step, what happens when these organisms give off waste material or die?

    . . . photochemical energy, which is used by plants in photosynthesis, fixed in carbohydrates and other compounds, . . . becomes fuel for [the] cool-burning cellular furnaces of living organisms.

    Robert L. Smith

The photosynthetic grasses and broad-leaved plants in the author's back yard provide food energy for this rabbit. The rabbit is a first order consumer (herbivore) in the "lawn ecosystem". Photo courtesy H. Hungerford.

The photosynthetic grasses and broad-leaved plants on the Oklahoma prairie provide food energy for these young prairie dogs. The prairie dog, like the rabbit, is a first order consumer (herbivore) on the grass-land. Photo courtesy H.R. Hungerford.

Enter the coyote! This fella would be more than "happy" to eat either the prairie dog or the author's rabbit. The grasses and broad-leaved plants provide food energy for the coyote too, but it must first be processed by the prairie dogs and the rabbit. Thus, the coyote is a second order consumer - a carnivore in the ecosystem. Photo courtesy H. Hungerford.

Dead organisms and their wastes have to "go" somewhere. Think about it for a minute. If all of the fallen twigs, branches and dead leaves in the forest didn't "go" somewhere, we would soon be up to our "whatevers" with twigs, branches and dead leaves. The same holds true for animal wastes and the bodies of coyotes, mice, birds, and so on. Here the **decomposers** take over.

Decomposers are typically fungus plants like decay bacteria or molds and mushrooms. The decomposers obtain energy by breaking down the complex molecules of wastes and dead bodies into simpler chemicals - chemicals that can be used in their own lives. And, some of these chemicals are returned to the soil or water to be recycled, once again, by green plants. Rather amazing, isn't it?

This photo shows a dead tern on a beach on Florida's Gulf Coast. Scavengers and decomposers are already at work, the decomposers breaking down the tissues that were once a part of the living organism. The nutrients, which were locked up in living tissue and were not available to be used by green plants, will be chemically converted by decomposers to a usable form. Photo courtesy H. R. Hungerford.

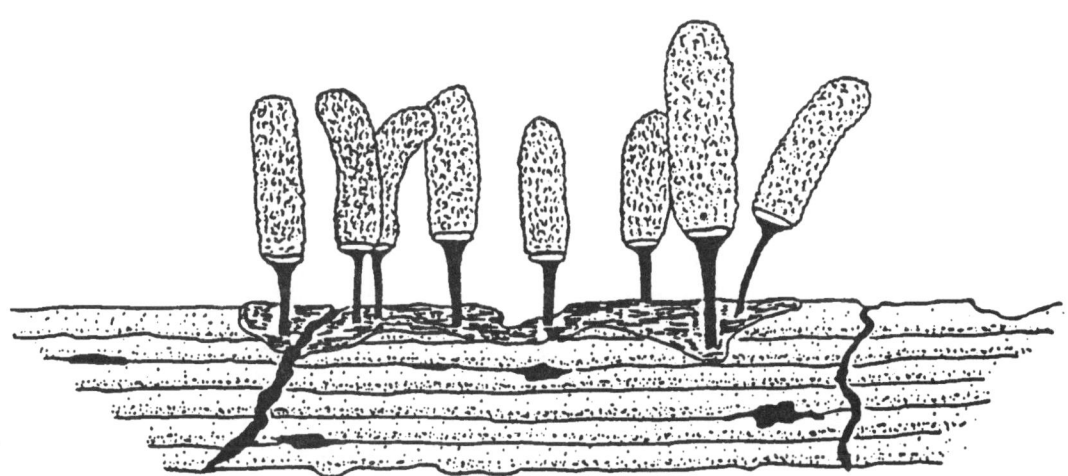

Slime mold growing on a decaying tree trunk. The slime mold is a decomposer in the forest food web, breaking down dead tissue and returning nutrients to the ecosystem.

Bison [buffalo] manure or dung on an Oklahoma prairie. The solid wastes and urea from mammals in any ecosystem act as a potential source of nitrates which can be used by green plants. However, solid wastes are also used by numerous insects including a variety of beetles and flies. Important parts of some life cycles take place within or in association with the dung. Even so, bacteria and fungi also work on the manure or chemicals produced in the manure, converting it to nitrogen compounds that can be used by plants. Some of it, of course, can also be lost into surface or ground water. Photo courtesy H. R. Hungerford.

Ecosystem Pathways for Energy and Nutrients

Both energy and nutrients move through ecosystems. Below, you will find a figure which diagrams how energy and nutrients move through ecosystems. This is a very simple diagram and the writer wants you to have full command of it.

Note that the flow of energy is directional (very important!). Note also that nutrients are cycled over and over. So, we have a **one-way street** with energy and a **two-way street** with nutrients.

Now, let's see how this lays out in a phenomenon called a **food chain**. On the facing page, you will find a diagram of a simple prairie food chain. This diagram "shows" photosynthesis being conducted by a prairie grass plant (the **producer**). Some of the food energy stored in the green plant is used by the prairie dog (the **primary consumer**). The prairie dog, in turn, might be killed and eaten by a ferret (the **secondary consumer**). A hawk just might get lucky and catch the ferret (the hawk being the **tertiary consumer**). In this particular food chain, the hawk meets an early death and its tissues are broken down by **decomposers**. Some of the chemicals produced by the decomposers are recycled by the green plant (some might call this fertilizer). By the way, the green plant may still be living after all of the food chain has been completed.

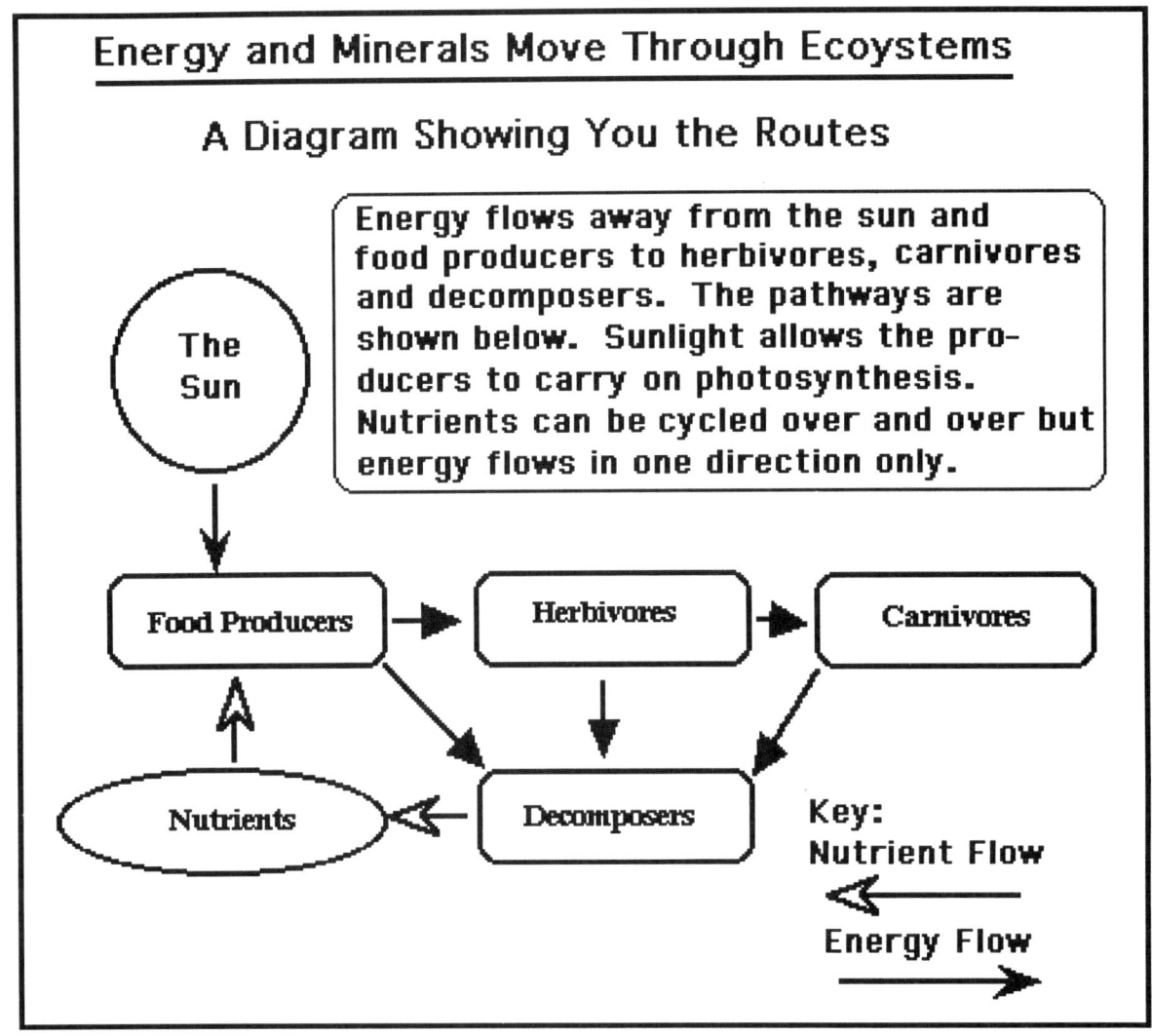

80

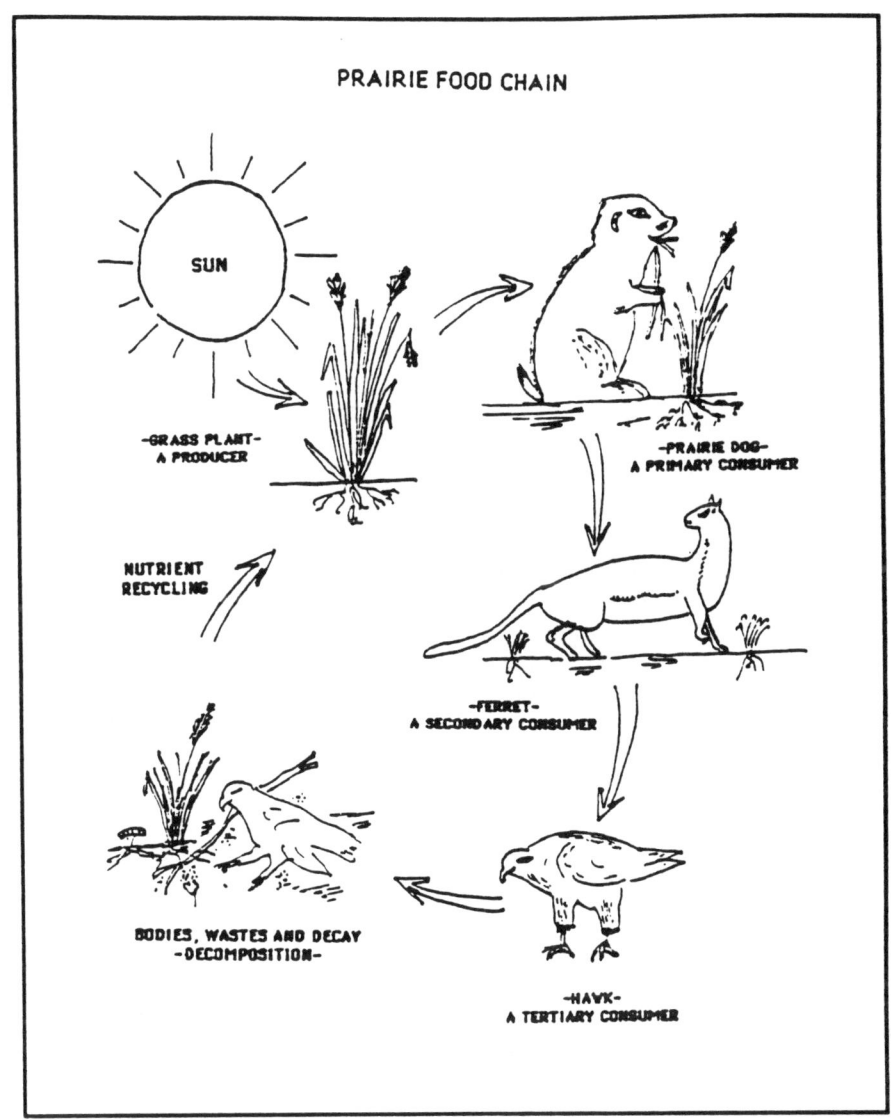

PRAIRIE FOOD CHAIN

Needless to say, the food chain (energy movement) is rarely this simple. Do only prairie dogs eat on grass plants? No! Grass plants are visited and at least partially consumed by mice, grasshoppers, beetle larvae, and other primary consumers. Needless to say, many different organisms eat mice and many different organisms eat grasshoppers. The underground beetle larvae, feeding on the roots of the grass plants, could well be eaten by a mole. On and on!!! So, **energy flow** can be quite complex but it **is always away from the green plant**. When complex interactions between energy producers and energy consumers take place (as in this example), we call the phenomenon a **food web** (or energy web). On one of the following pages, we have attempted to diagram some of the complexity that is in a food web.

At the beginning of this section you read, "Energy drives ecosystems"! If you cannot explain that quote you either need to reread this section or berate the writer for not helping you conceptualize this - or both! Please, please try to understand the importance of energy to ecosystems and how energy flows through ecosystems. And, take a few moments to think of some legitimate examples of both food chains and food webs.

Ecologists have learned that mangrove forests are very important ecosystems around the world. The mangroves seen in these photographs are in Florida.   As can be seen in the photos, mangroves can create almost impenetrable forests which provide a habitat for a number of marine and coastal species.   The importance of the mangrove as part of a food chain was not known until after the middle of the Twentieth Century.   What is interesting about this food chain is the fact that it is a detrital one, beginning in the leaves that fall into the tidal zone below the plants.   Huge numbers of these leaves fall making for a large reservoir of organic material.   Within hours, bacteria and fungus plants begin to colonize the leaves. These organisms digest the detritus and make chemicals available to very small animals, e.g., worms, snails, clams, oysters, etc.   These animals, in turn, become food sources for larger marine animals such as crabs and fish which are, in turn, fed upon by larger animals.   Some of the animals associated with the mangrove forests are threatened or endangered. The reason for this endangerment lies, in part, with the desire of developers to develop coastal areas into human dwellings.   Realization of the ecological importance of the mangrove forests has slowed the development of the mangroves. Photos courtesy H. R. Hungerford.

Example of an Incomplete Grassland Food Web

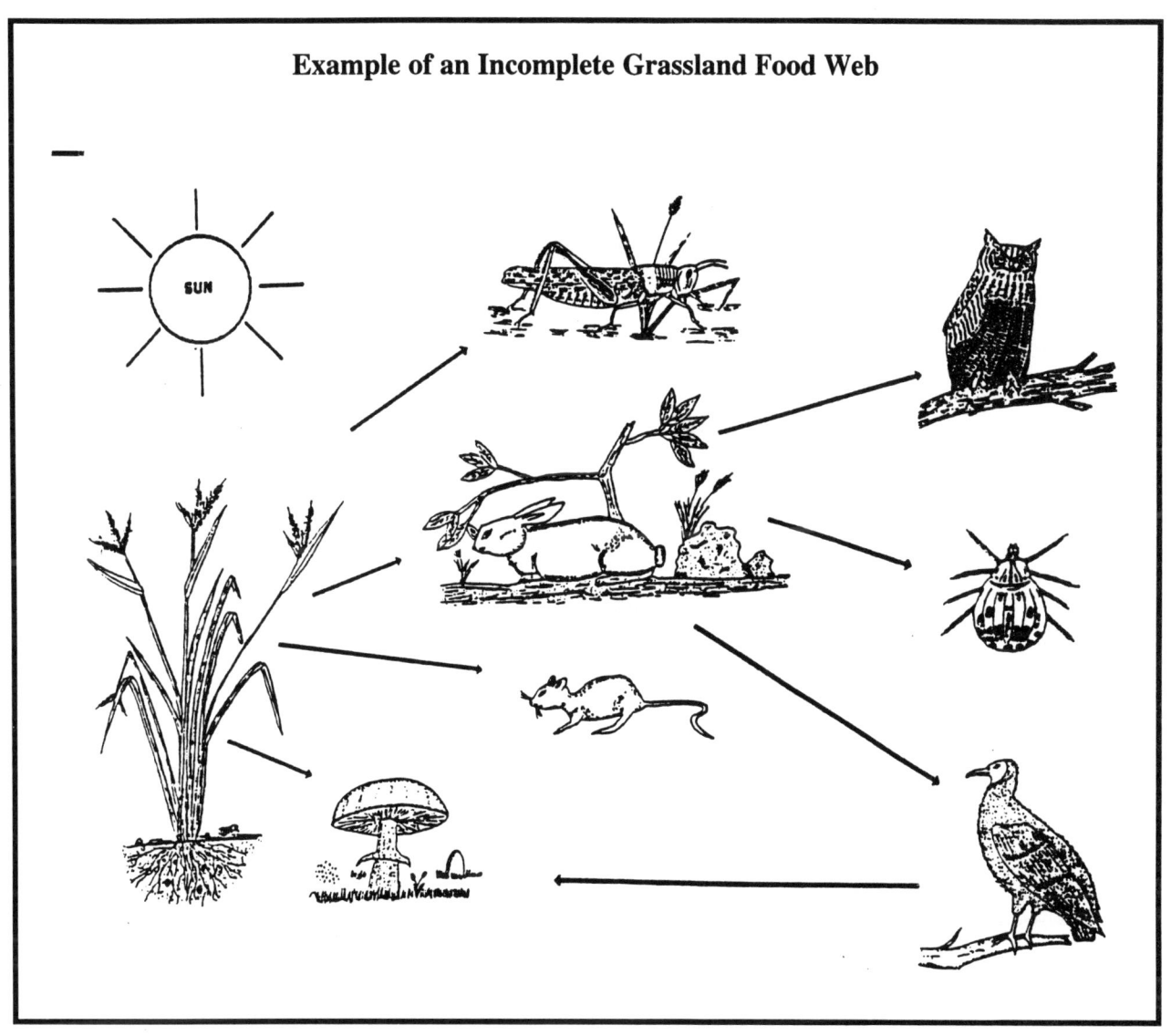

The Energy Pyramid:
Remember, You Don't Get Something for Nothing

Back to the grass plant. That grass plant is carrying on photosynthesis every day that there is enough warmth and light. That is a great deal of photosynthesis. And, when you multiply that food production by the number of grass plants on a prairie, you have a lot of food being produced. But, does the grass plant simply sit there and store food? Certainly not! That grass plant must carry on its own life processes. Some of that stored food is converted by the grass plant itself to provide energy for its life functions. So, some of that energy is converted to other things needed by the plant and some of it is simply "burned" up during respiration. Because respiration produces heat energy, measurable amounts of heat are lost into the atmosphere.

Now, let's shift to the cow pasture. Enter our cow once again. Remember, this is the cow your brother-in-law is going to butcher and eat. The cow eats the top off of the grass plant. The cow must process the grass and convert it to usable energy, use that energy for its life processes or convert the chemicals in the grass to meat, bones, hair, etc. The cow moves over the pasture,

83

burning up energy. Heat is given off by the cow. Just how efficient is the cow in capturing the energy that was stored in the grass? Pretty efficient, eh? Nope, not very efficient at all.

The cow will consume about ten (10) pounds of grass in order to put on one (1) pound of "flesh". This 10:1 ratio is fairly common in nature although some organisms (like the catfish) are considerably more efficient.   Anyway, your brother-in-law eats the cow. How efficient is he in converting "cow" to "human"? Once again, not very efficient! Beginning to get the picture? All along the way, energy is lost as one organism feeds on another. Below you will see a diagram of what is called an "energy pyramid".   This diagram uses a different example but the phenomenon is the same - lost energy along the pathway of the food chain. Remember the first law of energy? You really can't get something for nothing!

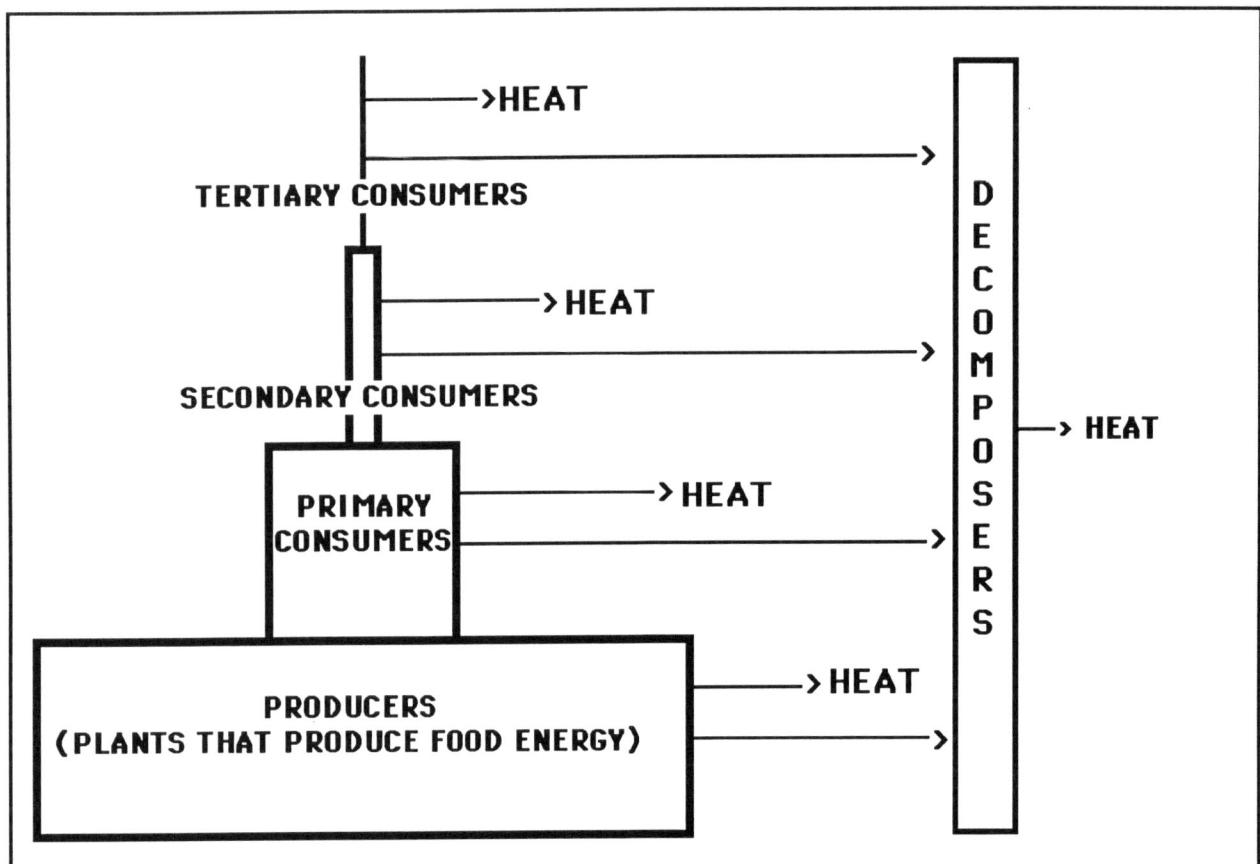

FIGURE: DIAGRAM ILLUSTRATING AN "ENERGY PYRAMID".

Examples of energy pyramids can be found in all ecosystems. Some energy pyramids have even more levels than this one. An example of such an energy pyramid could well begin with an oak tree in a southern Illinois forest (the producer). The primary consumer could be an insect such as an aphid. The secondary consumer could well be a bird such as a migrating warbler. The tertiary consumer could be another bird, such as a kestrel. All of these organisms yield waste materials (or could die). In both of these instances, the material would be utilized by decomposers.

Of greater importance than an example is the concept itself. Note that there is less usable (available) energy at each ascending level. Most of the energy produced at each level is used for the processes involving "living". These processes involve the loss of great amounts of heat energy which is radiated away from the organism. Can you see implications for man's food chains in this diagram?

We probably should take a moment to consider the implications of this. Your brother-in-law probably would not want to feast on a cow that was fattened solely on grass. He would demand "corn-fed beef"! In order to provide corn-fed beef, the rancher/farmer would have to grow corn and then fatten the cow on the corn. Would we see the same inefficiency there? Sure we would. Ten pounds of corn to one pound of cow and ten pounds of cow to one pound of brother-in-law. We can't get something for nothing here either. The point is, when people eat meat, the efficiency of the situation is in serious question. Why not eat fresh corn instead? Would that be more efficient? It certainly would be. Are there implications here for humankind as a whole? What does it say for our American eating habits? And, which would be cheaper to boot? There are a lot of questions needing some pondering here.

Are all meats so heavy with energy inefficiency? As we noted before, the catfish is much more efficient. Some say that the catfish has a return ratio of less than 5:1. Certainly there are fish that come in with a fancy consumption to storage ratio. So, would we be better off, energy-wise, eating beef or catfish? You should be able to answer that question by now.

Net Primary Productivity

Let's get right to the definition. Net primary productivity refers to **the rate at which green plants produce food energy minus the rate at which they use it**. So . . .

> ### Net Primary Productivity = Production - Use

Back to our grass plant again. You have already seen how the grass plant produces more energy than it consumes. It has to be this way or the prairie dog would go hungry, the mouse would go hungry, and the grasshopper would go hungry (let alone your brother-in-law's cow). The grass plant simply produces more than it uses. The difference between these two points is net primary productivity. Important? You bet it's important and you will be able to explain its importance at the end of this section (won't you?).

How do we express net primary productivity? It is usually expressed in **kilocalories per square meter per year**. What is a kilocalorie? It is the term for 1000 calories. That's not too difficult a concept. And, a square meter? That's a bit bigger than one square yard. So, when we speak of net primary productivity for a particular area, we are talking about 1000 calories of **net conversion** of **sunlight** to **stored food energy** per **square meter** per **year**. The net primary productivity of agricultural land is about 2800 kilocalories per square meter per year. These are the kilocalories (in corn, soybeans, wheat, rice, etc.) that a square meter of agland can produce in one year's time.

The ecologist uses net primary productivity to assess the potential of various biomes (and other areas) for producing food energy to support food chains for humans and other animals. On the next page you will find a diagram of the net primary productivity of some of the major ecosystems (adapted from Miller, 1988). Be sure you read this diagram correctly. Do not interpret it to mean that this represents the ratio of total production from one ecosystem to another. It simply shows how much productivity one can expect from a given ecosystem.

The Net Primary Productivity of Some of the Major Ecosystems

Types of Ecosystems

Types of Ecosystems	Productivity
Marine Estuaries	///
Swamps and Marshes	///
Tropical Rain Forest	///
Temperate Forest	////////////////////////////////////
Agricultural Land	/////////////////////
Temperate Grassland	///////////////////
Lakes and Streams	///////////////////
Tundra	/////
Open Ocean	/////
Desert Scrub	///
Extreme Desert	//

0 1000 2000 3000 4000 5000 6000 7000 8000 9000 10000

Approximate and Average Net Primary Productivity (kcal/m^2/year)

The figure above gives you an idea of how productive plants are in a number of the major ecosystems around the world. There are several important ideas for you to think about with this figure:

1. The three most productive ecosystems are ones that are in very short supply around the world. They are also ones that we are losing at an alarming rate.

2. There is more ocean that any other type of ecosystem. The net productivity of the ocean is very low, as you can see in the figure. However, since oceans cover such a large area of the globe, they account for more overall production than any other single ecosystem. Unfortunately, the earth's oceans are being polluted at an alarming rate.

3. Humans and all other animals depend upon net productivity for their very survival.

Now, consider how much of the earth's surface is covered by the various ecosystems shown in the diagram. How much of the earth's surface is covered by estuaries? Not much. How much of the earth's surface is covered by swamps and marshes? Not much and these ecosystems are decreasing due to man's ability to drain wetlands. How much tropical rain forest? There used to be a lot of it but we are losing it at a dramatic rate due to its being cleared for timber and its conversion to grasslands to meet the demand of man for beef cattle and hamburgers (yes, that's true!). Well, these are the three most productive ecosystems. These are either in short supply or they are disappearing rapidly.

You can see from the diagram that the oceans are very limited in their ability to produce energy on a net basis. But, if we looked at a diagram which displayed the role of each ecosystem in terms of **total production** (not net primary productivity) we would see the ocean at the top of the list. This is simply because so much of the earth's surface (over 70%) is covered by marine environments. So . . . why not just harvest marine plants and convert them to food for mankind? Just consider the energy expenditure necessary to do this. Do you think that this would be efficient? How would humans react to this food supply (unless they were literally starving to death)? It is interesting that many writers look to the sea for providing food for the world's exploding human population. But, even if we consider the fisheries of the sea (remember that fish are consumers and not producers) we also must realize that many marine fisheries have already been over-exploited by commercial fisherman from a number of nations.

So, what's the answer to the question concerning the continued productivity of the world's ecosystems for producing food energy needed by all of the food chains in the biosphere (including man's)? Do you think that humans are making food production decisions based on ecological data? Do you think that ecological data should be seriously considered when we drain wetlands, convert estuaries to homes and commercial enterprises, cut tropical rain forests for timber and conversion to beef production, permit the oceans to be polluted, put up with the continued loss of topsoil from agland, and argue about what the eventual uses for the forests of the continents should be? It would appear that ecological knowledge is not being considered when humans make decisions about the fate of the ecosystems which are directly or indirectly responsible for their own welfare. What do you think? Just what **are** the answers?

> To what extent are humans making food production decisions based on sound ecological information?

CHAPTER IV

A BRIEF LOOK

AT

POPULATIONS

AND

RELATIONSHIPS

Learner Objectives for Chapter IV

Subsequent to your interactions with Chapter IV (and prior parts), you should be able to:

1. . . . describe a species population as a unit (level) of organization in an ecosystem and explain the role of populations in ecosystems.

2. . . . infer why the space-time variable can be important when considering a population of organisms.

   (Note: You already know that populations are made up of individuals. Individual members of populations can be born or die, and they can emigrate and immigrate. Energy flows through populations and nutrients are cycled there. And, typically, the population is a self-regulating system that functions as an integral part of the ecosystem. You might want to consider these things in part or in whole when responding to Objectives 1 and 2.)

3. . . . define (and explain the relationship between) **biotic potential** and **environmental resistance**.

4. . . . diagram the growth curve represented by an **eruptive population**. Further, be able to explain how an organism's biotic potential can result in an eruptive population (and provide at least one example).

5. . . . define the term **carrying capacity** and discuss the role of carrying capacity in population stability.

6. . . . using the "Kaibab Deer Saga" as an example, explain how the deer population became eruptive, why the population declined dramatically, and why the eventual carrying capacity was lower than the original one.

7. . . . explain the difference between an **optimum population density** and a **maximum population density** (carrying capacity).

8. . . . explain why optimum density is a much "safer" level than maximum density for the survival of an organism.

9. . . . explain why a population is a dynamic unit or organization rather than a static one (and provide examples).

10. . . . describe the predator-prey relationship in population dynamics and explain the consequences of this relationship for both prey population and the predator population.

11. . . . define **density-independent** variable as it relates to population dynamics.

12. . . . provide at least three examples of density-independent variables and explain how they operate to impact upon populations.

13. . . . explain (providing examples) how humankind acts as a density-independent variable in population dynamics (or extinction).

14. . . . define **density-dependent** variable as it relates to population dynamics.

15. . . . explain how **food** operates as a density-dependent variable in population dynamics.

16. . . . explain how **behavior** acts as a density-dependent variable in population dynamics (and provide examples).

17. . . . discuss the role that density-dependent variables may play in the human population.

18. . . . discuss why it may be crucial for scientists to learn more about population dynamics from an environmental perspective (considering the populations of man and other organisms in the biosphere, as well as the fact that many ecologists feel certain that man is susceptible to many of the same variables that affect other organisms).

19. . . . describe several symbiotic relationships that exist between organisms and explain how each impacts the species involved.

An Anecdote

The old female Canada goose cocked her head to scan the sky as she felt the strong southerly wind flow over the March landscape. She grunted a low guttural sound that was heard by at least a few of the two hundred or so geese that made up the flock. All of the geese seemed nervous tonight as they swam slowly, rafted together on the southerly shore of Crab Orchard Lake in southern Illinois.

These geese and thousands more had wintered a fairly mild winter on this national wildlife refuge. The old goose had traveled here from Hudson Bay in Canada with her gander and two

yearling geese last November.   They had stopped in Wisconsin for a few days on the long trip southward because of a wind shift which slowed their progress and tired them out. She just didn't have the stamina she had when she was younger.

Her small family was still intact, having stayed clear of predators and the goose hunters during the long hunting season. Other family groups had not been so lucky and broken families were joined by bachelor geese or young females as all of the mature geese attempted to find mates during the late winter.

The lengthening days that told her winter was nearing an end, and an intense desire to reproduce on the same shore where she had been hatched nine years earlier, made her restless. The rest of the geese showed the same restlessness. A night sky full of stars to navigate by and a strong southerly wind were too tempting. With a loud "honk" she pushed herself forward in the water, wings beating furiously and her feet slashing hard against the water. In a matter of seconds she was air borne and the entire flock exploded from the lake to join her. Heading into the wind she gained altitude and then turned toward the north. She called over and over again and others in the flock responded as they organized themselves into a "V" formation. Higher and higher they climbed until the push of the wind was maximum. The old goose, at the tip of the "V", set course in the night sky and the honking from the flock could be heard as it passed over southern and central Illinois toward the Canadian border.

With a bit of luck and stamina, the goose might survive a few more trips and a few more winters. Whether she did or not is unimportant ecologically because her offspring will continue the long journeys of their parents and grandparents. Given the ability of waterfowl managers to protect the geese and the strength of the birds themselves, this event in nature could continue for many thousands of years into the future - just as it had happened for untold thousands of years in the past!

A BRIEF LOOK AT POPULATIONS

Introduction

As you already know, the species population is an important level of organization in the biosphere. And, you should also be aware that communities are no more than certain species populations **interacting** with each other. These two concepts give you a head start on understanding something about populations.

Now, you should be told that there are many concepts associated with populations and that these concepts, in the grand scheme of ecology, are both terrible important and, sometimes, very complex. Further, if you are to have a basic understanding of ecology, you must come to grips with some of the important ideas associated with populations and their regulation in the biosphere.

> **A thorough understanding of ecology includes key concepts concerning populations and their regulation.**

Once again, a *population* is a group of organisms (plant or animal) of the same species occupying a particular space at particular point in time (e.g., all of the white oak trees in Jackson County in 1988). The population, in addition, is an organizational unit (level) through which energy flows and nutrients are cycled. And, interestingly, it is a self-regulating system that helps keep the ecosystem (or community) in equilibrium (dynamically stable over time).

Populations also have birth rates, death rates, age structures, densities, growth patterns, and dispersion in both time and space (both dispersion within the ecosystem and to different ecosystems).

All of this appears extremely complex and it can be! However, Chapter IV will attempt to illustrate some of these concepts and make you feel more comfortable with them. There is always some danger in trying to simplify these concepts and it is recommended that you go from here to additional readings or field studies if you feel it important to do so.

Biotic Potential and Environmental Resistance

Every species population has a certain biotic potential for growth (i.e., the extent to which it can expand (grow) under the conditions that are present). Many organisms tend to have an amazing capacity for reproduction in an environment which has "unlimited resources" for them. If you take a look at the global human population you can get a glimpse of the validity of this idea.

The biotic potential of various organisms has intrigued scientists for a long time. Edward Kormondy reports that Charles Darwin calculated that a single pair of elephants would have over 19,000,000 descendants alive after 750 years if its biotic potential could be realized. Now, considering the long gestation period of the elephant, these numbers are astounding.

What about an organism with a short reproductive cycle? Again, Kormondy reports on the work of L.O. Howard who studied the common housefly. Howard determined that one housefly could result in seven (7) generations of flies per year. One female will lay about 120 eggs at a time. About 60 of these will be female. You can fool around with the numbers if you want but this biotic potential would result in 6,182,442,727,320 flies in one year. Folks, that's six trillion and that's a lot of flies! Try to get supper in the kitchen with all of these flies around.

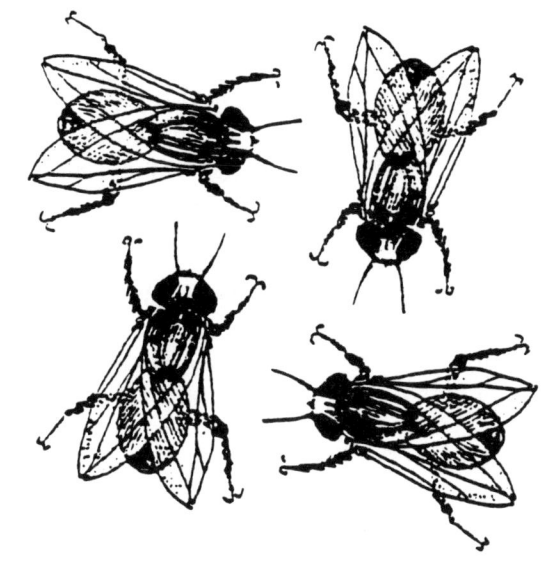

Now, it should be obvious that an unrestricted growth curve (unrestricted reproduction) on a graph should look like a rocket taking off. Let's call such a jump in a population *eruptive*. An eruptive population growth curve takes on the appearance of a "J-curve". The J-curve is diagrammed below.

Is the J-curve (the eruptive population) a reality in the biosphere? You bet! Ecologists tell us that when an organism exploits an unoccupied niche in an ecosystem, its numbers will often explode in this manner. In some organisms, like the housefly, this can take but a blink-of-an-eye; in others, years may be involved. Again, the human organism has taken decades to erupt. Still, when we talk of a century or two we are looking at only a small parcel of time, when we consider the age of the earth or the time during which living things have inhabited the earth.

So, we see that populations can, and sometimes do, erupt dramatically. Why don't we see this as a common occurrence in ecosystems? Enter *environmental resistance* (the extent to which the environment limits the biotic potential of a population)! First of all, resources for a population are really not unlimited. Resources are finite and play a terribly significant role in population regulation. Secondly, the population itself can contaminate its own environment if that environment is over-exploited (again, look at man as an example). And, too, the population can experience changes in temperature, moisture, isolation, chemistry, etc., etc. and can respond to these changes negatively.

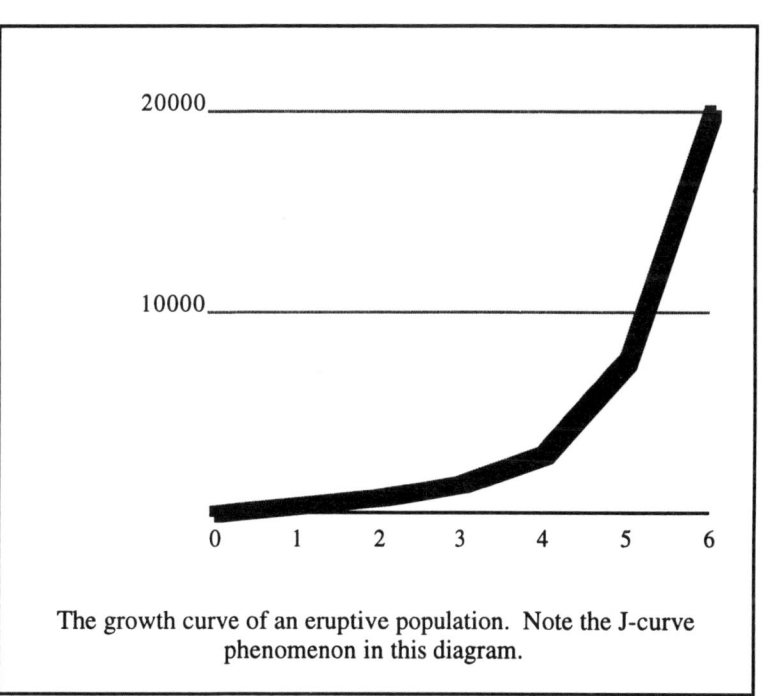

The growth curve of an eruptive population. Note the J-curve phenomenon in this diagram.

Under "natural conditions" a population tends to erupt until it reaches zero growth (See the diagram below.). Here it may be in equilibrium with its environment. Equilibrium is typically the upward limits for this organism in this environment. Oftentimes, this point is termed "carrying capacity". Under these conditions, the growth curve resembles the diagram on the following page, sometimes called the "S curve". It doesn't take too much thought to speculate that the carrying capacity can change from time to time and, indeed, this can be and is often the case.

There are times when certain species will normally erupt dramatically and then their populations will crash, again normally, in an equally dramatic fashion. There are other times when a population will erupt in an abnormal fashion due to some unusual or aberrant variable in the environment. Let's take a look at both of these conditions with examples.

In the illustration on the following page, you will see the growth curve of an insect population interacting with a deciduous tree population in a southern U.S. ecosystem (from April to the following March). Although the diagram is representative only, this condition is observable with many insects that are dependent on the food-producing capability of the deciduous tree.

A good example of this phenomenon would be aphids interacting with oak trees. The aphid population is very, very low during the winter months (as can be seen in the diagram) but when spring arrives and the leaves begin to appear on the oak trees, the population erupts in a J-curve manner reaching its maximum density between June and July. At this point the population begins to

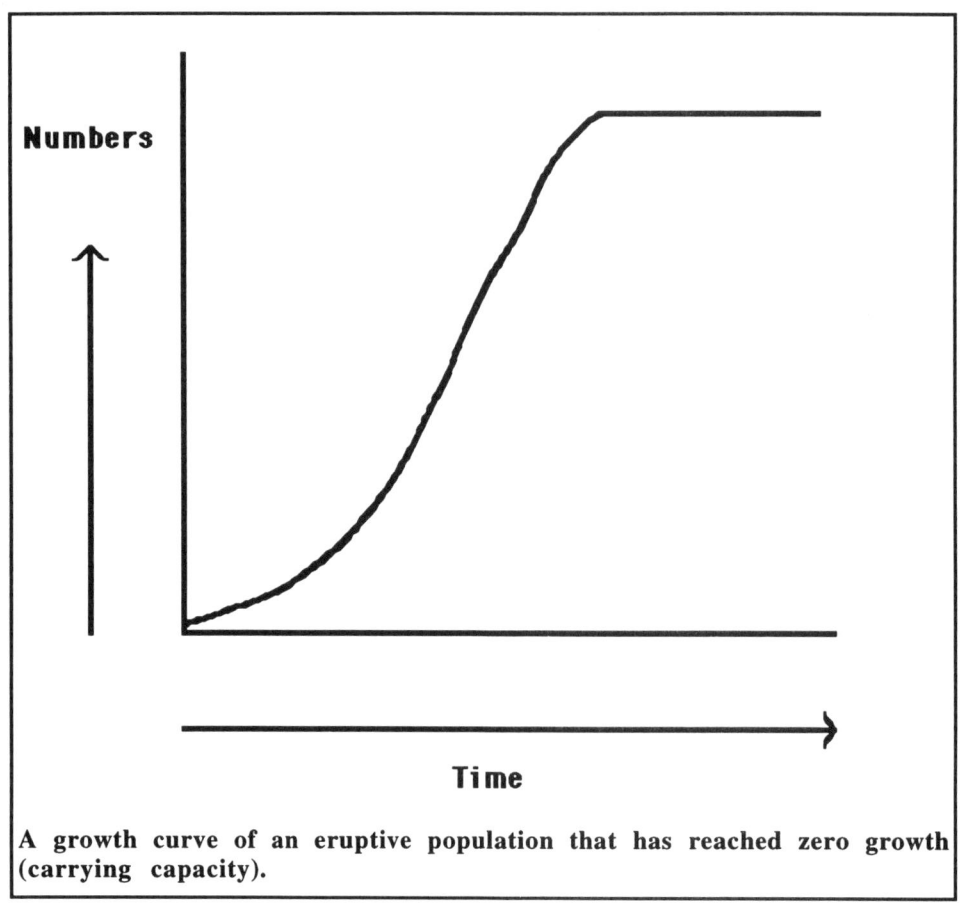

A growth curve of an eruptive population that has reached zero growth (carrying capacity).

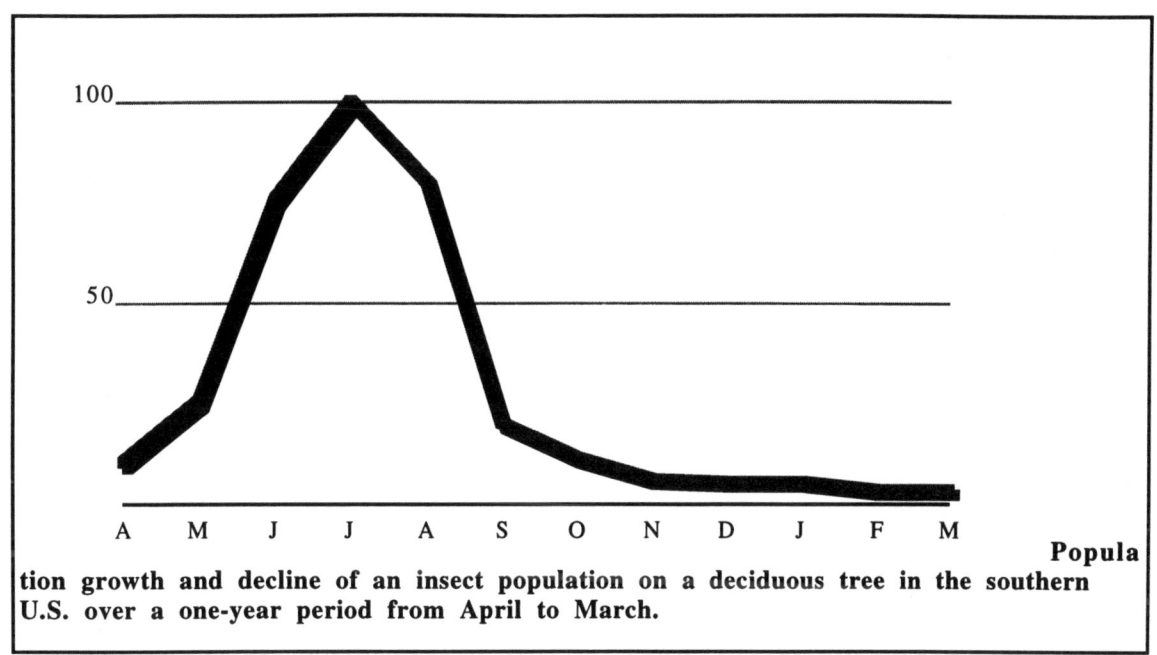

Popula-

tion growth and decline of an insect population on a deciduous tree in the southern U.S. over a one-year period from April to March.

decline and does so rapidly. The aphids can no longer exploit the niche as successfully as they did earlier in the summer. The aphids' environment becomes less and less hospitable in any one of a number of ways. How might the aphids' environment change? A few ideas come to mind. Sheer numbers could result in population stress from competition among aphids (population stresses are commonly observed in ecosystems). The leaves of the trees begin to age which might affect the availability and quality of the food produced. Predator populations could influence the aphid population dramatically (it usually takes a predator population longer to grow than the prey population).

In some instances, temperature is a major variable in the control of aphid populations. Some aphid species cannot tolerate high air temperatures. Some populations may even crash instantly to near zero when the air temperature reaches 100 degrees F. Our diagram does not indicate that this would be the case but high temperatures could still influence the insect population negatively. If the air temperature rose beyond the "optimum temperature range" for this species its population should begin to decline. Which variable is the key? Actually, it may be a combination of variables with some being more important than others.

You might think that this population fluctuation is simply the "normal state-of-affairs" for this insect species. Indeed it might be. But (and it's an important "but"), there is a cause-and-effect relationship in operation here and it is incumbent upon the student of ecology to try to ascertain what the variables are that impact upon this "normal" yearly fluctuation. And, remember, this kind of population growth curve is very common in the environment. Can we bring this

> **Species population: A group of organisms (plant or animal) of the same species occupying a particular space at particular point in time.**

situation home to the reader? Let's try. Are you a gardener? This kind of a growth curve would be more or less observable with cabbage worms, with corn-ear worms, with bean beetles, at times with grasshoppers, or with aphids on apple trees. Think about it! Or, as a homemaker, how about fruit flies in the summer and fall? There is always a high correlation between the fruit season and fruit flies. The writer suspects that the population growth curve of fruit flies would look very much like our hypothetical aphids on oak trees.

97

Well, how about the second example - that one focused on an unusual intervening variable that impacts heavily on a population? The classic example used to illustrate this phenomenon is the case study of the Kaibab deer. If you are familiar with this case study so be it. However, it is important to present this to those who may know little about it.

The Kaibab Plateau lies in northwestern Arizona, adjacent to the Colorado River and the Grand Canyon. Prior to 1907 the plateau had a deer herd that numbered about 4,000. This herd was healthy and largely stable as a function of predation by wolves, pumas, and coyotes as well as a good healthy habitat for them. However, there were those who decided that the deer could be benefited if their predators were removed from the plateau. Thus a campaign was initiated to do exactly that. The predator kill? Some 3000 coyotes, 600 pumas, and 11 wolves were removed from the plateau. Once the removal of predators was well underway, the deer population really began to expand and to exploit its environment. On came the J-curve and, by 1924, there were about 100,000 deer on the plateau. This population saturated the environment ,and the carrying capacity (about 30,000 deer) had been breached. The results were both saddening and dramatic. In 1925 and 1926 more than half of the deer starved to death because the habitat had been degraded so badly. The population continued to decline after 1926 and by 1939 was down to about 10,000 animals, far below the *original* carrying capacity. The animals' range was so badly damaged from overgrazing that, even then, more deer died from starvation than had been killed by predators.

The diagram on the facing page illustrates this situation and shows how dramatically a population can be impacted by improper wildlife management. Of great importance in this study is the fact that the deer so changed the environment as their numbers erupted that the changes did not permit as high a carrying capacity subsequent to the damage. There should be a lesson (or a number of lessons) there somewhere. Can you think of any?

98

The notion of "carrying capacity" seems rather simple, doesn't it? It involves the idea that an ecosystem has resources available which can support X number of a given species, e.g., deer, foxes, skunks, oak trees, aphids, toads, garter snakes, poison ivy, etc.

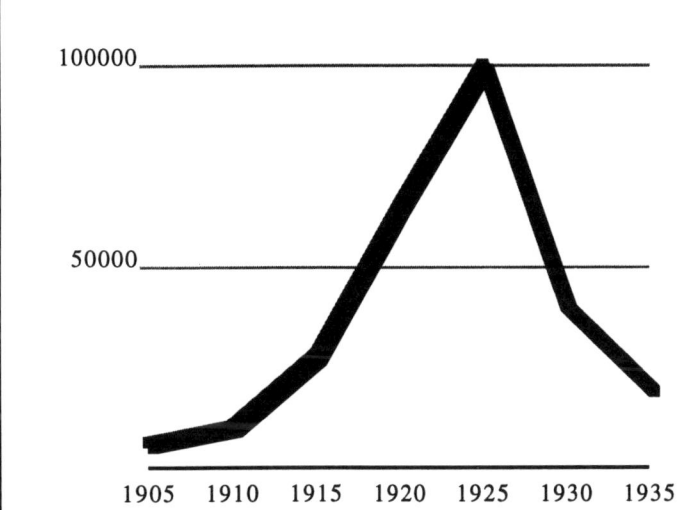

The Kaibab deer saga! As predators were killed, the deer herd increased dramatically. This was followed by heavy browsing of available food sources. As the population peaked, there were signs of starvation. During the two years after the population peaked, 60% of the herd died from starvation. Note the decreased carrying capacity after all was said and done!

Not too difficult, eh? It makes a lot of sense and scientists have worked on this concept for a long time. However, enter a second aspect of this idea! Many ecologists claim, and probably correctly, that somewhere there exists, for each species in each ecosystem, something called an "optimum density". Optimum density would be that population level at which the ecosystem is not stressed, somewhat below the "maximum carrying capacity" which might be liable to some sort of disaster under certain environmental conditions.

We see this concept more or less illustrated on the Kaibab deer graph. Remember that in 1907, there were only about 4,000 deer on the Kaibab Plateau. This number was far below the maximum carrying capacity which was 30,000 animals. Was 4,000 the magic number for "optimum density"? We simply do not know. But, we can state rather emphatically that optimum density was probable somewhere between 4,000 and a number less than 30,000. That's a lot of space isn't it? And, this low 1907 population may have triggered the notion that the removal of predators would be a positive variable for the deer. You could easily go back to the Kaibab graph and guess that the optimum density should be somewhere around 20,000 animals. And, it is entirely possible that careful management practices could have increased the deer heard to that number without seeing the J-curve disaster come about. But (!), *after* the disaster on the Kaibab Plateau, scientists determined that the carrying capacity had been reduced to about 10,000 deer. What would the "optimum density" be then? Most certainly, it would be below 10,000 (down from a higher number in 1907). You should now be getting the idea that a lot of variables interplay in the notion of "carrying capacity" and "optimum density".

Please do not assume (as many do) that this concept applies only to game animals. It is, indeed, applicable to all organisms whether or not they seem to have some value for humans. We are looking at overall population dynamics and

> **Optimum density allows room for environmental changes in the ecosystem which might otherwise threaten the population itself.**

not just wildlife management here. It appears as though every population has a point at which its numbers do not threaten either the ecosystem or itself. This is the *optimum density*, below the maximum carrying capacity of the ecosystem. Optimum density allows room for environmental changes in the ecosystem which might otherwise threaten the population itself. If environmental changes occur at the maximum carrying capacity, the population could be in immediate serious trouble and the consequences, for that population, could be disastrous.

Still More Basic Thoughts on Population

Population Makeup: Many students of ecology run around with the notion of a population as a group of individuals, i.e., they see individuals rather than the population per se. Sure, the population is made up of individuals but the population is, in reality, a unit separate and apart from individual organisms. The writer can see some of the readers grumbling about this right now! Why not individuals? Simply because the population is a "unit of organization" and as an organizational unit must be considered in its totality rather than as individual entities.

Let's work on this idea a bit. If a given population of opossums in a southern Indiana forest ecosystem is stable over time at about 100 animals, we must realize that there will be deaths, births, some emigration, and some immigration going on in that population. Of course, births and deaths (as well as emigration and immigration) involve individual opossums but it is the overall population in which we are interested. Ecologically, it is the species populations and its "dynamics" that are important in a scientific sense and not individual organisms.

Maybe another example would help. If a population of aphids on a oak tree grows from 50 to 50,000 during a summer, those 50,000 individuals which eventually make up the maximum population are *not* all individuals which have survived over that period of time. Aha!!! Sure, some individuals have died, some have been preyed upon, some have emigrated, and some have immigrated. New individuals, of course, have been born. So, if we tried to deal with these aphids as individuals we would go crazy! Therefore, we most certainly have to look at the unit population instead. Make sense?

Of course, one problem with this lies in our tendency for empathy with animals, particularly vertebrates, e.g., birds, mammals, etc. This empathy focuses on the rights and worth of individual organisms (e.g., a deer we see on the way to work, a fox that lives in a nearby woods, a nesting pair of wood ducks on a nearby pond). This preoccupation with something related to humanism and aesthetics can get in the way when we look at things in an ecological sense. Thus, it becomes imperative for us to try, at least, to separate our emotional tendencies from our scientific view of the biosphere.

The Population As A Dynamic Unit: All of this talk about population stability can also be confusing at first. When we talk about "population stability" we are not talking about organizational units which are static. We are, instead, speaking of an ecological entity which can be very dynamic. Sounds a little antithetical doesn't it? But, in reality, it isn't at all antithetical. We must realize that population fluctuations can and do occur but, overall, these fluctuations *usually* do not jump around haphazardly. Instead, these fluctuations are a consequence of population units responding to certain variables in the ecosystem. Thus, going back to our aphids again, the population cycle illustrated on the graph may, in reality, be a normal state of affairs, with the species responding each and every year to the same variables which result in growth curves more or less like every other year (with exceptions of course).

With most organisms, there are "good years" and "bad years" and, of course, populations respond to these. This phenomenon is widely documented. An example of cyclical population changes can be seen in the graph at the bottom of this page. This graph demonstrates cycles in the population size of the varying hare in Canada and Labrador.

The cycles represented in the graph are similar to the ones which seem to operate in the cottontail rabbit population in the U.S. Other examples of populations with cyclical fluctuations are: commercial marine fishes, rabbits in the Midwest, bobwhite quail in the Midwest and the South, the varying hare in Canada and Labrador, the lynx in Canada, and the sand grouse in Europe. Some of the variables associated with varying populations are well known and others are not.

A short discussion about the varying hare graph seems appropriate. The data indicate that, although the hare population fluctuates dramatically, some semblance of "order" seems to exist. Although the population of hares seems to erupt periodically, their numbers always seem to fall back to a subsequent low, only to increase once again. Why? Two sets of variables are probably

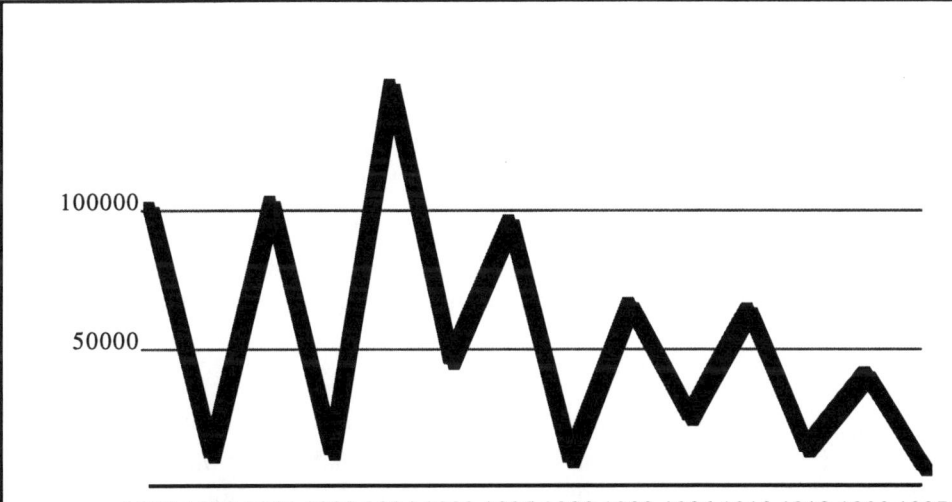

Estimated population fluctuations of the varying hare of Canada and Labrador. Note the wide variation in sizes of populations. These populations tend to cycle about every ten years. This is not an uncommon occurrence in some mammalian species.

responsible. One set of variables relates to environmental conditions such as food supply, harshness of weather conditions, etc. During "fair" periods of substantial food and years with moderate weather, populations respond by rebounding from their lows. As they rebound and grow, predation and disease (the second set of variables) are certain to increase. These two sets of variables operate together to act upon the population.

The preceding example introduces an important idea: predator-prey relationships have a great deal to do with population fluctuations. In the case of the varying hare, the lynx is a major predator Records from the fur industry in the far north show a dramatic relationship between the lynx and the hare.

> **Predator-prey relationships have a great deal to do with population fluctuations.**

Shortly after the hare population begins to grow, so does the lynx population. This may mean that, as the hare population increases, predator pressure builds. It continues to build as a function of increased numbers of lynxes until the hare population begins to collapse once again. Subsequent to the lessening of hare population, the lynx population also goes on the decline. Thus, the two populations are closely tied to each other and, perhaps, ecologically, interdependent. Can you see how this might be the case? Consider how the lynxes could be considered "good guys" from an ecological point of view.

When dealing with predator-prey relationships, it is interesting to note that prey organisms and predator organisms do not peak at the same time. The *predator organism peaks after the prey organism* and typically *begins to decline after the beginning of the decline of the prey species.*

Limiting Factors in Populations

Several major ideas emerge as we look at variables that seem to be associated with population dynamics:

(1) A population tends to arrive at some point of equilibrium (carrying capacity) and then to fluctuate around that number.

(2) We can look at a population in terms of its average density over time, a density which is appropriate for the environmental conditions in which it exists.

(3) A population is influenced by forces outside the population (density-independent forces) *or* by the forces within it (density-dependent forces). The overall control of the character of a population is most certainly a combination of these forces.

(4) Organisms of an individual species react to different variables and/or combinations of variables in their environment. Too much or too little of a particular substance or condition can severely impact a population.

(5) We do not know all of the forces that act on populations to regulate them nor do we totally understand those forces that have been identified.

The Law of Tolerance

Back in the early part of the 20th century a scientist by the name of Shelford came up with what is known as "the law of tolerance". This concept tells us that too much or too little of a substance or condition limits the ability of a species to survive. Current thinking, on the other hand, seems to modify this idea a bit by focusing on the interactions brought about by the intermingling of a number of conditions and/or substances. This of course can get quite complicated.

Before we leave "the law of tolerance", however, let us consider some factors which do, indeed, limit a species ability to maximize success in an ecosystem. For example, fish, amphibians, and reptiles are not able to regulate their body temperatures. Their temperatures vary with the temperature experienced in their environments. They are active during the warm seasons. However, the are usually inactive during the winter and seek pro-

The Law of Tolerance

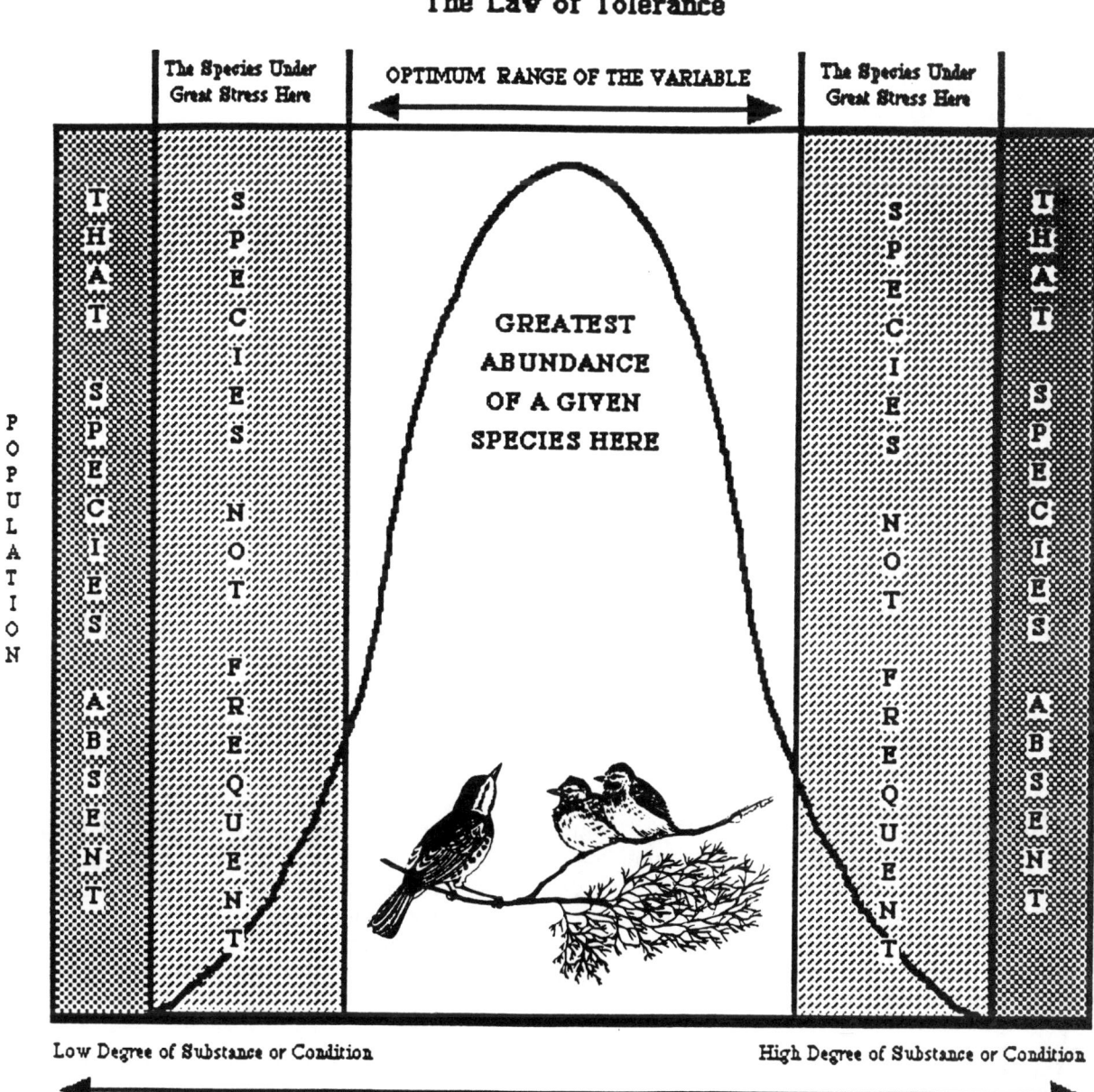

tection from very hot conditions during the summer months. In most cases, the temperature range within which they can be active is above 40 degrees F and below 110 degrees F. In addition, all organisms, both plants and animals, have an *optimum temperature range* within which they can be very successful (depending, of course, on the other variables within the ecosystem).

Moisture is another critical variable. In fact, moisture and temperature together control climate which, in turn, dictates the presence or absence of most ecosystems. Still other variables would include soil, wind, light, slope direction, and fire. You might want to consider species (and/or ecosystems) that might be impacted by these variables with respect to "the law of tolerance".

Let us now look at some of these variables (and others as well) from a different perspective. This perspective has to do with whether a population is impacted by variables that are "density-independent" or "density-dependent". Let's see how these discussions unfold.

Density-Independent Variables

Some variables operate independently of the density of a given population to influence population density. A few of these are described below.

| Weather | **Weather** is a very powerful density-independent variable. It can influence population growth and density both positively and negatively. A warm spring with adequate rainfall will result in successful flowering of oak trees and the subsequent production of acorns. Acorns mean food for many animals such as turkeys and squirrels. Their populations respond accordingly. A cold spring and an acorn crop failure can produce widespread starvation in these populations the following winter and, therefore, a sharp decrease in density.

| Snow cover | Can **snow cover** negatively influence organisms? One study showed that the number of months that the ground was covered with three or more inches of snow influenced populations of bobwhite quail. Mortality was as low as 4% during winters where 3 inches of snow covered the ground for less than a month and as high as 80% during winters where 3 inches of snow covered the ground for three months or more. A similar situation exists with deer in northern forests. Where there are 50 or more days of accumulated snow 24 inches deep or deeper, deer populations suffer dramatically. The reason is that it is difficult for the deer to travel to food sources. The fawns, in particular, are severely restricted in movement and as many as 5 out of every 6 fawns die as a consequence.

| Soil moisture | Yes, **soil moisture**! Southwestern deserts contain populations of Gambel's quail. Gambel's quail is very dependent on winter and spring rains and subsequent soil moisture in April. If there isn't enough soil moisture to produce rich populations of flowering plants the quail suffer. They rely heavily on these plants during the following winter for food. Interestingly, soil moisture in the desert also impacts on rodents. If green vegetation is not produced in quantity, the female rodents simply do not reproduce. Thus, the adults will survive but no new offspring are added to the population.

| Rainfall | Heavy spring **rains** impact on the reproduction and juvenile survival in such organisms as rabbits, quail, pheasants, and others.   So, we see that too little rainfall can be a negative influence on some populations and too much rainfall a negative influence on others. Moderate rainfall can positively impact on certain populations, etc., etc.!

Air temperature If average spring **temperatures** are below 53 degrees F, ring-necked pheasants have a very difficult time reproducing. This results in lowered reproduction and, therefore, less population density. As we noted earlier, certain aphid populations (e.g., the walnut aphid in California) will crash if the air temperature reaches 100 degrees F and stays there for any length of time.

Human beings And what of **human beings?** Humans can positively or negatively impact on populations. Sometimes they do both at the same time (but this means impacting on several species at once). Let's take the last situation - being both a positive and a negative influence. If Western forests are clearcut (all the trees removed at once), some animal populations are benefited and some are harmed. In this instance, populations like those of juncos and deer mice thrive and populations of nuthatches, squirrels, and voles disappear. One understands, of course, what happens to the fir tree population in a clearcut operation. The writer can only surmise that if you root for juncos and deer mice you would also then root for clearcutting firs. On a more serious note, humans have had a hand in some disastrous population declines and species extinctions. Let's look at a few of these. The poaching of rhinos (for horn) and elephants (for ivory) in Africa is criticized the world over by conservationists and others as well. The elephant population is in serious trouble and the rhino population may be doomed to live only in zoos and on game farms. Cutting of virgin forests in the southern U.S. resulted in the extirpation (extinction) of the ivory-billed woodpecker from North America.

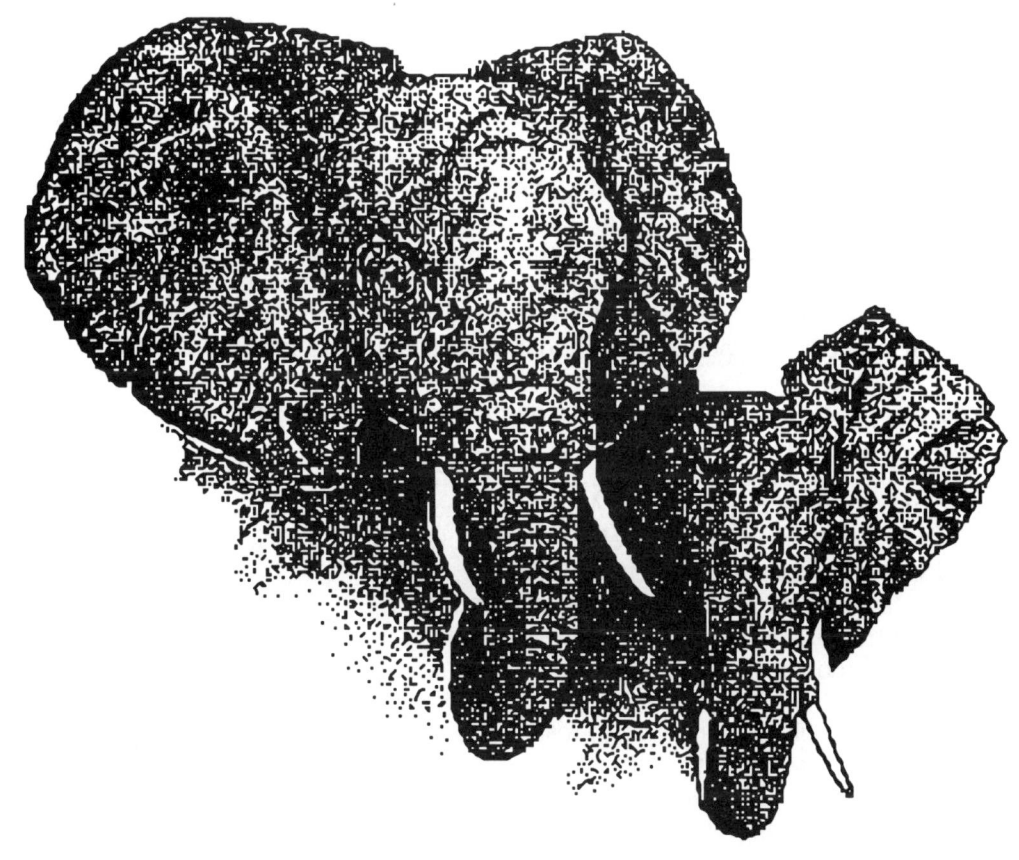

105

A combination of market hunting (which can also be density-dependent under certain conditions) and lumbering led to the extinction of the passenger pigeon. Market hunting in North America for hides, meat, and feathers has either sharply reduced or has exterminated populations of many birds, reptiles, and mammals. The drainage of wetlands across North America and, in particular, the Dakotas has resulted in drastically reduced waterfowl populations. The use of pesticides has threatened the bald eagle, the

> **Humans can impact positively or negatively on species populations! Extinctions of species populations have become rampant the world over!**

osprey, and others. And, too, land use management practices have serious impacts on many organisms, both plant and animal. The impacts of man on naturally existing populations in the environment are legendary. And they continue to this very day! But, the environmental side of the situation is another story for another time.

Density-Dependent Variables

Discounting the variables we have discussed above (i.e., all other things being equal), the regulation of population density seems to be tied up with stability - at least stability as we have defined it. This means that there are mechanisms **within populations (density dependent)** that control population size over the long term. Density-dependent variables seem to appear when populations reach a certain density and become low-key when populations sizes are lower. Also, density-dependent variables appear to be related, in some way, to competition between individuals within the population. This competition usually relates to some kind of resource, e.g., space and food.

Let's take a look at some of the density-dependent variables and gain at least an initial concept of how they work. And, too, some of these probably work with man as well which makes them most interesting. We must realize that many, many people do not like to think that they might be liable to built-in mechanisms that control reproductive behavior but there is a good deal of evidence to support this notion. However, much of the application of density-dependent variables in man is theoretical in nature simply because the ecologist can't take a population of humans and apply experimental techniques to it. So, you can think about these "human relationships to population regulation" and reject them, accept them, or choose to consider them further.

Food There is a good deal of argument among ecologists about **food** as a density-dependent variable. On the surface, it would appear that food might be a very logical density-dependent variable, i.e., the less food there is for a population the greater the risk for that population. And, in some cases this has been demonstrated very nicely. Think back on the Kaibab deer saga. The critical variable in the crash of the deer population was available browse (food). Remember, 60% of the 100,000 deer died from starvation in the first two years following the top of the J-curve.

North American deer have a tendency to respond to a rich food resource by reproducing with a vengeance. Unless population density is held in check through predation or hunting pressure, populations tend to grow large (again, remember the Kaibab deer). Once the food resource is over-utilized, starvation (particularly of the fawns) becomes a real threat. But, a lot of deer can still survive on browse that is nutritionally poor. Poor nutrition results in poor growth, poor reproduction, increased fawn mortality, and, of course, a lot of older individuals within the population (think about it). So, with American deer, food seems to be a key variable in controlling population density.

Oftentimes, food acts as a limiting variable in consort with some other variable (or set of variables). We see food as one important variable in some insect populations such as fruit flies and aphids. But, as we already know, aphids can also be "kicked around" by other variables such as temperature. Still, food resources do impact on a number of insect populations and scientists are quite certain that, with many species populations, food is an important density-dependent variable.

Now, what about human beings? If we go back in history, we can find numerous examples of famines. Famine is also no stranger to modern man. We read about famines in the newspapers and see them on TV. However, it is equally certain that famine has not lowered the human population in total (worldwide). So, can we say that food acts in a density-dependent manner in the human population? Like the deer, man can and does suffer nutritional stress (food related). Poor food resources and subsequent nutritional problems result in some high prices in terms of population "quality". Consider the results of poor nutrition. This list is a long one and includes nutritionally related diseases (e.g., anemia, rickets and others), delayed maturity, and increased infant mortality. It can and does result in mental retardation. What are the ecological implications of famine on a world-wide basis? Of course, we have not seen world-wide famine yet but what do you think the results might be? Would there be an ecological connection?

| Behavior | When we look at **behavior** as a variable, we look at the levels of tolerance and intolerance displayed by individuals of the same population. Many organisms have well defined levels of social behavior which tend to control population density. Social behavior in organisms tends to control the number of animals in a particular habitat, access to a food supply, and access to mates. As you can readily see, these are important considerations for individual members of a population.

| Territoriality | **Territoriality** is one of the very interesting density-dependent variables associated with behavior. Every elementary school child is taught (?) that song birds have territories. But, are they taught the relationships between territories and population density? And, are they taught that territories are held, typically, only at certain times of the year? Why territories if there isn't a reason for them?

Territoriality can be a very complex concept if we look at all of the variations on the theme. Consider the cardinal, the state bird of more than one state. If we feed cardinals in the winter they will often come to the bird feeder in rather large flocks, males and females mixed together. However, as soon as spring

> **Many organisms have well defined levels of social behavior which tend to control population density.**

arrives, and the reproductive urge begins to descend upon the species, you can find a male cardinal singing loudly from a conspicuous perch. Another can be heard some distance away. This display proclaims a territory which will be used during the breeding season for the nesting, mating, and feeding. And, the territory will be defended with vigor (and usually successfully).

And, too, the muskrat, like the cardinal, uses a territoriality mechanism to control mating, feeding, and rearing (nesting). Some other mammal species behave similarly.

The best folk wisdom tells us that these territories are established to protect the food resources of the reproductive individuals. We would probably see some real population problems if a number of pairs of cardinals sought food during the breeding season in the same prime habitat. The same holds true for the muskrat. However, it is probably more complicated than this. Ecologist observe that each species (e.g., the cardinal) has a certain habitat in which it can be highly successful. This habitat is finite (limited). Aggressive and reproductive (mated) individuals seek out prime habitat and establish territories. Other members of the population (some mated and some not) are forced into marginal or less than ideal habitat. Perhaps an attempt is made to rear young here and perhaps not - it all depends on circumstances. What is known is that, if a particularly good habitat (territory) is abandoned for some reason, an individual from the marginal habitat will move into it. We also know that mortality is typically higher in the marginal habitat while breeding success is higher in the good habitat. If numbers of individuals in the marginal habitat do not reproduce and are preyed upon, it seems logical to assume that territoriality is serving its purpose, i.e., keeping the population density within reasonable limits.

Ecologists have developed a number of theories to explain territoriality. We won't go into them here. However, you must realize that the scientists do not know precisely how territoriality works. What we do know, however, is that this behavior is exhibited in a number of ways in numerous species and appears to work toward controlling population density.

Social Behavior is, of course, often associated with territoriality. And, sometimes, the two are hard to distinguish. Even so, social behavior can be fascinating in its complexity and in its results. If we look at social behavior from a density-dependent angle, we can demonstrate that it does, indeed, tend to control reproductivity within the population.

The most fascinating example of social behavior from a density-dependent perspective for this writer lies with the wolf. Wolves live in packs which have been shown to be cooperative hunting units. However, that's about where cooperation ends.

A wolf pack usually consists of several social levels which serve to control reproductive behavior. The top "dog" in the pack is termed the alpha male. He is the boss. All others defer to him. But, there is also a dominant female and she is termed the alpha female. All other wolves in the pack are subordinate to her (excluding the alpha male). These other wolves are, quite logically, called subordinate males and females. But, beyond these subordinate animals are ones called peripheral males and females and they are kept out of the social structure of the pack although they are members of it. Quite complicated, isn't it?

Now, what goes on here? The alpha female controls mating within the pack. In typical habitat during normal years, the female will not permit any other female to mate (even though they will come into heat). Even when the alpha male prefers a subordinate female, the alpha female puts a stop to any "fooling around" on his part. He will mate with her and no wolf else! Interestingly, when she has pups, others wolves in the pack cooperate in litter rearing.

These behaviors rather effectively limit the population density of the wolves. What happens when the wolf population is low for some reason or another? When that happens, this particular social structure breaks down a bit and subordinate females may also bear young. So, when the population is stable, social behavior limits reproduction. When the population is low, another mode of social behavior increases reproduction. It would appear that, in part, the subordinate and peripheral females are actually acting as reservoirs of reproductive potential in the social organization of the wolf pack.

Social behavior is a well known phenomenon in nature and exists among some reptiles, some insects, and birds as well. Often, this social behavior acts in subtle ways to control reproductivity within the population. Interestingly, social behavior is often linked to other variables which can make the process quite complex.

And what of social behavior in man? At times in man's history, social behavior was well defined and not subtle at all. Prior to the Renaissance there were rigid social structures and people fit into those or suffered the consequences. A brief reflection on your history courses will bear this out. But, what about now? Does modern man have social structures? Ecologists are very interested in this phenomenon and believe that man does, indeed, act according to certain "pecking order" structures in manners similar to those in birds, wolves, etc. Are there not superordinates and subordinates in most human institutions? Certainly we can see them in businesses, in homes, in religious institutions, in prisons, and in "social affairs". Although we probably do not like to admit it, we can identify alphas, betas, and peripherals in human situations. Who has the power? Who has the prestige? Who has the money? Who has the most desirable mates? Fully integrated folk have all or most of these things. Those humans who are fully integrated into the "system" have much more flexibility (and often power) than those who are not. People not totally integrated into the "system" will most probably suffer the most anxiety, stress, and negative physiological response to the social "order".

Whether social behavior in humans controls population density is unclear but it probably does not. But, did it at one time in man's history? Quite probably it did - before many social structures were broken down by an "enlightened society".

Stress is a variable closely linked to territoriality and to social behavior. In fact, it has been noted in association with these variables before. However, it seems incumbent on us to consider stress separately to see what this density-dependent variable produces in certain situations.

Stress can be observed in both plant and animal populations. And, of course, you could probably write a very intelligent paper on the causes of and responses to stress in human beings. Large numbers of people make their livings by helping human beings deal with stress - mental, physical, and combinations of both. Although stress, at this point in history, doesn't control human population density, it does have negative effects on reproduction and the consequences of reproduction (e.g., premature births, infant mortality, etc.) and, therefore, on the population as a whole.

But, what about other organisms? In plant populations, an increase in density can result in a great deal of stress which is responded to in interesting ways. In some situations, resulting from competition for available resources, the entire population may react by slowing the growth of individuals. Another response is increased mortality. And, still another is decreased reproduction. Some plant species will discontinue seed production if the population density reaches a certain level.

Some animal species respond dramatically to stress. This happens both in captivity and in the wild. Ecologists have done numerous experiments in the laboratory and have found that some animal populations like rats, mice and rabbits show marked reactions to high densities. Rather than deal with these animal species one by one let us, instead, comment on some of their responses to density-produced stress. In high densities, ecologists have observed serious involvement of the endocrine system. Glands involved included the pituitary and adrenal glands. This led to abnormal growth patterns and a curtailment of reproduction. In some animals, no females reached sexual maturity. And, in those which did reproduce, abnormal behavior could be observed, e.g., cannibalism, aggression, abnormal sexual behavior, etc.

In the wild, similar situations have been observed in rodents with high reproductive potential. High density causes stress which results in both physiological and psychological responses. Certain body functions fail (e.g., kidneys) and massive mortality results.

These observations have led ecologists to theorize that high population densities lead to stress which, in turn, leads to decreased reproduction and increased mortality. These variables tend to reduce the stress on the population by decreasing density which allows the population to return to a higher level of reproduction. The logic seems sound. But, just how generalizeable this theory is remains to be seen.

Other variables also play a role in population regulation. One example! We see some organisms responding to population pressures by **dispersing**. The history of the cattle egret is a classic case in point. Originally from Africa, it arrived in South America in 1937. From there it spread through Central America and can now be found as far north as the Great Lakes in the U.S.A. There is no doubt that the egret is very successful in these new areas because it fills a niche which has few competitors. Dispersal can also be dramatically recalled as one investigates the history of the European starling and the English sparrow in the U.S. Both of these birds were introduced by man. Because they found few enemies and an ideal habitat here they spread like "wildfire" across the continent.

And the Important Points Are?

Populations do vary across time. And, it appears as though there are cycles involved. Whether these cycles are controlled by environmental conditions surrounding the populations or by variables within the populations themselves is largely a moot issue. Of course, in some instances, both may play a role (and there are cases where this appears to be true). Population dynamics in the natural scheme of things is a reality - regardless of the prime mover.

Although we know relatively little about population dynamics it remains an important and fascinating part of ecology. What has been presented here only scratches the surface of this topic. A visit to the library and some time with ecology texts, field biology texts, better college level biology texts, and other sources can flesh out a great deal of information for the reader. If you are interested in these concepts, do not hesitate to look for additional information.

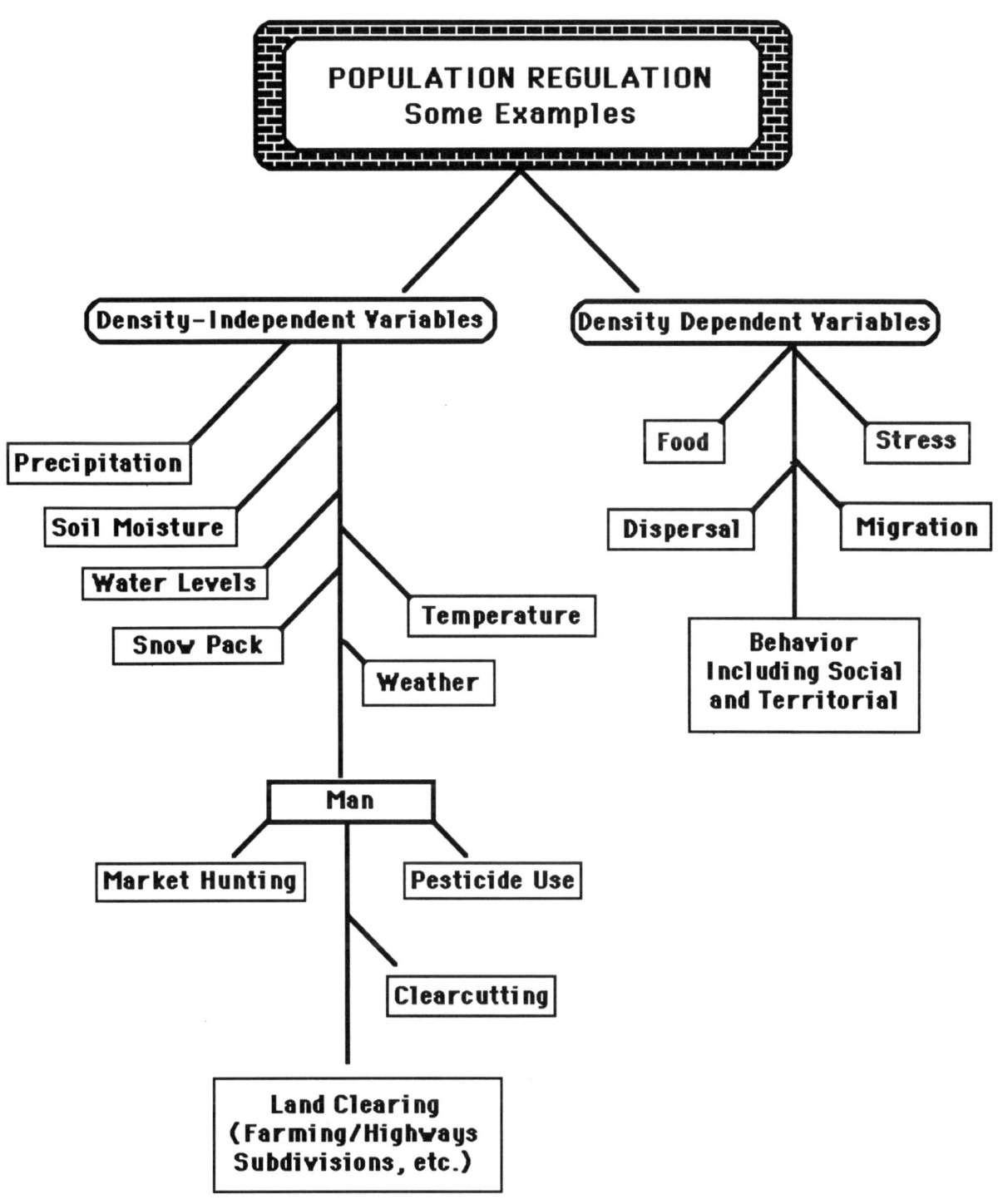

This diagram illustrates a number of variables which appear to influence population density. Still, there is a lot to be learned about population regulation. Because ecology is a fairly youthful science, the number of studies involved are limited. Are the primary causes of population regulation density-independent or density-dependent? There is argument.

Some Very Special Relationships In Populations

This topic, for the writer, has always held a great deal of fascination, for here we enter the world of *symbiosis* - as Smith would define it: "the living together of two or more species." Further, these two or more species must have some sort of a relationship between them. This relationship can benefit one of the species or it can benefit both. Or, it can be very detrimental to one of the members in the relationship. It all depends. Sounds like it can be kind of exciting doesn't it? Well, it is, but maybe not for the reasons you think!

The notion of symbiosis can be a difficult one to deal with. On the surface things seem rather simple and we will attempt to keep them that way here. However, when one digs deeply into the topic we find evidence that experts don't always agree on all of the facets of the topic. Further, a number of ecologists look upon some of the more complex relationships - ones that have developed over long periods of time - as a phenomenon called coevolution, i.e., one or two of the species changing their life functions in some manner and becoming interdependent, with one or both dependent on the other for survival.

We are not going to worry about the "what was" part of these special relationships long ago. It is quite enough to be concerned with the "here and now" of the relationships, and so it will surely be most, if not all, of the time. Just what are some of the examples of symbiotic relationships? And, can we describe who is benefited and why or why not? This is, sometimes, where it gets really interesting. It is not always easy.

One example: Commensalism. Here is a symbiotic relationship in which one of the species is benefited and not of any particular benefit to the other. If we walk into that Florida swamp, surrounded by cypress and ash trees, we would probably find ferns, orchids and/or bromeliads growing from the trunks of these trees or colonizing a branch. These plants are provided with a support which involves gaining light energy above the ground or water's surface. This relationship may also involve the collection of nutrients that accumulate at the base of the plant and it most certainly keeps the plants out of the water. It is easy to see that the ferns, orchids, and/or bromeliads are benefited. What of the tree? It doesn't seem to benefit or harm the trees at all. This example of symbiosis is commensal. Another example would be that of the remora fish and the shark. The remora attaches itself to the body of the shark and gets a free ride around the ocean and, perhaps, scraps of food when the shark feeds. What does the shark get? It might get a bit of an irritation from the attachment of the fish but, basically, it is unaffected while the remora seems to get all of the goodies.

These are pretty "simple examples"! But, what about the concept of predator-prey relationships? Isn't one species benefited and the other unaffected? Well, maybe! It depends upon the species involved. Oftentimes we find that the prey population may, in fact, be benefited by having the old and diseased individuals culled out of the population by the predators. This is often the case with the large predators - the cats - come to mind right away. This relationship could well be something else and we will talk about "mutualism" later. In a predator-prey situation where the prey species is largely unaffected, we would call it commensalism. Of course, the *individual being eaten* might not agree wholeheartedly with our inference. Things are not always as simple as they first appear.

Another example: Mutualism. In a mutualistic relationship, both species benefit in some manner. A very common example is that of the lichen, the oftentimes green, crusty plant which grows on rocks and fallen logs and even damp building materials. The lichen is really a composite of two plants, a fungus plant and an alga species. The fungus provides a habitat for the alga as well as moisture and some protection. The alga, on the other hand, provides food via photosynthesis and, therefore, both prosper or benefit. This relationship appears to have become inseparable so we might be tempted to say that the two plants are forever combined into one.

One fascinating relationship between animal and plant is the one that has developed between the yucca plant and the small white moth, not too surprisingly called the "yucca moth." The yucca tends to bear its many flowers all at once in the spring on a vertical stalk. The yucca moth has become a very special pollinator for the plant. The pupa of the moth resides inside the plant throughout much of the year, emerging as an adult moth about the time the plant blooms. Soon after emerging, the moth gathers pollen and carries it from one pistil to another, insuring successful seed production. The moth then proceeds to the base of selected flowers where it lays its eggs. The eggs hatch, burrow into the ovary of the flower and begin munching on the maturing fruit. Needless to say, for these special flowers, the seeds are history. However, in exchange for the moth's reproduction, many yucca flowers become pollinated and fruit successfully. Large numbers of seeds are therefore available for dispersal when the seeds are mature.

In fact, insect pollination of flowers tends to be mutualistic. Both parties benefit in some manner. For example, bees gather nectar and pollen and the flowers get pollinated - often cross pollinated which would tend to enhance the genetic survivability of the seeds being produced. You might want to investigate very unique examples of insect-flower relationships. Some very peculiar ones exist among the orchids and with other flowers as well.

Another example of mutualism? Another very interesting relationship exists within the termites' bodies. As you know, termites eats wood. The problem is, the termites cannot digest wood! How is this rather important problem solved? Inside the gut of the termite resides a very important protozoan which digests the wood for the termite, allowing nutrients to be absorbed into the termite's body. Both the termites and the protozoans benefit . . . mutualism.

Many, many other examples exist.

Another example: Parasitism.

Parasitism exists when one organisms benefits and the other is harmed in some manner. The very best parasite does not kill its host. Many parasite-host relationships have developed over time and there are animals that exist as hosts for numerous different parasites. They may be harmed but seldom killed. Consider the dog with fleas, ticks, and tape worms! All parasites! Unusual? Not really when you consider the feral, wild, and poorly cared for animals.

Theoretically, the very best parasite is one that allows its host to live - at least long enough for the host to reproduce, therefore giving the parasite a continued existence and food supply. Some believe that a highly developed parasitic relationship might actually be commensal. Humans often harbor a wide selection of yeasts and bacteria which, under normal conditions, seem to do no harm. Are these really commensal with us or, in fact, parasitic? This is interesting to think about and it also makes science even more intriguing and complicated.

We said earlier that the idea of symbiosis is not always a simple one. Here is something for you to think about. Human beings eat plants and animals. Are humans, then, being parasitic? Predatory? What do you think? Typically, human beings eat those plants that they propagate and the animals that they propagate as well. Do the plants and animals benefit? Taken on an individual basis the chicken you are eating would not think so. However, on a population basis the decision might be different. Humans benefit from their domestic plants and animals. They provide a safe and continued food source. And the animals and plants continue to survive as a variety or population. It is interesting to think about.

In the photos that follow, there are examples of more than one kind if relationship. Try your hand at identifying them.   On one photo we see a giraffe eating leaves from a thorn tree in Tanzania.   In another photo we see a colony of "ant galls" on the thorn tree. These galls are caused by ants which have a close association with the trees and live inside the hollow structures.   The ants get very, very hostile when a branch is jiggled by a giraffe trying to get at the leaves.   Whenever this happens, the ants race to the offending giraffe and sting its face.   The giraffe, not wanting more abuse, moves on to another tree where the process can happen once again.   Of course, the giraffe gets to eat some leaves from each tree but is unable to strip the branch bare due to the attacks made by the ants. There is at least one excellent example of mutualism here. What are its components? Any other relationships that you can think of? Photos courtesy H. R. Hungerford.

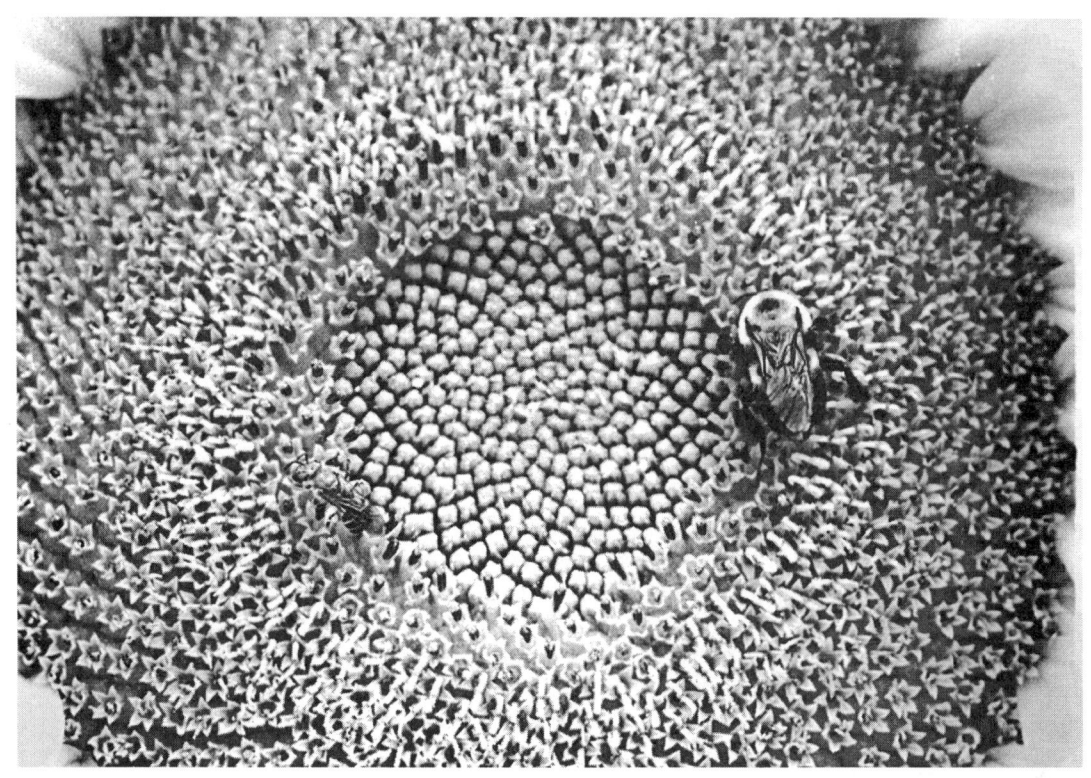

This is the head of a giant Russian sunflower. You will note two different bees feeding on some of the many individual flowers making up this flower head. The flowers are very attractive to bees and other insects. Sometimes there are a dozen or more insects "working" a single sunflower on a warm sunny day. What is the relationship between these animals and the plant? Why do you think so? Photo courtesy H. R. Hungerford

Activity 4.1

Observing An Eruptive Population: The Very Sexy Fruit Fly

The J-curve becomes a very real phenomenon if you can observe an organism producing offspring at a rate that accomplishes that. One that can do exactly that for you is the common fruit fly (*Drosophila melanogaster*). Not only that, the fruit fly is easy to culture at home, school, or just about anywhere that its tolerance range can be accommodated.

There are four stages in the life cycle of the fruit fly: the egg, the larva, the pupa, and the adult fly. In a warm environment the fly will produce new adults in about two weeks. The adults can live for weeks.

Wild fruit flies can be captured easily in many places in the U.S. during late summer and autumn. They can be captured out-of-doors or even inside where they have become established around fresh fruit.

If you want to capture wild flies, place a section of ripe banana or part of a very ripe peach (or other fruit) in a jar. Place this "trap" in an area known to have fruit flies in the environment. As the fruit ferments, the flies are attracted to the culture. When a number of flies are observed within jar it can be covered with a porous cloth secured with a rubber band. The flies can then be transferred to more stable culture bottles. Transferring flies can be accomplished by placing the culture in the refrigerator (NOT the freezer) and cooling them to the point that they will not fly out of the jar when it is uncovered and the flies removed. Needless to say, the transfer must be done with dispatch because as soon as the flies warm up they are up, up and away!

You can prepare fruit fly cultures in many different glass containers from standard vials purchased from biological supply houses to half pint milk bottles (becoming harder to find all the time) to baby food jars, etc. You can raise fruit flies on sections of banana (and other fruit) that has had yeast sprinkled on it. As you might imagine, these cultures can mold and liquefy causing problems for the flies. However, if this is all you have available, use this culture medium.

If you can, purchase culture materials from a biological supply house. All of the major supply houses sell materials for culturing fruit flies. One such supplier is General Biological Supply Co. at 2700 York Road in Burlington, NC 27215 or 19355 McLoughlin Blvd. in Gladstone, Oregon 97027. From these suppliers you can purchase flies for general use at under $20.00 per culture. Improved medium which is very easy to use can be had for as low as $5.00.

If you have the time and patience, a great activity is devised by creating new fruit fly cultures every ten days or two weeks. A sequence of three or four of these timed cultures allows one to observe cultures of different ages. The study/discussion questions that follow are based on this strategy.

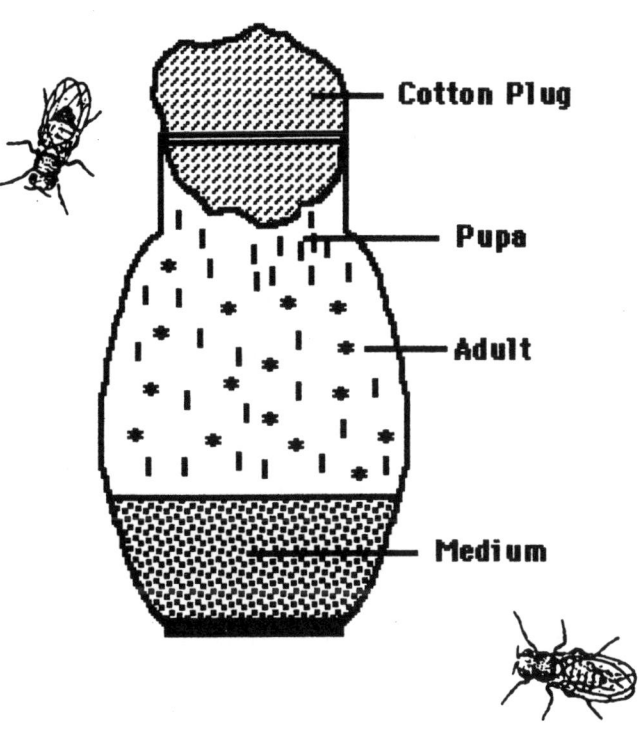

Cotton Plug

Pupa

Adult

Medium

Questions:

1. What differences can you observe between populations in a culture that is at least two weeks old compared with one that is one week old.

2. What differences can you observe between populations in a culture that has gone through three generations compared to one that is only one week old?

3. Estimate the number of flies that you can observe in two week, three week, and four week cultures. What are the proportions? Are the fruit fly populations headed for the J-curve phenomenon? What is your evidence?

4. The fruit fly cultures represent environments that are, in at least some ways, closed. By this we mean that the food supply is finite and there is no place for waste materials to go. Thus, food diminishes and waste products collect. Eventually, the population will diminish. How long does this take in your cultures? Once it begins, how long does it take for the population to crash?

5. You are observing eruptive populations of the fruit fly. The human organism is also an example of an eruptive population. Are there any implications for man that can be drawn from the fruit fly observations? If so, what are they? Think this through carefully.

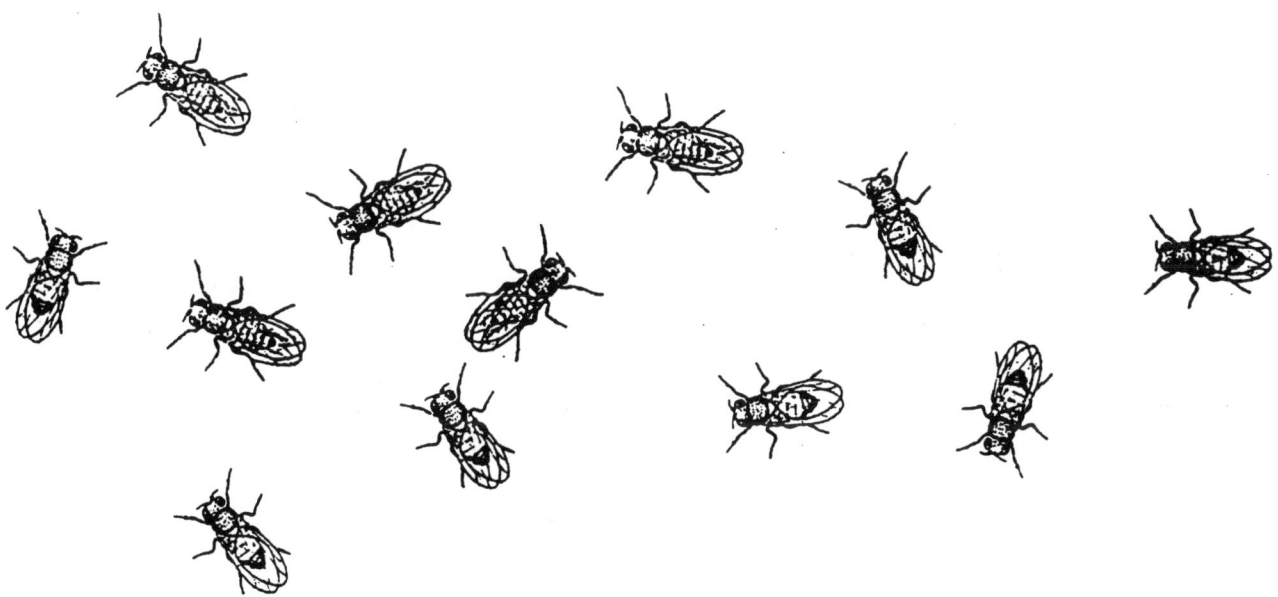

Activity 4.2

The Pop Concert: Species Population Observations

Intent of this activity:

The intent of this activity is for you to become an observer of a species population and its interrelationships in the ecosystem. A carefully structured set of observations in a given location over time should result in much clearer concepts of what is meant by the **species population** and by **interrelationships**.

Procedures:

Search for and choose any species population that appears to you to have some *dynamic qualities*. This could be either a plant population or an animal population. However, should a plant population be chosen, many observations may have to result in inferences about interrelationships that have taken place over time rather than being able to directly observe current dynamics.

A few examples of species populations which could be available for study in many regions include: (1) an ant colony; (2) cockroaches; (3) plant lice (aphids); (4) potato or bean beetles; (5) honey bees; (6) paper wasps; (7) fireflies; (8) Norway rats; (9) barn swallows; (10) weaver finches and (11) germinating (young and vigorously growing) garden plants.

Choose an arbitrary time span over which to make observations. Keep good records. Prepare a paper which synthesizes what you have observed over time concerning this species population. If you choose to make inferences concerning these observations make certain that they are supported with data. Similarly, try to refrain from being anthropomorphic.

Some variables you may wish to consider while making these observations are:

1. The space involved, i.e., the space in which the population was observed. This could be a population of doves at a winter feeder, a nesting population of swallows, or an ant colony.

2. The time involved, i.e. what periods of time and at what times during the day?

3. What are the relationships that appear to exist between the space-time variables and the observations made? For example, observations made of a species population of blackbirds during the winter will yield far different results than those made during the nesting season.

4. What specific interrelationships can be observed between the organism and its abiotic environment?

5. What interrelationships can be observed between members of the population?

6. What interrelationships can be observed between members of this population and members of other populations?

7. What activities seem to be carried on by the population as a whole?

8. How may the interrelationships observed influence the survival of the species population?

9. What observations, if any, tend to support the idea that the species population is a dynamic pattern of life in an ecosystem?

Chapter V

SUCCESSION:

ECOSYSTEMS

CHANGE

OVER

TIME

Learner Objectives for Chapter V

After your interactions with Chapter V, you should be able to . . .

1. . . . communicate an accurate definition of "succession".

2. . . . communicate the basic principles or "rules" of succession, e.g., "The climax community is the last stage of succession and remains fairly stable over long periods of time unless severely disrupted."

3. . . . explain why the climax community tends to be stable over long periods of time unless severely disrupted.

4. . . . provide several examples of ways in which a climax community differs from those preceding it. You might also wish to be able to explain how these examples impact on stability (see No. 3 above).

5. . . . distinguish between primary and secondary succession and provide examples of each.

6. . . . explain why primary succession is often an unsuccessful phenomenon in nature in terms of reaching a climax situation.

7. . . . conduct a succession "laboratory" and communicate scientifically valid conclusions and inferences related to the data sets produced.

8. . . . describe, in some depth, the role of the human organism in modifying successional patterns - both terrestrial and aquatic. In addition, evaluate this pattern of modification and make very specific recommendations on what actions should be taken to remedy the situation (if you agree that a remedy is called for).

> . . . few communities are free from disturbance, and the greatest cause of disturbance is man himself. He has greatly modified natural communities the world over. . . . To provide food for himself, man has cleared away natural vegetation and replaced it with simple, highly artificial communities of cultivated species, adapted to grow on disturbed sites.
>
> **R. L. Smith, 1974**

An Anecdote

The old man rocked a bit as he got out of the car but his cane bit into the gravel on this back country road and he was able to steady himself. At eighty-five years of age his hair was snow white but he was shadow thin - and not too good on his feet any more. On top of this he had a touch of arthritis and today it was bothering him a bit more than usual although he didn't quite know why.

His daughter sat quietly in the car and smiled a caring smile. She knew that her father really wanted to come back here and visit the place where he grew up and where his children were born. She remembered it too. They owned the small 120 acre farm for many years and tried their best to make a go of it. If it hadn't been for the garden and live-stock - the hogs, the cattle, and the chickens - they would have gone hungry many cold winters.

She also remembered the chores every morning and every evening. All of the kids had their chores and this undoubtedly helped keep the family and the farm going. It was a shame that things didn't work out. Mom died back in 1945 and the family and the farm kind of fell apart after that. Sure, they all tried to keep things going the but the kids, one by one, left home and the economy of the times just didn't seem to fit into their style of farming. Dad had moved to town to get a job in a defense plant during the war and the farm just seemed to go down hill. The soil was pretty well worn out having suffered many years of erosion and low fertility. This wasn't rich black prairie soil like the farmers had 100 miles to the north. This was the dull brown soil that was converted to agriculture when the forest was cut and cleared.

She remembered the day that the government man had made a visit to her father back in '48. He was from the national forest and offered to buy the farm and put it into the national forest system in the region. It was a good offer at the time and her father had accepted it. Dad moved off the farm permanently. Later, after the war, he moved many miles away where work was available. It had been over 30 years since he had visited the area.

Her father's face was expressionless as he gazed over the land his family had once owned. He remembered every acre, every fence and every fence row. But it looked much different than it did when he sold it to the government. A forty year old forest grew where corn rows once glistened in the summer sun.

Because he had grown up on this property, he had come to know the trees of the region very well. He could pick out the tall persimmons and the scattered sassafras trees. The tulip poplars, resting on stout trunks, thrust their thick green crowns skyward. In between all of these trees were oaks of a number of species and hickory trees as well. A wild black cherry, in fruit, attracted a number of birds as they tried to find every small round cherry. There were mockingbirds, cardinals, starlings, red-winged blackbirds, and titmice - all after the cherries. He wondered if the apple and pear trees had survived where they had been abandoned forty years earlier. If so, the animals would love to visit them in the fall of the year. He could remember deer coming up near the house to feed on fallen apples even when the family lived there. But, the pear and apple trees were probably gone, replaced by the same wild things that now grew before him.

He was wise enough to realize what was happening before his very eyes. Where corn and clover once grew a forest was in the making. In another forty or fifty years the persimmon, sassafras, and wild cherry trees would mostly be gone also. In their place would be tall, mature, robust oaks and hickories, representing the major forest type of the region. In years to come the U. S. Forest Service would probably sell the timber here and another forest would begin anew. This is the way things happened in the national forest. And, maybe this was the way things ought to be. The land wasn't really meant to be farmed. Heaven knows, he learned that the hard way.

He eased himself back into the car without saying a word to his daughter. She knew better than to attempt a conversation either. Many of his thoughts were in the past, intermingled with those of the present. A memory-filled tear flowed slowly down his cheek as a

female quail with three young ones crossed the road in front of the car. The land now belonged to the wild things - particularly the things of the forest - on the land where he once worked so very hard.

As his daughter eased the car down the rough gravel road away from the old homestead he knew that he would never come back. He had made his pilgrimage, the one he wanted so desperately to make. It was done! Things change and he had been forced to change with them.

SUCCESSION

Ecosystems change over time! If there was one overriding generalization to express "succession" this is the one. But, as with most generalizations, there is more to it than this. This progressive change involves both the species makeup in the ecosystem and energy energy flow through the ecosystem. It is the gradual and ongoing replacement of one kind of plant and animal community by another until the community itself is replaced by another, usually one that is more stable and complex that the previous one.

> **Succession is the *progressive change in the structure of an ecosystem* over time.**

What is absolutely fascinating about succession is the fact that a community in the successional process modifies itself so very much as to make the physical environment inhospitable for itself. Yes! The ecosystem gives "birth" to and develops a habitat in which it cannot survive but one which is very suitable for exploitation by another group of plants and animals, i.e., a different ecosystem!

One needs to understand, however, that the change from one ecosystem to another does not take place on a particular day or in a particular season. It takes place gradually, over time, as the composition of an ecosystem changes. Early stages in certain successional patterns might evolve over a relatively short period of time - say a decade. Later successional stages may take much longer to evolve into new and unique ecosystems - say five decades for example.

The "Rules" of Succession!

Perhaps it would be wise to lay out a series of statements that tend to characterize succession - statements which we will call "rules" for or the principles of succession. These are found on the following page:

Principles of Succession

1. Succession can be viewed in a time - space frame of reference. Time changes and space usually remains constant.

2. Ecosystems involved in succession produce environments (habitats) which lead to their own destruction, i.e., they are replaced by new and substantially different ecosystems.

3. The stages in succession can be predicted with a high rate of accuracy.

4. As succession progresses, the ecosystems that develop tend to become more and more complex (increasing species diversity) and, thus, more stable and able to survive longer.

5. The final stage of succession is called the "climax community" - the development of an ecosystem that tends to remain in existence over very long periods of time.

6. If the climax community is severely disturbed (e.g., by grazing, wind storm, lava flow, fire, clearcutting, etc.), succession will begin anew.

Stages in Aquatic Succession

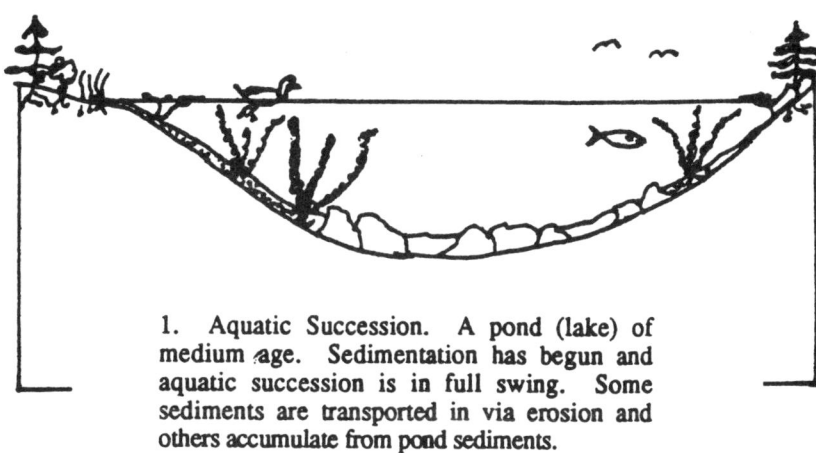

1. Aquatic Succession. A pond (lake) of medium age. Sedimentation has begun and aquatic succession is in full swing. Some sediments are transported in via erosion and others accumulate from pond sediments.

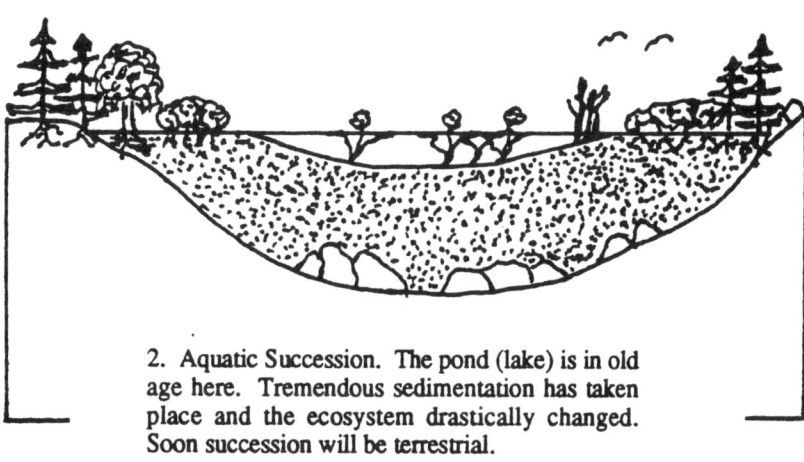

2. Aquatic Succession. The pond (lake) is in old age here. Tremendous sedimentation has taken place and the ecosystem drastically changed. Soon succession will be terrestrial.

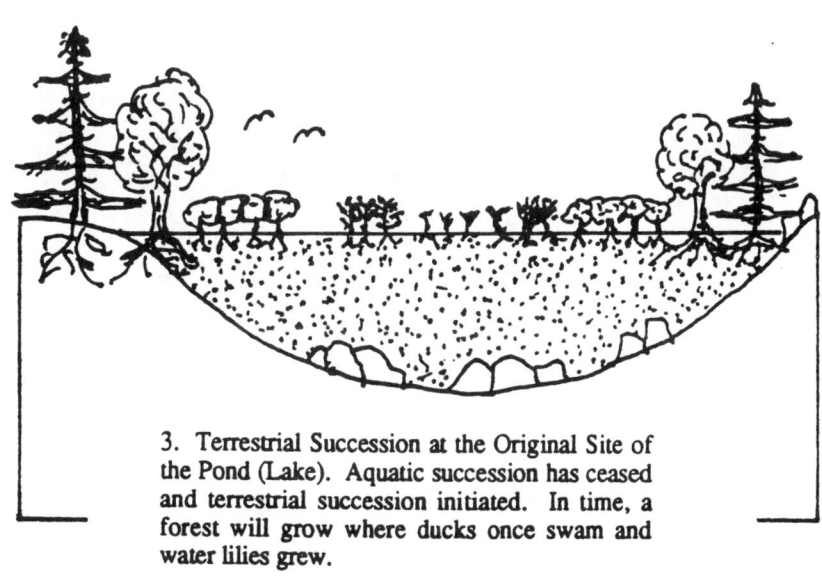

3. Terrestrial Succession at the Original Site of the Pond (Lake). Aquatic succession has ceased and terrestrial succession initiated. In time, a forest will grow where ducks once swam and water lilies grew.

127

A Midwestern Example of Succession

In the anecdote you read at the beginning of this chapter, the old man made a pilgrimage back to the land that he or his father or grandfather had cleared for farming. You will recall that, where corn rows once existed, there were now a rich variety of trees - wild cherry, tulip poplar, persimmons, and sassafras, etc. interspersed with some oaks and hickories. So, how did these trees replace a corn field?

In the Midwest, hardwood forests were the original ecological inhabitants that pioneers and others cleared for farming. The farms were often worked until the forest soil wore out or eroded badly (as it did in many hilly areas). Once the soil would no longer produce a viable crop, the land was - and still is - often abandoned. When this happens, a phenomenon called "secondary succession" is initiated and continues until a climax forest once again grows in that same space. What causes this to take place?

The corn field is typically abandoned in the fall of the year. This produces an environment which is characterized by bare soil, covered in part, by corn stubble. In the spring of the year, as the soil warms, "weeds" germinate in large numbers. These "weeds" may be annuals, biennials, as well as a few perennials. Most typically, though, have short life cycles - they germinate, grow, flower, and produce seeds quickly.

The seeds of these weeds may have rested in and on the soil for years as many species have tremendous survival potential through their seeds. Other seeds are blown in by the wind, e.g., milkweeds. Some are transported in on the fur of coyotes, opossums, mice, foxes

The month is June in southern Illinois and tens of thousands of "weeds" have germinated in a field that grew corn the year before. Even though the corn stalks have not decayed, succession is certainly under way. There will be animals here already . . . rodents, snakes, many insects, spiders, etc. Numerous food chains will be observed. Left to succession's own devices, an oak-hickory forest will grow here in a century or so. Photo courtesy H. R. Hungerford.

and other mammals. Still others are deposited as birds and mammals defecate in the field. The plants to colonize the area are those that can do so in open, sunlit areas. Some of the plants we might find in the lower Midwest include lamb's quarters, goldenrod, mustard, burdock, chicory, and nettle.

The ecosystem produced by these "weeds" may mature in three or four years and evolve into another which contains many plants with longer life cycles. Grasses and more perennial weeds begin to appear as do certain woody plants like blackberry, poison ivy, and wild rose. Soil tends to be stabilized and shaded by these plants. The animal life expands similarly and comprises a fairly rich variety of animals, particularly insect herbivores although longer food chains are certainly present. Skipping the numerous arthropods, just a few of the animals associated with these ecosystems would include field mice, voles, shrews, moles, a variety of snakes, meadowlarks, foxes, coyotes, rabbits, quail, and the occasional deer.

In a few years trees begin making an appearance. The ones to grow successfully are those that are sun-tolerant, i.e., they can begin life and be successful in the open. In the lower Midwest these are often winged elm, sassafras, persimmon, and sumac. And, depending upon the seed sources nearby, one may find tulip poplar and one or more of the oaks as well.

Over time, these hardwood tree species out compete the "weeds", (grasses and perennials) and create a habitat in which they, themselves, find it hard to reproduce. In this more moist, shaded environment germinate the seeds of those trees that will eventually grow into a climax forest - red and white oaks as well as a variety of hickories.   This process may take a century or more to unfold in totality but that is usually no problem because succession seems to be a most patient and persistent process. Uninhibited by fire, cattle, chain saws, and ploughs, an oak-hickory climax forest will one day grow where the old man tried to grow corn and raise a family!

Needless to say, the oak-hickory forest is dramatically different from the weedy field that appeared after the farm was abandoned. Compared to earlier successional stages, the climax ecosystem is characterized by large plants, slow plant growth, complex food chains, many decomposers, a high species diversity, lots of biomass, a large number of specialized niches, and high energy efficiency.

Even after reading the characteristics of the climax ecosystem, you might still wonder why the oak-hickory forest is able to maintain itself over long periods of time. The answer is relatively simple: *The oak-hickory forest is tolerant of the environment it itself creates!* This is true of all climax communities. It might be interesting to consider just how important that phenomenon might be in a broad, global ecological sense.

Other Possibilities Growing From the Corn Field?

Are there possibilities other than the oak-hickory climax forest successional pattern in the Midwest? There are always other possibilities but the oak-hickory scenario is very typical. However, were the field to be extremely dry (unlikely for a corn field), one could observe a different oak ecosystem develop - one made up of oaks which are adapted to extremely hot and dry conditions, e.g., post oaks. These oaks are able to survive in extremely hot, dry environments. Conversely, if the soil was very moist much of the year, the successional pattern might develop into a beech - sugar maple climax forest. Once again, however, it is unlikely that this would occur because these environments are typically not cultivated to corn. And, too, these very moist conditions are likely to be found toward the bottom of slopes or in broad depressions between parallel ridges. These are, again, very unlikely places for a corn field.

However, if we forget the corn field for now, we should keep in mind that, although the oak-hickory ecosystem is typical of the lower Midwest, other hardwood ecosystems exist there too. The beech-maple ecosystem is just one example.

In this photo we see a southern Illinois field that has been abandoned for perhaps a decade. Early successional trees can be seen in the photograph. Here they are sweet-gum, wild black cherry, sumac, and cedar. Grasses are still evident along with a number of broad-leaved plants such as the common milkweed. Often, secondary succession scenes in this region will look quite different with sassafras, persimmon, sumac, and winged-elm crowding each other as well as the grasses and broad-leaves plants. However, the end result will be the same under most circumstances. If undisturbed by humans, an oak-hickory forest will grow here many decades hence. Photo H. R. Hungerford.

Secondary succession in the Pacific Northwest. In the state of Washington, clearcuts like the one seen above are common. Every tree is removed. The clearcut is allowed to re-seed or it is planted by hand. If allowed to re-seed naturally, this would be another example of secondary succession. In the highly managed forest seen in the photo, the trees are harvested every 60-70 years. However, if allowed to continue to develop for several hundred more years an "old growth" forest of huge conifers would result. One can be seen below. These old growth forests have been the source of great controversy of late due to their rapid disappearance and the endangered species and other organisms they support. Photo courtesy H. R. Hungerford.

And What of Primary Succession?

We must take a few moments and discuss another form of succession which is called "primary". Primary succession is unlike secondary succession in that there is no soil available in which succession can begin. Primary succession is initiated in conditions which find little or no soil present, e.g., highly disturbed areas such as bare rock outcrops, newly formed sand bars, sand dunes, and raw glacial till. One might be quick to infer that succession in these conditions might take much, much longer to unfold. This inference is correct!

On bare rock, the first colonizers are crustose lichens and certain mosses. These plants appear sporadically in patches and do not form a complete mat. However, a few higher plants can grow in association with the mosses and small "bare rock gardens" can appear here and there on the rock surface. Now, we tend to teach students that the lichens and mosses modify the environment so that a soil can form and other plants can begin growing there. This may not be true. There is little evidence to support this somewhat romantic idea.

What actually happens is that, over time, soil is washed into the area from outside sources, it becomes trapped in crevices and depressions (or in and around the lichens and mosses) and begins supporting other plants which invade the area. These other plants are usually species from surrounding areas as well as the typical rock species themselves.

Primary succession may take centuries to produce a climax community! Sometimes a thin layer of soil forms and the area becomes fairly stable over time permitting the development of shrub and/or tree ecosystems to take over. Often, however, the ravages of wind and water take their toll and the primitive ecosystems become highly disturbed keeping the area in a constant state of flux Even so, you might ask if the area would not - some day - see a mature forest growing there. This would be entirely possible and even anticipated. It is all a matter of time! Where the corn field became a mature forest in a couple of centuries, the bare rock complex may not fulfill its destiny for many centuries. Succession is famous for its "patience"!

> *. . . the greatest cause of [ecosystem] disturbance is man himself. He has greatly modified natural communities the world over. . . . Nowhere is land change more complete than in industrial and urban areas, a climax-type of human succession that has its own developmental stages. This succession is accompanied by air and water pollution from industrial and human wastes. . . . Attempts to restore the areas are not wholly successful.*
>
> *R. L. Smith, 1974*

Structures of human origin may appear to be immune from succession. However, on a long term basis even these structures can disintegrate. In this photo we see plants growing from cervices in a sidewalk made of bricks and concrete. The bricks and mortar have weathered enough to permit water to collect and to freeze and thaw creating cervices that collect a rudimentary soil. At least three species of plants have begun to colonize these crevasses. This interesting situation is much like primary succession. Photo courtesy H. R. Hungerford.

Activity 5.1

The Forest Succession Dry Lab:
How Do Ecologists Study Hardwood Forest Succession?

Ecologists use a variety of techniques for studying succession. One standard strategy is the use of the quadrat. A quadrat is a carefully measured space within which ecologists make counts of the species there.

On a grassland, the ecologist may lay out a quadrat one meter square and count the number of individuals of every species within that space. Prairie plants are so thick that a one meter square space will work. In a forest, on the other hand, the ecologist may lay out a space which is ten meters wide and ten meters long. This produces an area of 100 square meters. Because forest trees do not grow as close together as prairie plants, this larger area works very well.

Within the quadrat, the ecologist may plot every tree in the canopy as well as every understory tree and every seedling tree. In this way, he/she knows what the dominant canopy trees are and what trees are growing under them as well. Using data from a number of quadrats in a forest, the scientist can tell a great deal about the ecosystem. He/she can determine if the forest is stable or if succession is taking place. He/she can make conclusions about the general health of the ecosystem as well. For example, in western Kentucky, there are areas in oak-hickory forests where there are few seedling trees. Deer have eaten most of the seedlings out of the forest. Thus, ecologists know that the forest is in serious trouble because few replacement trees grow in it.

Using a quadrat study, scientists can also make management decisions. Again, in western Kentucky, foresters are recommending the reduction of the deer populations in order to bring the forest back to a healthy long-term condition.

You Can Study Forest Succession

If hardwood forests exist in your region, your instructor may choose to take you outside to study forest succession first-hand. Toward the end of this chapter you will find a Data Collection Worksheet which you can use. For those of you who will not be going out-of-doors, we have included several typical quadrats that could be observed over time in a Midwestern successional pattern. On the following pages you will find five (5) quadrats. These represent what you might observe in one quadrat over a 100 year period.

Let us assume that a Midwestern farm is abandoned. It is allowed to revert to the ecosystem representative of the biome. As you know, this will take time. In a few years, trees will begin to appear where there was once fields of corn, soybeans, or wheat. The first quadrat (Fig. Q1) illustrates this quadrat after five (5) years. There are only five trees here and they are small ones. There are three sassafras seedlings, one sumac seedling, and one persimmon seedling. Thus, the sassafras represents 60% of the trees in the quadrat. The remaining 40% is equally divided between sumac and persimmon.

Over the years, this 100 square meter quadrat will change dramatically. Your task is to count each species in each quadrat and determine the percentage of each species for each quadrat. These data can be recorded in the table provided with this activity. Once you have all of the data placed in the data table, think about and respond to the problems at the end of the activity.

Tree Seedlings Found in Quadrat
After Field Was Abandoned Five (5) Years

Fig. Q1

		P							S
&									
	&								
&									

Tree Species	Number	% of Total
S - Sumac	_____	_____ %
P - Persimmon	_____	_____ %
& - Sassafras	_____	_____ %
Totals	_____	_____ %

Tree Species Found in Canopy
After Thirty (30) Years

Fig. Q2

		P					S	S	S
						S	S	S	S
						S	S		
	E						S		
		&							
&		&	&						
	&						E		
&		E				E			
									P
	E					&	&		

Tree Species	Number	% of Total
S - Sumac	_____	_____ %
P - Persimmon	_____	_____ %
& - Sassafras	_____	_____ %
E - Winged Elm	_____	_____ %
Totals	_____	_____ %

Tree Species Found in Seedling Layer
After Thirty (30) Years

Fig. Q3

WO		E		D			D		TU
	PH	&			S			S	
D		WO		P				S	S
		SO				S			S
	SO			& &	RB		E	SH	WO
P	WO			&		P			&
E			WA		E E				
	&	D		SO		E		E	
PH				PH			E		
WO	TU		D		&	& &		WO	E E

Tree Species		Number		% of Total	
S	- Sumac	_____		_____	%
P	- Persimmon	_____		_____	%
&	- Sassafras	_____		_____	%
E	- Winged Elm	_____		_____	%
RB	- Red Bud	_____		_____	%
D	- Dogwood	_____		_____	%
TU	- Tulip Poplar	_____		_____	%
WA	- Walnut	_____		_____	%
WO	- White Oak	_____		_____	%
SO	- Scarlet Oak	_____		_____	%
SH	- Shagbark Hickory	_____		_____	%
PH	- Pignut Hickory	_____		_____	%
	Totals	_____		_____	%

Tree Species Found in Canopy
After One Hundred (100) Years

Fig. Q4

		WO							
								SH	
WO									

Tree Species	Number	% of Total
WO - White Oak	_____	_____ %
SH - Shagbark Hickory	_____	_____ %
Totals	_____	_____ %

Tree Species Found in Seedling Layer
After One Hundred (100) Years

Fig. Q5

D					SH				
		WO						SH	
				SO					
								WO	
	WO				&				
				PH			SO		
PH								WO	
	SO								
					SH			YO	YO
WO			D					WO	&

Tree Species		Number	% of Total
&	- Sassafras	_____	_____ %
D	- Dogwood	_____	_____ %
WO	- White Oak	_____	_____ %
SO	- Scarlet Oak	_____	_____ %
YO	- Yellow Chestnut Oak	_____	_____ %
SH	- Shagbark Hickory	_____	_____ %
PH	- Pignut Hickory	_____	_____ %
	Totals	_____	_____ %

Quadrat Data Table

FIG. Q6

Tree Species	PERCENTAGES			
	30 Year Canopy	30 Year Seedling	100 Year Canopy	100 Year Seedling
Sumac				
Winged Elm				
Persimmon				
Sassafras				
Red Bud				
Dogwood				
Tulip Poplar				
Walnut				
White Oak				
Scarlet oak				
Yellow Chestnut Oak				
Shagbark Hickory				
Pignut Hickory				
TOTALS				

Data Collection Worksheet
For Studying Succession in the Out-of-Doors

Tree Species	Number	% of Total
	_____	_____ %
	_____	_____ %
	_____	_____ %
	_____	_____ %
	_____	_____ %
	_____	_____ %
	_____	_____ %
	_____	_____ %
	_____	_____ %
Totals	_____	_____ %

Problems and Discussion Questions

1. Find and describe the 100 year succession pattern that has emerged on your data table.

2. What might account for the low number of trees in the five (5) year quadrat?

3. In every instance, there will be more seedlings present in a quadrat than canopy trees. Why?

4. Predict what this quadrat will look like at 150 years. What is the basis for your prediction?

5. Would you consider the 100 year old forest to be a climax ecosystem? Why?

6. Two sassafras seedlings appear in the 100 year seedling quadrat (Q5). Only under very special circumstances could they survive to become canopy trees in this quadrat. What might these circumstances be?

7. If we walked into a quadrat like the five year old one on a warm, sunny day in June, we could observe a very warm air temperature and a warm soil temperature. One hundred years later, in the same quadrat, on an identical day in June, the air and soil temperatures would be much cooler. Why?

CHAPTER VI

HUMANS

AND THE

ECOLOGICAL

CONNECTION

When birds die off in unnatural numbers, . . . what we are seeing is not just a warning of impending degradation, but a part of the degradation itself - a tearing of the ecological web that keeps the planet's health in balance.

Howard Youth, *World-Watch*,
January/February 1994, p. 11.

Learner Objectives

During or subsequent to any and/or all interactions with this Chapter, you should be able to . . .

1. . . . communicate, in some depth, an understanding that human beings are:

    a. integral parts of ecosystems themselves.
    b. critical ecological variables in those ecosystems.

2. . . . communicate the differences that exist between what are called monobiotic (one species or a single crop) ecosystems and naturally-occurring ecosystems. Further, be able to state why monobiotic ecosystems are not stable over long periods of time if not tended carefully by human beings.

3. . . . communicate some of the ecological effects on naturally-occurring ecosystems of man's efforts to maintain monobiotic ecosystems. Use good examples throughout.

4. . . . describe the differences that exist between the term "ecology" and "environmental science" and/or "environmental education". Also be able to describe in some detail why these terms are so very interrelated.

5. . . . communicate at least a moderate understanding of the critical interrelationships that exist between human population, resource use, technology, environmental degradation, and pollution.

6. . . . sharply differentiate between "environmental problems" and "environmental issues".

7. . . . explain why human population growth may be the single most important variable in the population <-> resource use <-> technology <-> environmental degradation <-> pollution model.

8. . . . communicate an understanding of the relationships between "classes of issues" and "ecological concepts". Further, be able to inspect issue scenarios and identify the "classes of issues" reflected in those scenarios as well as the "ecological concepts" associated with those issues.

9. . . . successfully analyze issues and identify the players, their positions, the associated beliefs, and the values reflected by those positions and beliefs.

10. . . . infer and communicate what might be a successful "ecosystem approach to the management of the earth" as recommended by R. L. Smith.

An Anecdote

People, Tomatoes, and Ground Water

He was middle-aged - forty-five to be exact. His bronzed face and arms appeared even darker in the slanting rays of a sun due to set within the hour. The many hours of work in the sun of south Florida would tan one in a hurry. His tan, unlike the sunbathers on the sandy beaches to the east, extended only from his biceps to the tip of his fingers. The rest of him, except for his face and neck, was a stark white because he always wore a work shirt with the sleeves rolled up. This to protect his upper body from the cancer-causing rays.

The man raised his hand to his hat, removed it from the crown of his head and wiped the sweat from his brow. It was still hot this May evening. But, he wasn't concerned about the sweat nor the bronze of his arms - he was thinking about the visit the environmental protection people had paid him earlier in the day.

He stared intently at the long rows of tomatoes that lay before him. They stretched almost to the horizon. The crop would be ready to pick in about ten days. It would then be shipped to places far away, places he had never visited or even heard of. His contract with the distributor left the distribution of the tomato crop to someone else.

What the EPA official told him bothered him greatly. Who was to know that the evolution of the truck farming business would lead to this? His father had started the truck farm fifty years ago when the war effort made truck farming very attractive financially. In those years, tomato farming was very labor intensive, demanding the services of an army of migrant workers. They did everything from manual cultivation to irrigation chores to picking, sorting, and packaging the ripened crop.

Today's labor force was much smaller. Heavy machines planted and cultivated the field. Other machines sprayed pesticides on the crop to keep a horde of insects and other plant eaters out of the field. There were even machines to pick the tomatoes. The tomatoes were still sorted and hand packaged but it took fewer people to do it. The money went mostly for machinery and chemicals.

Who would have thought that the chemicals he used on the field would show up later in the ground and surface water in the park to the west? He wouldn't have dreamed that his fields were contaminating the drinking water from wells to the south. He knew that the pesticides he used were potent ones but they were supposed to break down in the soil. Evidently they were not doing this. What was the answer?

He couldn't just stop growing vegetables for human consumption. Although he had been a very ethical man all his life, his future and the future of his family depended on the income from the fields he saw before him.

There was a lot at stake and he knew it. He still had a large loan at the bank. This crop wouldn't - couldn't - pay it off. His investment in the irrigation system and the other machinery ran into the hundreds of thousands of dollars. More than one family of laborers depended on him for their living as well. And too, this was the heart of the vegetable growing region for this part of the United States. The EPA man had told him that the same water contamination was being observed in fields to the east and even in central Florida.

But, by the same token, the park's wildlife was being threatened. The well water that people were using for drinking and bathing should be clean and uncontaminated. He brooded over what seemed to him to be a serious environmental problem - perhaps even an ecological calamity. There were lots of things to think about. Was there a nice, clear-cut answer? How would his father have handled such a situation? What were his options? What were the legal implications? He felt certain that he understood some of the ecological implications. Just what would the answer turn out to be? He shook his head as if in conversation with someone else. Then, ever so slowly he turned and walked to the pickup truck parked behind him. Tomorrow would turn out to be a long day with lots to think about.

A 48 Year Old East Texas Poacher in a 1993 Conversation With H. R. Hungerford

" . . . ya, I hunt ducks sometimes . . . when they come in to roost [chuckle]. But mostly I hunt deer. I got this here thirty-oh-six [30-06 caliber rifle] and, when I sight it in it'll make a hole in a pack of cigarettes at 150 yards. I must of killed 200 deer with that rifle. The last 'un cost me sixteen hundred dollars ($1600.00). I was pretty drunk and only about a mile off the highway back in the woods. I killed this 'un and got careless. I throwed it in the back of the truck with my dog and headed for the highway. They was waiting for me there [law officers]. . . . I didn't get to eat the deer [laughter]! Hell, I wouldn't have no luck at all if there weren't bad."

Humans And The Ecological Connection

Comments On - And A Preface To - This Chapter

Many were the times that I pondered this chapter both prior to and during the process of writing it. And there were times when it seemed wise in one sense to back off and not include it at all. Why? . . . simply because this topic is enormously complex and entirely too difficult to present in one chapter. The content is not *ecology* per se and, although the content is science-related it exists, for the most part, in the realm of the social studies. Still it seems irresponsible to write a book on ecological concepts and ignore, for the most part, the human ecological connection. Thus, the reader will find here what I fear is an entirely too shallow treatment of this very, very important connection.

Undoubtedly there are readers who will wonder what the connections are between the principles of ecology and the presence of human beings in ecosystems. That question is simple to answer. Human beings are ecological variables! Conversely, there may also be some value in such a chapter for those who are a bit more sophisticated about ecology and the environment. It is here that we view some of the impacts that the human organism has had on the world's ecosystems.

What is intended in this chapter is to present a few of the major ideas inherent in a treatment of "humans and the ecological connection". Throughout this book there have been included some human-related anecdotes which might make the concepts easier to assimilate and sustain. The very first chapter describing the soil <-> grass <-> buffalo <-> Indian relationship is one of these. Also, this particular anecdote goes right to the heart of the matter because, as we shall see, one of the major ideas here rests with the notion that if we mess with one variable in the ecosystem there stands a very good chance that other very important ones will be effected. This is what happened in a big way in the soil <-> grass <-> buffalo <-> Indian relationship.

Another closely related and major idea that should come from working through this chapter is the understanding that human beings, themselves, are members of ecosystems. And, in the long run, we are subject to the same checks and balances as other organisms in those ecosystems regardless of how dedicated and initially successful we are in modifying these same ecosystems for our own ends.

In reality this chapter is a select mix of ecological concepts wrapped in an environmental science and human responsibility dimension - if you will, a focus on at least some of the major interrelationships between humans and the ecosystems with which they interact. The resulting issues are, of course, the heart of the matter. And there are entirely too many of them! How you view them in a personal responsibility dimension is, of course, up to you. I do ask, however, that you *not* view them and disregard the ecological connection!

We begin with a short overview of humans and their impact on the environment over time written by a highly respected ecologist from West Virginia University - Robert L. Smith.

Thoughts on Humans and Their Role in the Environment

for the Last 2,000,000 Years by Robert L. Smith

In his nearly 2 million years of occupancy of the earth, man has been molding the planet to his own designs. For much of his existence he was part of the natural scheme of things. He was a part of the nutrient cycle, and like the other consumer organisms with which he shared the earth, he received his portion of natural energy flow. As his technology developed and his mastery over the environment increased, man destroyed natural ecosystems of which he was part and replaced them with simplified ecosystems. Their components became domesticated plants and animals shaped to man's needs and without whose protection and care they could not exist. Man directed the flow of energy toward his own ends by reducing or eliminating plant and animal competitors. His interference interrupted nutrient cycles, so he supplemented or replaced natural cycling with fertilizers. . . . To increase yields even more he added energy input from draft animals, and later replaced them with power supplied by fossil fuels. When the bulk of human population became concentrated away from the source of food supply, man had to develop mechanisms and institutions for the distribution of foods. This process moves the nutrients in food far from their source and introduced excessive wastes into aquatic ecosystems. . . .

Now man in his domination of the earth finds himself on the verge of an ecological catastrophe. At the same time that he is causing his environment to deteriorate and is exhausting exploitable resources, he is allowing his population to push upward to the ultimate carrying capacity of the earth, and there is no place into which it can expand. The result is that man the organism may find it difficult to adapt to an environment he is rapidly changing. . . . man must develop an understanding of and respect for natural ecosystems. If man is to exist he has to work within the framework of ecosystems of which he is a part. In other words, he needs to develop an ecosystem approach to the management of the earth.

Adapted from: Robert L. Smith, *Ecology and Field Biology* published by Harper & Row, Publishers, 1974. pp 26-27.

If we might review what Smith is trying to communicate, the following points seem appropriate:

- Humans drastically modified ecological systems (patterns of life or ecosystems) when we learned how to domesticate plants and animals.

- The domestication of plants and animals led to very simple (sometimes called monobiotic) ecosystems which demanded high inputs of husbandry along with nutrients in the form of animal, then industrial fertilizers.

- The ability to sharply modify ecosystems and produce food monobiotic ecosystems led to our moving toward the city concept in which food energy had to be transported into those cities.

- Large populations of human beings living close together resulted in waste material being concentrated in these cities and then discharged into aquatic ecosystems which has a very negative effect on those ecosystems.

- Our ability to adapt in so many ways has also led to a population explosion which approaches the carrying capacity of the earth.

- It would appear appropriate for us human beings to develop an ecosystem approach to the management of the earth.

Discussion Questions:

(1) What would a successful *"ecosystem approach to the management of the earth"* involve, i.e., what are the things that might make such an approach work?

(2) What important (and critical) variables might stand in the way of developing an ecosystem approach to the management of the earth?

(3) Why do you think that your responses are correct, i.e., on what do you base your conclusions?

A Photo Essay and Activity

What follows is a photo essay taken in an authentic pioneer village/farm from the 1850's. It is found on the Kentucky-Tennessee border in the region known as Land-Between-the-Lakes. Please consider each photo in your conceptualization of life during the period just prior to the Civil War. You will be asked to make some comparisons between the 1850's life style and that of the 1990's in much of the United States.

MIDWESTERN LIFE: THE 1800's

A Photo Essay and Activity

Life for western Kentucky residents in the 1850's was, in many ways, harder than in the 1990's. However, it was also easier in some ways and certainly less consumptive. Photo courtesy H. R. Hungerford.

The photos on this page illustrate some of the ways humans made use of local resources. Fences, barns, homes, barrels, furniture, toys, and tools were made of wood locally obtained. Stone steps came from creek bottom sandstone - clothes from cotton and wool. Photo courtesy H. R. Hungerford.

Agriculture was definitely energy intensive but much of the energy came from human calories, not petroleum. Tools were hand made - metals forged from western Kentucky iron ore, handles from Kentucky ash trees. Fields were plowed with oxen and planted by hand. Photo courtesy H. R. Hungerford.

Surprisingly, some 1850 western Kentucky residents had lawns - made up of native grasses and "weeds" and mowed by domesticated sheep and goats. Fertilizer was no problem but one had to demonstrate a certain agility while walking on the lawn. Photos courtesy H. R. Hungerford.

Activity: An Analysis of Life in the 1850's

The photos on the previous pages demonstrate how the Tennessee Valley Authority is trying to show citizens of the 1990's how people lived in the years before the civil war. The setting is the 1850's Home Place south of Golden Pond, KY in Land-Between-the-Lakes (TVA).

Consider for a few moments the resources you can identify (observe) directly from the photos and those you can infer. Below, list those resources on the left. On the right, list the comparable resources that the people of the 1990's use in their own homes and in agriculture.

Resources Used	
The 1850's	**The 1990's**

Having made two lists, decide which lifestyle is more energy intensive. Can you judge this or would you have to decide what kind of energy is being expended (or the source of that energy)? Think about this carefully before you answer.

More importantly, perhaps, are the differences in the ecological impacts that can be inferred from your analysis. You might want to consider ecological differences in resource management, differences in energy consumption, differences in resource consumption (other than energy), differences in population density and dynamics 1850 vs 1990, and differences in the human struggle for survival in the existing ecosystem(s).

Would you want to return to an 1850's lifestyle? Could you duplicate the lifestyle of this era if you wanted to? Are the same resources available? What about the level of competition for those resources? Would the struggle be the same? Different? The "creature comforts"? Life expectancy? And, what of the ecological consequences? Are the ecosystems of the 1850's identical to those in existence now? And what of the condition of existing ecosystems?

152

Some Ecological Impacts Of Human Beings
At The End Of The Twentieth Century

As you have learned, life in the 1990's is vastly different than it was 140 years earlier in western Kentucky. In the preceding activity, you were asked to make some rather dramatic comparisons which included resource management, energy consumption, human population density and dynamics, and the impact on natural ecosystems.

Upon close investigation, the ecological consequences of Man's activities seem bewildering complex. Indeed, in many ways they are! However, before one can synthesize even a partial picture of these consequences, a look at some specifics might prove helpful. Throughout this book, some mention of the human ecological condition has been made even though the intent was to look at basic ecological concepts and not get directly into many of the ecological problems facing Mankind today.

What follows is a very incomplete photo essay which reflects many of the ecological enigmas facing human beings, especially in the United States. This essay, alone, will not provide the desired synthesis, but it will be one step in that direction. The reader is asked to view this essay critically and look for ecological implications throughout, i.e., what ecological impacts can be identified from each scene?

As humans moved farther and farther away from the sources of available energy, they needed to transport energy farther and farther. Here is an excellent example! This is one of the transcontinental pipelines which transport hydrocarbons from the Southwest to urban and suburban consumers. This is a pipeline as it crosses the Mississippi River in southern Illinois. If you note the man painting it, you will get some perspective on its size. Photo courtesy H. R. Hungerford.

The technological ability to change the planet's surface to accommodate personal or corporate desires is legendary. The ecological implications of these activities are staggering. Here several acres of what was once an oak-hickory ecosystem later transformed into a monobiotic agricultural field are now being transformed into a Wal-Mart Super Store (1993). One must realize that once tens of thousands of living interactions took place where now there will be asphalt, concrete blocks, cement, steel, and retail sales. This huge space will be ecologically "dead" in terms of a native "pattern of life". Photo courtesy Dave Hagengruber.

This photo illustrates the same concept as the one above but from a different perspective. Here we still see the agricultural application of, again, what was once an oak-hickory forest. In fact, such a forest ecosystem can be seen in the distance. One hundred ten acres are for sale. The sign says that the seller will develop it to suit the buyer. We know not what this monobiotic ecosystem will become but the possibilities are certainly numerous. If we remember that naturally existing ecosystems are finite in number and size, we then begin to appreciate the impact that this and other sales are having on the biosphere. Photo courtesy H. R. Hungerford.

The photos above and below are related to those on the previous page. Here we see different perspectives of what is (or was) for sale in and around Destin, FL. A close inspection of the photos reveals that the "soil" is sand. In one instance we are looking at undeveloped beach property on a primary dune on the Gulf Coast. In the other, property in Destin itself. Environmental scientists have known for a long time that primary dunes behind ocean beaches should not be developed. The rationale for this opinion is not altogether ecological - part of it focuses on the fact that hurricanes can wreak havoc on structures built close to the sea. Recent hurricanes on the east coast of the U.S. have borne out this perspective leading to major issues for coastal political agencies. Photos courtesy H. R. Hungerford.

155

The great floods of 1993 along the Mississippi and Missouri Rivers will remain in memories and history for many years. The devastation brought about by these floods was colossal and, in places, almost beyond belief. Human suffering was enormous. Damage to agricultural lands was severe. These floods could have been - and were - predicted. Periodic flooding of this magnitude has happened before and will happen again, if not on the Mississippi and Missouri, elsewhere. Why? There are three reasons: (1) people persist on living on flood plains or in flood plain communities, (2) engineers have tried and tried to build levees to "tame" the Mississippi which only aggravates flooding when it does come, and (3) as noted earlier, periodic flooding of this magnitude simply happens every so often. Photos taken in Ste. Genevieve, Missouri with the assistance of Bob and Delores Roth - courtesy H. R. Hungerford.

Pictured on this page are two of the most endangered species in the world, the Florida panther and the black-footed ferret. The panther suffers from lack of habitat and by being struck by automobiles. Only a few remain and these are genetically weak. Last ditch efforts are being made to salvage at least part of the gene pool. The ferret, on the other hand, was thought to be extinct! However, a few were discovered in 1981 in Wyoming. These have been bred in captivity and are being released back into what is hoped to be a compatible environment. The ferret is a small creature of the vast North American prairie and totally dependent on prairie dogs which are hated by a variety of human beings including ranchers. When the U. S. Forest Service began poisoning prairie dogs about 80 years ago, the ferrets were seemingly doomed. In both cases - panther and ferret - the problem is an ecological/human problem although complex in both cases. Panther photo by Darrell Land courtesy Florida Fish and Game Commission. Ferret photo courtesy U.S. Fish and Wildlife Service (no photographer credited).

Market hunting has always been a mainstay of those who would profit from taking wildlife for dollars. Although market hunting is on the wane, hundreds of thousands of dollars - mostly illegal - are obtained each year by poachers taking game commercially for meat and trophies. The photo here may not be a market shoot at all but, as the caption reads, a two day hunt near Ewing, Nebraska in 1900. The turn of the century still saw skies darkened by flocks of migrating waterfowl and bags like this were common. Photo courtesy the Nebraska Game and Parks Commission. Photo credited to Mr. and Mrs. Francis Wood of Oakland, California.

This photo is of a dead raccoon along I-24 west of Paducah, KY. Although there is little research on the "road kill" phenomenon except in terms of deer-vehicle collisions, the death toll is enormous. Where road kills are studied, they are tallied in deaths per mile per day, week, month, or year. Birds, coyotes, foxes, opossums, deer, panthers, snakes, amphibians and numerous other animals are killed by vehicular traffic. Photo courtesy T. L. Volk and D. Hagengruber.

On one hand we kill millions of creatures on highways. On the other, we introduce animals which are not members of native ecosystems. We have done this with cats, dogs, the English sparrow, the starling, the nutria, the Norway rat and others. All of these create havoc in the environment unless kept in check by humans. Feral cats are far more destructive than many realize. The cat shown is the author's - not at all feral but closely related to the millions that are! Photo courtesy H. R. Hungerford.

Problems associated with non-native species are extreme in Hawaii. Here on the "big island" of Hawaii in the Bird Park called Kipuka Puaulu, the native forest is so stricken with exotic species that harsh measures have been put in place in order to try to remedy the situation. This notice at the entrance to the park is straightforward and to the point. Managers are trying to control the destructive species! Photo courtesy H. R. Hungerford.

It seems as though human beings are committed to polluting ecosystems. Even though some businesses and industries have begun to take pollution seriously and responsibly, many problems continue. Serious pollutants still getting into the environment include heavy metals, sulfur dioxide, particulate matter, nitrogen dioxide, carbon dioxide, pesticides, municipal solid waste, untreated or poorly treated sewage, and noise. The scenes on this page are simply two examples. In the top photo, citizens of Hawaii have produced an illegal dump in a sugar cane field on the island of Oahu. The bottom photo was taken on a beach near Fort Walton Beach, Florida. Photos courtesy H. R. Hungerford

Olympic National Park, state of Washington. Photo of a temperate rain forest of hemlock, spruce, etc. Photo courtesy H. R. Hungerford.

A clear-cut on a tree farm near Olympic National Park, Washington. Photo courtesy H. R. Hungerford.

The transport of freshly cut logs out of the commercial tree farm seen in the above photo. Photo courtesy H. R. Hungerford.

A "mountain" of logs being readied for overseas shipment on the docks in Port Angeles, WA. Photo courtesy H. R. Hungerford.

Concepts Concerning Ecology, the Environment, and Problems and Issues Resulting From Human Involvement

An Introduction

The photos you have seen on previous pages in this chapter reveal a number of serious environmental problems, all of which are embroiled in multiple issues. A very simplistic list would contain problems associated with solid waste management, forestry management, pollution, poaching/market hunting, threatened and endangered species, flooding, land use management, and energy use/distribution.

> **An environmental problem is related to some resource, either renewable or nonrenewable, when something about that resource that is of value to human beings is threatened or at risk.**

To try to describe the roots of environmental problems/issues in a simple manner is an extremely hard thing to do. However, we will try to do that very same thing here. But, first, let us think about two terms that we should seriously consider when talking about environmental problems and issues.

What is an environmental problem? *An environmental problem is related to some resource, either renewable or nonrenewable, when something about that resource that is of value to human beings is at risk.* Examples: A volcano erupting, an earthquake, a flood, a forest fire - any or all of these putting something(s) of value to human beings at risk. And an environmental issue? *An environmental issue arises when human beings or their institutions differ about what should be done about an environmental problem.* Issues result from differing positions, beliefs, and values. Examples: Raging arguments over the management/disposal of low-level radioactive wastes, very serious arguments over the management of old growth forests of the U.S. Northwest, differences of opinion as to whether to rebuild all of the Mississippi River levee system after the great floods of 1993, differences of opinion concerning the ecological impact of golf courses in Hawaii and elsewhere, arguments concerning whether zoos should be repositories of gene pools of critically endangered species. On and on!

And so humans enter the ecological arena as a critically important environmental variable. How so? Simply because, without Man as an ecological variable, there would be no issues - the problems would be resolved by natural means, i.e., "solutions" without any interference by the human or-

> **An environmental issue arises when human beings or their institutions differ about what should be done about an environmental problem.**

ganism. Conversely, we must understand very clearly that Man is the cause of many of the environmental problems and all of the environmental issues. It is really that simple. However, simplicity ends with this concept! Man's involvement is far from simple.

Wiser scholars than I have determined that this whole scenario is, in reality, the result of *interrelationships between human population, resource use, technology, environmental degradation*, and *pollution*. Yet other scholars believe that the consequences of these relationships, in turn, result in enormous stress within human populations. And, too, there is a great deal of evidence from research into population dynamics and eruptive populations to allow scientists to draw very somber hypotheses concerning serious societal problems - both current and future ones.

An Oversimplified Diagram Of The
Population <> Resource Consumption <> Technology <> Environmental Degradation <> Pollution Model

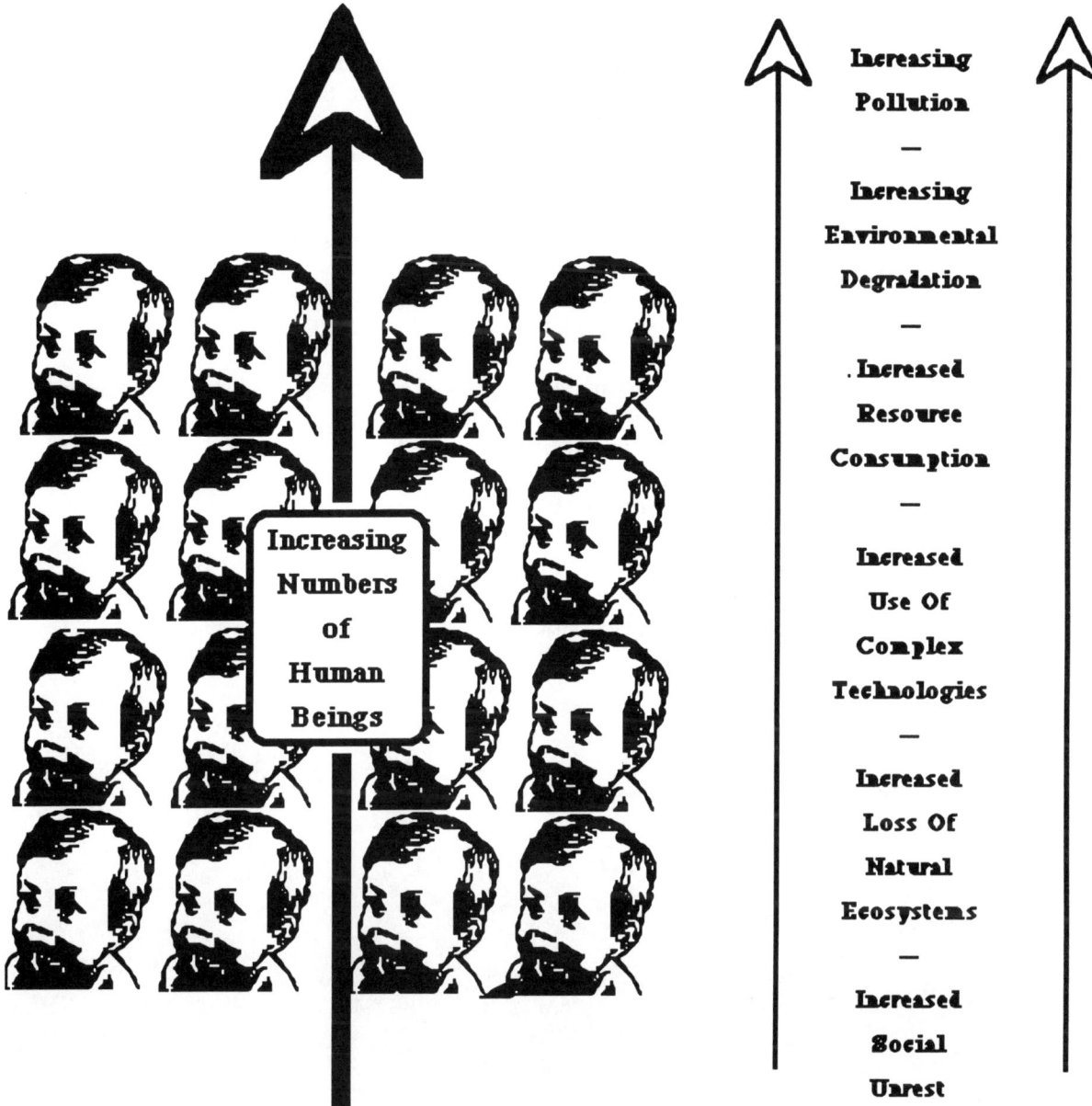

Increasing
Numbers
of
Human
Beings

Increasing
Pollution
—
Increasing
Environmental
Degradation
—
Increased
Resource
Consumption
—
Increased
Use Of
Complex
Technologies
—
Increased
Loss Of
Natural
Ecosystems
—
Increased
Social
Unrest

It could be both worthwhile and very interesting to list evidence of stress within human populations, and to discuss the elements in this list. What societal evidence is there? Could this stress become more serious over time? What is the evidence?

Where Do We Go From Here?

Thus far in this chapter we have looked at a fictional anecdote about people, tomatoes, and ground water and an explanation (by R. L. Smith) of how the human organism has evolved from a dynamic part of the natural scheme of things to being on the verge of an ecological catastrophe. We have, hopefully, thought through some of Smith's comments before looking at the photo essay on Midwestern life in the 1800's. We then tried to make a lucid comparison between resources used in the 1850's and those used in the 1990's. Considering the ecological impacts of resource consumption in the 1990's you were asked to consider, again, the 1850's lifestyle and how it differed from those in society today.

Subsequently, we viewed numerous examples of how human beings now impact the environment toward the end of the Twentieth Century. Referring back to these examples, you were introduced to the concept of an "environmental problem" and that of an "environmental issue". Given the apparent role of all of us as ecological variables, we introduced the notion that this whole scenario is, in one way or another, a function of *interrelationships between population <-> resource use <-> technology <-> environmental degradation <-> pollution*.

If we analyze the interrelationship model highlighted above, we can list a number of "classes" of issues, i.e., issue headings that would house numerous discrete or subordinate issues. A number of these headings might be:

Important Classes of Issues

Human Population	Noise Pollution	Municipal Wastes
Energy Consumption	Aesthetic Pollution	Water Resources
Land Use Management	Pesticides	Endangered Species
Air And Water Pollution	Toxic Wastes	Feral Organisms

Forest management in the United States is a hot bed of issues. Among them is the issue surrounding the practice of making openings in the hardwood forest's canopy. This forest fragmentation damages the ecosystem as a whole and promotes other problems such as the disastrous parasitism of neotropical song bird nests by the brown-headed cow bird. Photo courtesy H. R. Hungerford.

164

Now, if we go back through the Table of Contents for the first five chapters of this book, we can identify a number of ecological variables some of which would be, in one way or another, related to these classes of issues. A conservative number of these headings might be: the ecosystem (included here would be the notion of "habitat" as well as biome, community, and microcommunity), the species population, adaptations, energy production, energy exchanges, biogeochemical cycles, population dynamics, limiting factors in populations, and succession.

Ecological Concepts

The Ecosystem	Energy Production	Population Dynamics
The Species Population	Energy Exchanges	Limiting Factors
Adaptation	Biogeochemical Cycles	Succession

From here we move to examples of environmental problems and issues and describe several in an all too abbreviated manner. Each summary will focus on a separate problem or issue. Most (perhaps not all) will have a direct connection with one or more of the "Classes of Issues" as well as with one or more of the "Ecological Concepts". We will ask you to identify the classes and the concepts associated with each. Remembering that there will be times when your identification will have to be arbitrary, it is important to be able to defend your selection(s).

The first summary issue will focus on problems associated with public beaches. We have identified both the Classes and the Concepts for you. Remember, these selections are somewhat arbitrary but, in this case, they could be defended in a discussion. What do you think of the issue and concept decisions regarding the beach closings?

A Few Comments On Beach Closings

". . . there are thousands of ocean beach closings every year in the United States due to unhealthy levels of water pollution, but no national oversight to track the magnitude of the problem and no national standard to ensure that all swimmers are fully protected. . . . there were more than 2,600 occasions in 1992 when ocean and bay beaches were either closed or subject to advisories against swimming. Most of these were due to high levels of bacteria indicating the presence of human or animal waste. The principal sources of this pollution include inadequate sewage treatment plants, raw sewage discharges from outdated 'combined' sewers (which handle both sewage and rainwater), and polluted storm water runoff."

Source: *The Amicus Journal*, Fall 1993, p. 3.

Select the "Class of Issue(s)": *Air + Water Pollution ; Municipal Wastes*

Select the "Ecological Concept(s)": *Biogeochemical Cycles*

Identifying Issue Classes and Ecological Concepts in Real Issues

And now we visit the Mississippi flood plain after the great flood of 1993. If you live there or near there you know about many of the very important issues that followed the flood. The summary that follows deals with the issue surrounding converting floodplain land into wetlands. See what you think!

Floodplains-Into-Wetlands Plan Runs Into Opposition

"A proposal to turn floodplains into wetlands is for the birds, officials with the Upper Mississippi Flood Control Association said. . . . members criticized a Clinton administration task force report that recommends against rebuilding some levees damaged in last year's flood. . . . [The report] calls for renewed emphasis on converting floodplains into natural wetlands.

'We don't believe the answer is to vacate the floodplain,' said John Robb, an Illinois farmer who chairs the Upper Mississippi group's board of directors. . . . The association instead is encouraging Congress to rebuild levees on the Mississippi, Missouri and Illinois rivers to levels high enough to protect against a 500-year flood. Robb said rebuilding the levees to 500-year levels would cost about $1.8 billion.

The task force . . . did seek a new approach in which the states and corps [Army Corps of Engineers] would look at every alternative - including levees, wetlands creation and relocation - to improve the environment and reduce the impact of floods.

Robb said that the environment is better served by the current system. He said floods kill underbrush and vegetation that animals feed on, so turning the floodplain into wetlands would drive wildlife away."

Source: *Southern Illinoisan*, Wednesday, June 8, 1994. p 6A.

Select the "Class of Issue(s)": _____

Select the "Ecological Concept(s)": _____

The issue here is largely one of wetlands vs. agricultural lands on the floodplain of the Mississippi, Missouri, and Illinois Rivers. The Upper Mississippi Flood Control Association wants to see levees constructed that would protect farmland against everything including 500-year floods - gigantic floods that occur only once in every 500 years. In other circles, there is a strong groundswell of opinion that recommends against rebuilding many of the broken levees simply because they have been shown to be ineffective in many cases and they modify the environment greatly. A major levee system also increases the damage caused by floods when they do occur by forcing water onto far less of the flood-plain than might otherwise be the case. Fewer levees would, in fact, reduce the damage of the flood overall because more of the flood plain would be flooded. All of this aside, Mr. Robb's closing statement is interesting in an ecological sense. What do you make of this situation ecologically?

The issues surrounding marine fisheries are many in number. One of them focuses on the practice of "biomass fishing", a strategy which attempts to catch everything in an area in order to produce feed for fish farming. Let's look at this issue and consider its ecological consequences.

Interactions In A Few Marine Fisheries
or
In Ecology You Simply Cannot Impact On Just One Thing
When You Do Something To An Ecosystem

. . . there is the growing practice of 'biomass fishing,' in which fishers in some countries take all the fish they can catch with fine-mesh trawling equipment. Much of this cleansweep catch goes to meet the growing demand for feed for fish farming. In the most entropic possible disregard for the values of biological diversity, hundreds of interdependent species are ground up into a mash to feed a few monocultured fish.

As fishers remove an ever greater proportion of the biomass from the marine environment, entire ecosystems begin to suffer. In the Shetland Islands, Arctic terns, puffins, and other nesting birds failed to breed in the mid and late 1980's, apparently due to overfishing of the sand eel, a small shoaling fish caught for fish meal and oil. The birds normally fed young sand eels to their chicks, but the fish's population declined with the commercial catch, which peaked at 56,000 tons in 1982 and then slid to 4,800 tons in 1988. In a similar collapse, off the coast of Peru, guano birds abandoned their young when the Peruvian anchovy fishery collapsed. In the North Pacific, Steller's sea lion, dolphin, and bird populations apparently have declined in recent years due to heavy fishing of Alaskan pollack. And in Kenya, researchers found that heavy fishing of triggerfish on coral reefs allowed the proliferation of rock-boring sea urchins that were endangering the entire ecosystem.

. . . the phrase 'there are always more fish in the sea' begins to sound rather quaintly and sadly dated, now that we are seeing just how finite the oceans' biological systems are.

Peter Weber for *Abandoned Seas: Reversing the Decline of the Oceans*, World-Watch Paper No. 116, November 1993, pp 35-39.

Select the "Class of Issue(s)": _____

Select the "Ecological Concept(s)": _____

Sometimes we humans mess with an ecosystem in so many different ways as to make the entire situation look chaotic. An interesting, but tragic, example of this lies with the native mussels of Illinois. See what you think of this situation!

Mussels Endangered in Illinois

"At last count, 29 of [Illinois'] native species of freshwater mussels were on the state endangered species list. Four others are classified as threatened in the state. . . . Reasons for their decline: . . . water pollution, over-harvest, dredging of lakes and waterways, sand and gravel mining in lakes and rivers, siltation, levying, construction, and unexplained mussel die-offs."

By: Fred Tetreault,
Outdoor Highlights, March 19, 1990.

Select the "Class of Issue(s)": _____

Select the "Ecological Concept(s)": _____

Let us consider for a moment a moral question! Do we as members of ecosystems have the right to modify those same ecosystems so as to endanger other species or drive them to extinction? The quote by Fred Tetreault tells us that, in 1990, 33 species of freshwater mussels in the state of Illinois were either threatened or endangered. Although some of the reasons were unknown, Mr. Tetreault is able to identify seven (7) very specific human-caused reasons. There are those who believe that our total disregard for the species with which we share this planet is immoral.

Since the 1973 enactment [of the Endangered Species Act], 550 domestic species have been listed as endangered. Another 3,000 species recommended for listing are awaiting protection. In the past decade, 34 species became extinct while on the waiting list.

National Wildlife,
February-March 1992, p. 34.

Hog Wild

A humorous title is probably inappropriate for this summary because hogs are so very destructive in many ecosystems. Feral hogs are found in California, Tennessee, Texas, Georgia, Alabama, Mississippi, and Hawaii among other states, and are a curse to many wildlife biologists and ecologists. Even though there are many ecologists who worry about the effect of feral hogs on ecosystems on the mainland, it is in Hawaii where feral hog controversy rages. Not only is the issue a hot one, it is complex.

Two kinds of pigs were brought to Hawaii. A small variety was brought to the islands by the early Polynesians. The impact of this animal on natural ecosystems was marginal. However, in the late 18th Century, Europeans introduced hogs that can weigh 300 pounds or more. These hogs, once they became feral, were extremely destructive. Their descendants still uproot rare, native vegetation and contribute to severe soil erosion. The soil that washes into the sea impacts negatively on coral reefs. The hogs eat the eggs and young of ground-nesting birds (like the nene). They spread disease among animal populations. They effectively change the environment to the point where alien weeds replace native plants. Native plants and animals are being driven to extinction. Ecologists have tried to control the damage by fencing out hogs, by live-trapping them, by hunting feral animals, and by using snares in critical habitat in remote rain forests to catch and kill the hogs.

So . . . one of the issues involves trying to save native ecosystems from the ravages of the feral hogs. Yet another issue revolves around the use of the hog by native Hawaiians as a food source. Many subsistence hunters do not want the hog population decimated. Still another issue focuses on the use of snares to protect critical habitat.

The use of snares in special circumstances is supported by almost every conservation and environmental group in Hawaii. However, People for the Ethical Treatment of Animals (PETA) believes otherwise. This organization questions the ethics of using snares and condemns their use to capture pigs. The Nature Conservancy writes, "For PETA the issue is black and white: Nothing can justify a human act that might cause any animal to suffer, even if that means allowing many other creatures to experience starvation, crippling diseases, the killing of their nestlings, destruction of their habitat and - the ultimate suffering - extinction. The Nature Conservancy views the issue as more complex, and seeks to minimize the suffering of all the forests' species."

Select the "Class of Issue(s)": _____

Select the "Ecological Concept(s)": _____

Information from personal interviews with Hawaiian players in the issue
as well as a fine article in *Nature Conservancy*, May/June 1994. pp 38-39.

169

The Nene: A Bird On The Critical List

Hawaii! The land of enchantment and paradise. People arrive on 747's from all over the world each and every day to golf, snorkel, fish, sun-bathe, get warm, and simply lie around under palm trees. However, Hawaii amounts to only 0.2% of the land mass of the United States. But it has about 75% of the documented plant and bird extinctions. And tragically, 40% of all endangered bird species in the United States are from Hawaii.

One of these birds is the Hawaiian Goose or Nene. The nene is the largest Hawaiian native land bird. Its closest relative is probably the Canada goose. These geese can fly but spend much of their time walking and climbing at rather high altitudes on the islands. They can fly between the islands but do so rarely.

Early in the 19th Century there were thousands of these birds. However, by 1990 they were completely gone from the island of Maui and scarce on the island of Hawaii. By 1950 there may have been no more than 30 of these birds left. This goose was on the verge of becoming extinct. However, a large captive breeding program brought the population to about 500 geese as of 1993.

What happened to the nene? The nene is a classic example of an animal that could not adapt to changing conditions. Non-native animals wreak havoc on the geese and their eggs and goslings. Among these predators are the mongoose, feral dogs, and feral cats. Other culprits are feral goats and pigs.

The situation for the nene is still questionable. If left alone [without careful management and a captive breeding program] the nene would probably become extinct by the middle of the next century.

Adapted from several sources but largely from an Eric Tong essay in:
Threatened and Endangered Animals,
Stipes Publishing Company, 1993. pp. 50-51.

Select the "Class of Issue(s)": _____

Select the "Ecological Concept(s)": _____

The Dramatic Decline In The Populations Of
Neotropical Migratory Birds

Please give the following pretest your best effort. If should take less than 60 seconds to complete.

The Pretest on the Decline of Neotropical Migratory Birds

The following list contains variables that may contribute to the worldwide decline in populations of neotropical migratory birds - birds that spend the summer and reproduce in temperate regions of the world and winter in tropical regions. Check all of the variables that apply as reasons for the decline of these animals:

   ___   over hunting of song birds for food

   ___   deforestation of tropical rain forests

   ___   forest fragmentation of temperate deciduous forests

   ___   overgrazing of grasslands

   ___   desertification in Africa

   ___   draining wetlands

   ___   the domestic cat

   ___   oil spills

   ___   toxic pesticides

End of Pretest

One could write a very long summary on this topic. However, I will attempt to be brief. Oh yes, if you checked all of the above, you are correct. Each of these variables impacts on the loss of the neotropical birds. You could do your analysis of this issue with only the information you have above. Even so, let's take a brief look at a few of these variables.

The domestic cat: People who have seriously observed domestic cats roaming out-of-doors for any reasonable length of time will know how effective they are as predators. Wildlife biologists are very concerned about the effects that the domestic cat can have in ecosystems. We often hear people who have cats (and let them roam) say that they don't worry about their cats being a problem because they are well fed. The wildlife biologist will tell you, however, that a well fed cat is a better predator than many natural predators simply because it is well fed. Many cats do not kill for food. They kill because they are genetically coded to kill. That is what they have done for millions of years.

Research into the effects of domestic cats on wildlife is beginning to grow. Some sobering statistics have come from some of that research. In Wisconsin alone it is calculated that there are well over 1,000,000 free roaming cats taking 400,000 game birds and 28,000,000 song birds each year. These figures don't even take into account the millions of small mammals killed and the three or four million rabbits taken.

As human numbers grow and subdivisions spread so do cats. And, in a number of areas there is great concern about the impact free-roaming cats will have on already endangered species - mammals as well as birds. Of course, many are the wildlife biologists who wonder just why folks let their cats roam!

Toxic Pesticides: The story of DDT is perhaps the most well known of all of the variables that one might discuss related to this issue. DDT was found to be a real menace to birds like eagles, falcons, and pelicans in the 50's and 60's. Ingested as part of the food chain, the mature birds were unable to lay sound eggs and reproduce. Once DDT was banned, many of the hardest-hit species rebounded. The bald eagle is a wonderful example. If we have seen a victory over the DDT issue in the U.S., why then are we discussing it here? Simply because it is still very popular in Africa and has been shown to damage a number of African birds-of-prey. And, too, DDT is not the only chemical that can damage or outright kill neotropical birds. Other chemicals that can damage bird populations would include lead, mercury, and selenium.

Forest Fragmentation: Interestingly, the severe decline of neotropical song birds may not be due so much to a net loss of deciduous forests but, instead, to how the remaining forests are managed. How so? The key to the deciduous forest situation is something called "fragmentation". Fragmentation occurs when large tracts of forest are opened up or cut up into smaller and smaller units. This occurs when highways are constructed, when shopping malls are cut out of woodlands, when subdivisions are constructed in oak-hickory forests, when golf courses are constructed or when power lines cut through a forest. Research shows that fragmentation permits a very serious parasite to invade the areas. This is the brown-headed cowbird which normally does not parasitize nesting birds in dense, unbroken forest land. The cowbird lays its eggs in the nests of others and then abandons the egg to the foster care of the parasitized species. Some song bird species will show a 90% rate of parasitism! And, in those nests which contain the cowbird egg, only the cowbird youngster normally survives!

The hunting of songbirds: Yes, there are cultures which kill and eat songbirds! One wonders about their value as a food source compared to their contributions to the ecosystems in which they live. Yet, millions upon millions of songbirds are eaten in the south of Europe alone each year.

Needless to say, this business of the neotropicals is extremely complicated. However, in North and South America we could see populations stabilize and extinctions less predictable if we would simply manage our forests, grasslands, and wetlands differently in both continents (and keep our cats at home).

Neotropical Birds Issue(s)

Select the "Class of Issue(s)": _____

Select the "Ecological Concept(s)": _____

Desert For Sale

A Two Page Problem/Issue Essay

The Sonoran Desert near Tucson, Arizona. Photo courtesy H. Hungerford.

A number of deserts can be found in North America. These are represented by the Great Basin Desert, the Mohave Desert, the Chihuahuan Desert, and the Sonoran Desert. All of these deserts except one are "hot deserts". The Great Basin Desert is classified as a cool desert.

Of all of the North American deserts, the Sonoran is the richest in terms of vegetation and animals. The vegetation is the most dense and the height most diverse. Small flowering plants are numerous and grow in association with the older trees and shrubs which hold an accumulation of soil in which the smaller plants can germinate and grow.

The richness of the Sonoran Desert vegetation brings with it a host of animals as well. In certain seasons the desert swarms with insects - including bees, crickets, grasshoppers, ants, wasps, butterflies, moths, and beetles. Even some amphibians are successful here. Some animals are active the year round. There are numerous lizards, snakes, rodents, and other larger mammals including mountain lions, coyotes, peccaries, coatis, and others. The desert tortoise roams here as well. Numerous birds - quail, woodpeckers, hummingbirds, swifts, finches, sparrows and others - are also common inhabitants.

The climate of the Sonoran Desert also attracts the human organism. Historically, the region was overgrazed by cattle barons. This overgrazing eliminated the grasses which accelerated the loss of topsoil through wind and water erosion. Development - cities,

174

highways, subdivisions, golf courses, airports, and a variety of others - has also substantially reduced and/or damaged the desert ecosystem.

The photos below illustrate one aspect of what can happen to the Sonoran Desert ecosystem. The "For Sale" sign is only a prediction of what is to come. The other photo illustrates one thing that can happen when the desert is sold for development. Habitat is reduced and increasing numbers of plants and animals become threatened and endangered.

It is important to consider what environmental problems and issues are associated with "selling the Sonoran Desert for development". What might some of these be? Are there similar issues elsewhere (beyond the Sonoran Desert)?

A part of the Sonoran Desert which will be sold for development purposes in approximately one acre tracts. Photo courtesy H. R. Hungerford.

This photo was taken almost across the road from the one above. What differences can you observe from the pictures? Photo courtesy H. Hungerford.

The "Desert for Sale Issue(s)

Select the "Class of Issue(s)": _____

Select the "Ecological Concept(s)": _____

175

The Anatomy of Issues:
Their Players and Their Positions, Beliefs, and Values

Issues can become complicated. Issues usually contain "players". **Players** are the individuals or organizations involved in an issue. Each of the players in an issue has a point of view about what should be done to resolve that issue. This point of view is called the player's **position**.

Let us return to the article entitled "Hog Wild" which is found a few pages back. Ecologists believe that feral hogs are an ecological disaster. They feel that the hogs need to be controlled. This is their position on that issue. The subsistence hunters want the hogs in the ecosystem as a food source. This is their position. PETA wants no hogs killed for any reason. The Nature Conservancy is adamant that hogs must be controlled in order to salvage native species of plants and animals.

The chart below summarizes what you have learned about the events, problems, issues, players, and positions in the Hawaii feral hog issue. Please study it carefully.

Issue Components	The "Hog Wild" Example
The Event	Introduction of large European hogs to Hawaii. Some escape.
The Environmental Problem	The feral hogs are creating ecological havoc among native plants and animals.
The Environmental Issue	Should the hogs be eliminated, thoroughly managed, or left alone?
The Players	Ecologists PETA Subsistence Hunters The Nature Conservancy
The Players' Positions	Ecologists: Control the damage done by hogs. Either eliminate or manage them. PETA: No snares - they cause suffering. Leave the pigs alone. Subsistence Hunters: The hog population must not be decimated. The Nature Conservancy: The hogs should be managed.

On to Beliefs and Values

You have become familiar with a number of new terms and their definitions. Let's review some of them.

> **Problem**: A situation or condition in which something or someone is at risk.
>
> **Issue**: A problem about which two or more people or organizations disagree.
>
> **Player**: Those persons or organizations who have a role in an issue or its solution.
>
> **Position**: The stand or posture taken by the player in regard to the issue or its solution.

Issues are complex. The ideas presented above are not enough for someone to completely understand the issue. In this section we present two new ideas which will help you understand environmental issues. Those new ideas are **beliefs** and **values**. Beliefs and values are both related to a player's position on an issue.

A **belief** is an idea that a person holds. The person thinks or believes that the idea is true. It might or might not be true, but the person believes that it is. Often a person's beliefs are strongly related to his or her values.

> **A belief is an idea that a person holds to be true.**

> **Values are specific ideas which help an individual decide what is important or worthy.**

Values are specific ideas which help an individual decide what is important or worthy. A **value** is the worth a person places on something. Everyone has personal values which are based on their past experiences. These values might involve money, status, beauty, religion, or a number of other things.

Values help shape the beliefs that an individual holds on an issue. They also help determine that individual's position on that issue. For example, the ecologists who want to preserve what remains of native Hawaiian plants and animals believes that the integrity of the ecosystem is important and that native species should be protected. The subsistence hunters do not necessarily disagree but they do not want to see the hog population reduced to the point where subsistence hunting is no longer possible. Interpreting values is a tricky business.

> **Values help shape the beliefs that an individual holds on an issue.**

Value Descriptors

The descriptions below attempt to name and define values that might be held by individuals. These definitions, as well as the list itself, are incomplete.

Value:	Definition:
Aesthetic:	the appreciation of form, composition, and color through the senses.
Economic:	the use and exchange of money, materials, and/or services.
Ecological:	the maintenance of natural biological systems.
Educational:	the accumulation, use, and communication of knowledge.
Egocentric:	a focus on self-centered individual needs and fulfillment.
Environmental:	the interactions between human activities and natural resources, e.g., plant and animal species, air, water, soil, etc.
Ethical/Moral:	present and future human responsibilities, rights and wrongs, and ethical standards.
Ethnocentric:	a focus on the fulfillment of ethnic/cultural goals.
Health:	the maintenance of positive human physiological conditions.
Legal:	relating to regulations, laws; law enforcement; law suits.
Political:	the activities, functions, and policies of governments and their agents.
Recreational:	leisure activities.
Religious:	the use of belief systems based on faith or dogma.
Scientific:	process of empirical research; knowledge gained by systematic study.
Social:	shared human empathy, feelings, and status.

Values and "Environmental" Statements

Directions: Below you will find a list of statements which relate somehow to ecology or the environment. You need not agree with the statements. Even so, you might want to analyze each for the value it represents. You can write the name of the value in the space provided.

1. Humans have a responsibility to protect natural ecosystems.	
2. Whale watching brings over $3,000,000 to the state of Hawaii each year.	
3. The Bible states that Man is meant to have control over the earth.	
4. We were taught how Native Americans used the bison to survive on the Great Plains.	
5. I like to watch bald eagles because they are beautiful birds.	
6. Fire was an important part of grassland plant and animal systems.	
7. If you want to become an ecologist, you should get a college degree.	
8. My family has always taken care of its farmland, and it is important for me to do the same thing.	
9. Many valuable medicines have been discovered in plants found in tropical rain forests.	
10. It is against the law to dump toxic chemicals into the Mississippi River.	
11. Only the government can enact laws to protect endangered species.	
12. Many bird watchers travel to Florida to see the birds that live there.	
13. The gray wolf is an important forest predator.	
14. I don't care if the duck season is closed or not, I'll hunt ducks any time I want to.	
15. My friends and I all enjoy sitting out at night and watching "shooting stars".	

Analyzing an Environmental Issue

You have now learned how to identify an issue, the players, and the players' positions, beliefs, and values. It is now time for you to begin tackling real issues and analyzing them. Below, you will read a short article entitled, "The New Frontier?". This issue is a fictionalized account of real events. The names of the community and the players have been changed. The issue, the players, and their positions have been identified for you. Your task is to complete the table by attempting to identify the beliefs of the players as well as the values reflected in those beliefs.

The New Frontier?

Each year millions of acres of agland are consumed by ever expanding strip developments, shopping centers and subdivisions. The never ending search by business tycoons and developers for more and more land seems to have no limit. Many communities are beset by issues surrounding development and Alchemy, Ohio is no exception.

In 1993, three new Alchemy subdivisions were begun on farmland and a new mall was completed, also built on what were once soybean fields. A total of 265 acres was converted by these projects. In 1994 still two more subdivisions were in the planning stages and houses were being constructed on all three subdivisions begun the previous year.

Not everyone in Alchemy is pleased with these events. A coalition consisting of citizens from the local Audubon Society, the Sierra Club, and the Citizens for Conservation began protesting the wholesale conversion of farmland to shopping centers and subdivisions. Mr. Henry Blackstone, Chair of the coalition states emphatically that developers have taken entirely too much liberty with their sustained hunger for more and more land to turn into money-making developments. He claims that neither Alchemy or the nation, for that matter, can afford to use up its agland in this way. Too many nations depend upon the U.S. for food and population projections indicate that this is just the tip of the iceberg. Blackstone also cites the increased traffic on roads that were not constructed for this volume as well as new demands on utilities such as water, sewage, and electricity.

Another coalition member, Alice Clark complains bitterly about the wildlife losses being observed on local roads. Road kills appear to increase in direct proportion to the traffic and the roads seem littered with dead deer, opossums, raccoons, foxes, and birds of numerous species. She says that this carnage is a tragedy and that the situation is made even worse because the animals' habitat is being destroyed by the developers.

The head of the Sanderson County Builders' Association defends the developments saying that no laws have been broken and that the housing developments employ some 85 workers which is important in an area where unemployment runs nearly ten percent.

The Mayor of Alchemy, Rita Benston, in a rare interview with the local newspaper, says flatly that these business and housing developments are good for Alchemy - that they will provide work for many skilled workers and eventually contribute to the tax base of the community. Furthermore, she says that, if the do-gooders in the conservation coalition want the zoning restrictions changed that they should get to work and see that they are changed. However, she says that she would oppose any such move.

A local high school science teacher, Harry O'Conner, has also written several Letters to the Editor (of the local newspaper) complaining about the environmental consequences of the developments around Alchemy, and trying to inform the public as to what was going on in their community.

O'Conner's arguments were very similar to those mounted by Blackstone and Clark. However, he stopped writing when he began receiving threatening phone calls, some of them anonymous. One caller identified himself as the original owner of the soybean fields that were converted to the mall and told O'Conner that those farm fields were his and that he could do anything he wanted with them. He told O'Conner to mind his own business.

Issue Analysis Worksheet

The Issue: To what extent should the farmland of Alchemy be converted to shopping centers and housing developments?

The Players & Their Positions	Beliefs	Value
Henry Blackstone Stop converting farmland.		
Alice Clark Stop converting farmland.		
Builders' Association Keep on building.		
Mayor Benston Keep on building.		
Harry O'Conner Stop converting farmland.		

In Closing

By this time it is hoped that all of us see the human organism as an integral part of ecosystems. Man is totally dependent upon the biosphere that is shared with other plants and animals However, as a group, we definitely do not act like it.

The Alchemy, Ohio story is very typical of the nonchalance with which we deal with the planet. We know that the human population is already at critical levels and continues to grow exponentially (remember the J-curve?). Yet we bulldoze and asphalt the very ground that can grow soybeans, corn, wheat, or other crops that contribute so importantly to the human condition. Why do we do this? The values involved are probably egocentric and economic. At least one of these is probably borne of ignorance of the ecological implications. The other, egocentrism, is harder to deal with.

Not only do we build shopping centers and subdivisions on agland, we pollute streams, rivers, and oceans as well as our own atmosphere and senses. In so doing we kill mussels and other aquatic organisms. Fish advisories are put out and we cannot fish on long stretches of the Mississippi River. We cut down topical rain forests and fragment deciduous forests and force numerous species of neotropical birds to face extinction. We bring our "pets" to foreign lands and wind up seeing them destroy the native species that have no defense against the newcomers. People speak all the time about the natural process of extinction but fail to tell us that, by the turn of the century, 20,000 species will probably become extinct each year. In 1975 only 100 species became extinct each year. Such is the current impact of Man in the earth's ecosystems.

The intent of this chapter is to show Man as an ecological variable. Hopefully, this has been accomplished. It is not the intent of this chapter or this book to tell the reader how to behave ecologically or environmentally. This is up to each and everyone individually. However, it is hoped that this book will help shape those behaviors.

Activity 6.1

Where Did We Put the Mall?
The Subdivision?
The Highway?
The Parking Lot?

The idea that shopping malls, subdivisions, highways and parking lots have always been where they are is a common one among human beings. Actually, they have only been where they are in the wink of an eye compared to historic time.

The task in this activity is to select a developed area, one which is of particular interest to you, and investigate it. This area could be a shopping mall, a subdivision, an entire small community, or a particular stretch of highway.

Search out expert consultants who can help you determine what the original ecosystem was in this location. You can rest assured that, at one time, there was a natural ecosystem there. [Do not consider an agricultural field a "natural ecosystem" although this could have been the intermediate system between the original ecosystem and the development.] When you discover what that original system was, you might want to try to describe or reconstruct it in writing, with murals, with maps, and/or models.

Who can help you find out what the original ecosystem was like? The sources of information might differ in different communities. Thus, you have a detective task on your hands. People who might provide some help would include the County Clerk, the City Planning Office, the Zoning Commission, long-term elderly residents, a local Historical Society, or City Hall. You might also want to talk to officials of local environmental organizations. Most of these sources can put you on the right track even though one or more might not have the final answer.

When you are finished with your investigation, consider how many species can be found there now compared to how many lived there before. Decide whether the area should be considered to be a "natural area/ecosystem" or whether it has been changed too much. Were any animal or plant species in the region threatened or endangered because of this development? Was this area important to native plants and animals?

Was the decision to change the original ecosystem a good decision? Why or why not?

Activity 6.2

Completing an Issue Web

On the following page you will find what we call "An Incomplete Issue Web". The issue web is simply a strategy designed to illustrate the interrelationships that exist between issues and between classes of issues. Trying to complete one can be both fun and frustrating and, perhaps, even impossible.

In any event, in this activity you are asked to try and complete the issue web presented here of one similar to it. You might want to start more simply and work up a web that has only two or three closely related classes of issues on it, e.g., human population, land use management, and energy consumption.

In order to help you get started on the larger issue web, consider where the following issues would be placed. Also consider whether they would be interconnected with other issues. If so, connect the closely related issues as you see in the incomplete issue web.

Example Issues

Aesthetic Pollution

Arid Land Irrigation

Clearcutting Of Forests

Coal Fired Power Plants

Draining Wetlands

Drift Net Fishing

Eradication Of Prairie Dog Towns

Illegal [Garbage] Dumps

Nuclear Waste Disposal

The Black-Footed Ferret

The Desert Tortoise

The Gray Wolf

The Jaguar [North America]

The Spotted Owl

Toxic Waste Dumps

Whole Log Sales In Overseas Markets

An Incomplete Issue Web

How much can you add to this issue web? The possibilities are many! Not even all of the important issue classes will be found in this figure, i.e., classes such as toxic wastes, noise pollution, aesthetic pollution, etc.

185

Activity 6.3

The Two Versus The Three Child Family:
A Look At The Consequences

Many human beings are unconcerned about the ecological effects of their reproductivity! This activity is designed to demonstrate the population effects if a couple has two children and each of them has two children and there are two children born in each succeeding generation with each marriage. Subsequently you are asked to calculate the same phenomenon looking at the effects of a couple having three children and that pattern continuing over a three (and even a four) generation time span.

The worksheet for this activity will be found on the next page.

The following questions might help you organize the results of this activity in your mind:

1. How many children do you observe being born in the third generation of the "two child family"?

2. You have been asked to calculate the number of offspring that would be observed in the fourth generation of the "two child family". What is that number?

3. Mathematically, there ought to emerge a pattern in the number of offspring being born in each succeeding generation? Can you observe a pattern? If so, what is it?

4. Given the typical 20-year time span for a generation, how many years would elapse before one observed eight children being born in the fourth generation? Hold on to that figure and the corresponding concept!

5. If the average life expectancy in this "two child family" culture is 70, how many of the *total number of individuals* (this figure would include the marriage partners a well) would have died during the four generations?

6. Moving on to the "three child family" culture, how many children do you observe in the second generation? The third generation? What is the number you have calculated for the fourth generation?

7. How do the "three child family" numbers compare with the "two child family" numbers?

8. Again, there should be a mathematical pattern emerging from the "three child family" reproductivity. If you can observe this pattern, how would you describe it?

9. Can this "three child family" culture avoid having a negative ecological impact on the environment? If so, how? If not, why?

10. Given that there are cultures in the world that are still producing five, six, and even more children per union, can you speculate on the ecological impacts that these cultures are having on their environments.

The Two Versus the Three Child Family:
A Look at the Consequences

M = Male; F = Female

The Two Child Family Over Three Generations

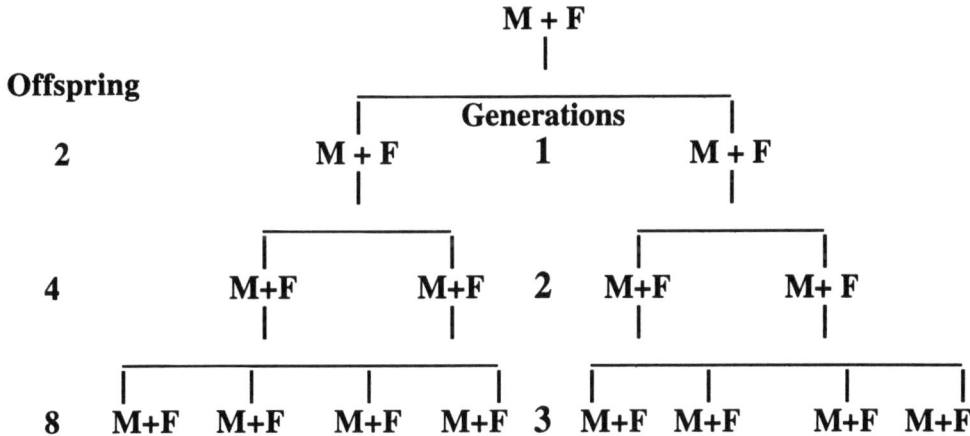

How many children would be born in the fourth generation?

═══════════════════════════════════

The Three Child Family Over Three Generations
[Complete the Chart]

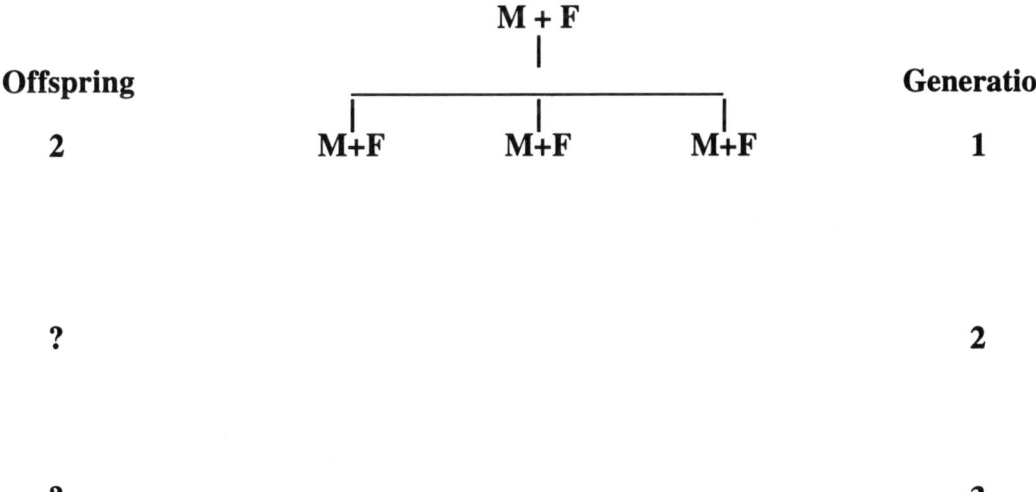

How many children would be born in the fourth generation?

188

Glossary Of Terms

Abiotic: nonliving; an abiotic variable in an ecosystem would be exemplified by such things as light, rain, moisture, heat, bedrock, and topography.

Acid Rain: rainfall (or fog) which is more acidic than normal, often caused by an infusion of sulfur and nitrogen compounds from vehicular exhausts and coal burning power plants.

Adaptation: a particular attribute which contributes to an organism's survival in a community, e.g., protective coloration.

Affective: relating to feeling, emotion, or desire.

Agrarian: pertaining to farming, agriculture. An agrarian society is one in which the economy and culture are tied mainly to agricultural (rather than industrial) enterprises.

Algae: usually microscopic plants that can carry on photosynthesis, often green, some single-celled, some many-celled.

Aquifer: a place where water is found within the earth's crust (this water known as ground water).

Atmosphere: typically thought of as the air that surrounds the earth.

Autonomous: independent, without outside control, self-regulating.

Bacteria: very small cellular organisms; most decomposers (along with the fungus plants) are bacteria.

Belief: that which a person holds to be true.

Biodegradable: any material that can be broken down in the environment by decomposers, e.g., paper products, human sewage, vegetable matter.

Biogeochemical cycles: those chemical cycles that are critical to the maintenance of ecosystems, e.g., nitrogen cycle, calcium cycle.

Biome: a very large ecosystem usually containing similar plants, e.g., deciduous forest biome, grassland biome, tropical rain forest biome.

Biosphere: that relatively thin "shell" surrounding the earth that supports life.

Biotic potential: the greatest extent to which a species population can grow under given environmental conditions.

Biotic: living, having life; a biotic variable in an ecosystem would be exemplified by a plant or an animal.

Canopy: the uppermost layer in a deciduous forest which receives the most light energy (sunlight).

Carnivore: an organism that kills and eats animals, e.g., lion, hawk, owl, snake.

Carrying capacity: the maximum number of organisms in a species population that the environment can support on an ongoing basis.

Clearcutting: a method of forest harvesting that removes all of the trees in a given area.

189

Climate: the average weather conditions in a given locale over a long period of time, e.g., several decades.

Climax ecosystem or climax community: that stage of succession that results in a relatively stable ecosystem, usually one with a wide array of species and habitats.

Cognitive: related to the mental processes by which knowledge is acquired; cognitive may relate to either an individual's knowledge or an individual's ability to process knowledge.

Community: in an ecological sense, an interacting and interdependent set of plants and animals, e.g., a prairie community, a pond community.

Competition (interspecific competition): when individuals of different species compete with each other for one or more resources. Example: lions and hyenas and vultures are known to compete with each other for meat in a kill.

Competition (intraspecific competition): when individuals of the same species compete with each other for one or more resources. Example: lions are known to compete with each other for meat in a kill.

Composting: the process of speeding up the decomposition of organic debris such as leaves and vegetable wastes in order to produce material that can be used as humus or fertilizer.

Conceptual: relating to mental images held by individuals and associated with events and objects; ideas.

Coniferous forest: a forest made up mostly of trees that are evergreen; trees having needles instead of leaves and reproducing with cones.

Consumer: An organism which feeds on a second organism, utilizing the food energy stored in the tissues of that other plant or animal. A first order consumer (herbivore) feeds on plant tissue. Second order consumers (carnivores) feed on first order consumers. Third order consumers may feed on both first and second order consumers.

Deciduous forest: the term given to a forest which contains trees that shed their leaves during the fall or winter.

Decomposer: An organism which obtains energy by breaking down the complex molecules of wastes and dead bodies into simpler chemicals.

Desert Ecosystem: an ecosystem that exists in very low annual precipitation, typically 10 inches or less per year; often, an ecosystem with widely spaced vegetation.

Desertification: the conversion of a productive ecosystem to desert through overgrazing, prolonged drought, or climatic change; often associated with man's activities.

Detritus: dead plant and animal material, body wastes, e.g., fallen leaves and twigs in a forest.

Dynamic equilibrium: a tendency toward homeostasis; stability over time with periodic fluctuations.

e.g.: symbol for "for example".

Ecology: the scientific study of the interrelationships that exist between organisms and between organisms and their physical environment.

Ecosystem: an aggregate of plants and animals which are interdependent plus the abiotic variables with which they interact; typically thought of as self-contained in the sense that many of the essentials for life can be cycled and recycled within that system.

Effluent: waste water from a sewage plant or industry.

Emigration: the movement of members of a population out of one locality into another; usually a permanent move.

Empathy: a feeling for; sympathetic identification with something, such as empathy for an endangered species.

Empirical: based on observation; founded on direct experience or experimentation; scientific.

Empiricism: the mode of thought which is typically scientific in nature, a philosophy focusing on the reality of observation and experience as the basis of truth; scientific method.

Endangered species: A species with very few surviving members; a species that could easily become extinct.

Energy flow: the movement of energy from one organism to another in a food chain or a food web.

Energy pyramid: the tendency for usable energy to be lost as it moves through a food chain; often a diagrammatic representation of available energy at various stages in a food chain.

Energy transfer: in ecology, the movement of energy from one life form to another in a food chain.

Energy: that which supplies the capacity for work or activity, e. g., plants provide the energy for herbivores to function in the environment.

Entropy: a measure of the degree of disorder brought about by an increasing complexity within a dynamic system; a thermodynamic measure of energy unavailable for useful work in a system undergoing change.

Environmental Impact Assessment: an evaluation of the extent to which certain activities will negatively impact/influence the environment.

Environmental issue: a problem with obvious environmental overtones surrounding which one can observe differing human beliefs and values.

Environmental literacy: that state in which an individual is environmentally knowledgeable and, above all, skilled and dedicated for working, individually and collectively, toward achieving and/or maintaining a dynamic equilibrium between quality of life and quality of the environment. (Paraphrased from Harvey, 1977)

Environmental resistance: the sum total of all factors that act in consort to limit the size of a population; intimately associated with carrying capacity.

Erosion: the processes by which the materials of the earth's crust are transported from one location to another by forces such as gravity, wind, water, and glacial ice.

Eruptive population: species populations that have unrestricted reproduction which can be symbolized by a J curve graph.

Estuary: the place where fresh and salt water mix along a coastline; typically an area of brackish water with vegetative zones dictated by water depth, soil type, salt content, etc.

Evaporation: takes place when a liquid such as water is changed to a vapor.

First law of energy: it takes energy to get energy, e.g., energy must be expending in the growing of carrots in order to provide for the energy that the carrots contain.

Floodplain: that land along a stream that collects the water when that stream overflows its banks.

Food chain: a linear pattern describing the flow of energy through an ecosystem; typically beginning with a food producing plant being eaten or partially eaten by a herbivore which is, in turn, consumed by a carnivore, etc.

Food web: a set of interrelated food chains within a given ecosystem.

Grassland: a very large biome found in regions with only moderate rainfall, over ten inches usually but under thirty inches - enough rainfall to support grasses but no extensive forests. In the U.S., much of the landscape from the Mississippi to Colorado would be classified as "grassland".

Groundwater: water that sinks into and through the soil to be stored underground. Large underground storage areas are called aquifers.

Habitat: that place where an organism can live and reproduce. That community or portion of a community where a species can be successful.

Herb layer: the layer in the forest that contains herbaceous plants and which lies beneath the shrub layer and above the litter/soil layer.

Herb: a non-woody (soft-tissued) stemmed plant that typically dies back at the end of a growing season.

Herbivore: an organism that eats plant material, e.g., rabbit, mouse, ground hog, deer.

Hierarchy: an organization of things arranged one above the other according to a logical order, e.g., a hierarchy of goals.

Homeostasis: the tendency to maintain normal internal stability in an organism or an ecological system, such as a hardwood forest, by coordinated responses of the system's components, compensating for environmental changes.

Humidity: a measure of the amount of moisture in the air.

i.e.: symbol for "that is".

Immigration: the movement of a population or a portion of a population into a particular area; usually a permanent move.

Incineration: the burning of something; often refers to a method of disposing of solid wastes in an incinerator.

Insecticide: that chemical or mixture of things intended to get rid of insects - often designed to kill insects.

Insolation: the amount of light energy that an area receives from the sun.

Interspecific competition: two or more species of organisms competing for the same resource in a particular ecosystem.

Intraspecific competition: two or more individuals of the same species or organism competing for the same resource in a particular ecosystem.

Issue: a problem about which there is disagreement by two or more individuals or groups (players).

J-curve: associated with the letter "J" which depicts the growth curve of an eruptive population or organisms, e.g., man.

Learner objectives: those objectives prepared for the student to learn/accomplish; objectives which will be met through instruction, usually stated in performance (behavioral) terms.

Legal action: any legal/judiciary action taken by an individual and/or organization which is aimed at some aspect of environmental law enforcement - or, a legal restraint preceding some environmental behavior perceived as undesirable, e.g., law suits, injunctions.

Limiting factors: in ecology, those variables which tend to put limits on the development of an ecosystem or on the activities of an organism; anything present in insufficient amounts so that an organism's survival and/or reproduction is restricted.

Lithosphere: that part of the earth's crust made up of solid material, as opposed to the "hydrosphere".

Litter/soil layer: the bottom layer of a deciduous forest containing animal waste, dead animals, and plant debris- the nutrients from which are returned to the soil by decomposer organisms.

Litter: the animal wastes, dead animal bodies, and dead plants, leaves, branches, etc. that lie on the forest floor.

Microcommunity: a relatively small ecological unit of interacting plants and animals. Examples would be a temporary pool in a forest, a fallen and decaying log, a tree hole containing water and housing breeding populations of insects such as tree-hole mosquitoes.

Monobiotic agriculture: growing only one crop in a relatively large area, e.g., a pine plantation, corn field, soybean field, rubber plantation.

Natality: refers to live births or birth rate.

Natural selection: the survival of a genetic form over time as a result of a particular adaptation favoring that organism.

Niche: an organisms' role in a community; not to be confused with where an organism lives.

Nitrogen cycle: that rather complex biogeochemical cycle that converts nitrogen from one form to another; responsible for producing nitrates which can be used successfully by plants.

Nutrient: any chemical that is needed by a plant or animal for growth and reproduction.

Omnivore: an organism that eats both plants and animals, e.g., grizzly bear, red fox.

Parameter: a limit; boundary.

Performance objective: See "learner objective".

Persuasion: an effort, verbally, to motivate human beings to take positive environmental action as a function of modified values, e.g., argumentation, debate, speech making, letter writing.

Pervasive: diffused throughout; to permeate.

Pesticide: any chemical or combination of things designed to get rid of weeds, insects, spiders, rodents or other organisms. Usually, the pesticide is designed to kill the target population.

Phenomena: events; happenings that may be observed. Singular: phenomenon.

Photosynthesis: that process that takes place in the presence of chlorophyll and light energy that allows water and carbon dioxide to be combined to produce oxygen and energy-producing carbohydrates.

"Player" (in an issue): someone involved in an issue, a person having definite beliefs (and a particular position on the issue) and certain supporting values.

Point sources (of pollution): a specific and definable point which serves as a source of pollution, e.g., smoke stack, sewage treatment plant.

Pollutant: a chemical whose concentration has built up to the point where it harms human beings, other animals, or plants. Can be found in air, water, soil, and other environments.

Population density: the ratio of individuals of a species population compared to available space.

Population dynamics: those interactions which can be observed taking place within a particular species population; population dynamics often refers to those variables which influence the population size of an organism over time in a given ecosystem/biome.

Position (on an issue): the stand or posture taken by a player in regard to an issue.

Predator: any organism that gains control over or kills another organism and feeds on part or all of it. The victim is called the prey organism.

Primary succession: succession that takes place in an area where there is no soil. Typically, this area has never had a plant community growing from it. An excellent example is succession on a lava flow.

Problem: a situation or condition in which something or someone is at risk.

Producer: typically, a green plant that can carry on photosynthesis. However, there are other primitive organisms that use other strategies to produce food.

Radioactivity: the property of being radioactive; the radiation given off as a consequence of radioactive decay, e.g., the radioactive decay of plutonium.

Rainforest: a dense forest in a tropical region which receives at least 100 inches of precipitation annually.

Recycle: to use again, in some productive manner, materials which are often considered as solid wastes by segments of a human population, e.g., aluminum, paper products, glass, plastics.

Remediate: to remedy, to restore, cure.

Scenario: the outline or synopsis, step-by-step, of a plot or an event; contains all the details of a plot or an event.

Second law of energy: a system tends toward increasing disorder with respect to energy, e.g., when energy obtained from plants by herbivores is used, about 90% of that energy is used for the animal is metabolism and is lost as heat and only 10% of the energy is used for life processes.